Articles on

CALVIN
and
CALVINISM

A FOURTEEN-VOLUME ANTHOLOGY
OF SCHOLARLY ARTICLES

edited by

RICHARD C. GAMBLE
CALVIN THEOLOGICAL SEMINARY

A GARLAND SERIES

Contents
of Series

VOLUME 12

CALVIN
and Science

edited by

RICHARD C. GAMBLE

GARLAND PUBLISHING, INC.
NEW YORK & LONDON
1992

Library of Congress Cataloging-in-Publication Data

Calvin and science / edited by Richard C. Gamble.
     p.   cm. — (Articles on Calvin and Calvinism ; v. 12)
    Includes bibliographical references.
    ISBN 0-8153-1053-6 (alk. paper)
    1. Calvin, Jean, 1509-1564—Views on science. 2. Religion and science—History—
16th century. 3. Science—History—16th century. 4.Copernicus, Nicolaus, 1473-
1543. I. Gamble, Richard C. II. Series.
BX9418.A74 1992 vol. 12
284'.2 s—dc20
[261.5'5'092]   92-29576
                                     CIP

Printed on acid-free, 250-year-life paper
Manufactured in the United States of America

Contents

Introduction

The sixteenth century brought not only a revolution in religion, but also great social upheaval in the areas of economics and politics, as well as changes in science. The newly invented printed books provide a convenient source of evidence for the state of science in the sixteenth century. At the beginning of the century, knowledge was still rudimentary and largely dependent on confused digests of ancient and Arabic sources. By mid-century there appeared works that surpassed the best of their predecessors. In astronomy, there was the *De revolutionibus* (1543) of Nicolaus Copernicus, a technical masterpiece as well as a revolutionary treatise on cosmology. In anatomy, the Belgian Andreas Vesalius created a new approach to anatomical research and teaching in his *De fabrica* (1543). In mathematics, the Italian Gerolamo Cardano advanced algebra (providing the general solution of the cubic equation) in his *Ars magna* (1545). This volume explores the relationship between Calvinism and the rise of modern science.

Ten   The Reformation and the Rise of Modern Science: Luther, Calvin, and Copernicus

The first half of the sixteenth century witnessed two revolutionary movements in the intellectual history of the West. Twenty-six years after Luther's theses on indulgences had shaken the Western church (1517), the strange theories of Nicholas Copernicus were published at Nuremberg (1543) and called in question the medieval picture of the cosmos. Neither event was a revolution in itself. Copernicus was fully aware of his forerunners in the ancient world, and his heliocentric theory required the criticisms and observations of his successors before the scientific revolution was complete. Others, before Luther, had tried to reform the Roman Church; and it could be argued that, viewed in the context of European intellectual history as a whole, his religious "revolution" was not much more than a minor disturbance within medieval thought. Not until the Enlightenment were Christian ways of thinking about God and man radically transformed. Still, the Protestant Reformation and Copernican astronomy were, at the very least, parts of two incomplete revolutions, and their coincidence in time invites inquiry into the relations between them. The later development of Copernican astronomy and the wider question of Protestantism's place in the modern world may be left outside the limits of this inquiry.

The relations of religion and science in the Reformation era were not confined to astronomical matters. Andreas von Carlstadt, for example, had his doubts about medical science and suggested that the sick should turn to prayer, not to the physician.[1] Again, the man who discovered the pulmonary circulation of the blood, Michael Servetus, was burned in Protestant Geneva.[2] Of course, he was not condemned for his physiological opinions. But one may still wish to argue that Calvin's religious fanaticism delayed the physiological advances that might have resulted from the discoveries of Servetus.[3] Moreover, if there was nothing in the Christian revelation to contradict the pulmonary circulation of the blood, one of the charges brought against Servetus was that he had cast doubt on revealed geography: whereas the Old Testament called Palestine a land

163

1

flowing with milk and honey, Servetus reproduced a statement of Ptolemy's according to which Judaea was notoriously barren.[4] In his widely read work, *A History of the Warfare of Science with Theology in Christendom*,[5] Andrew Dickson White quite properly took note of such aspects of his subject. It is only for reasons of manageability that attention is focused, in the present essay, on Luther and Calvin and their attitudes toward astronomy. Other reformers and other sciences could have been chosen.

Even when the theme "the Reformation and the rise of modern science" has been so circumscribed, opinions about it are sharply divided. On the one side, it has been argued that the Continental Reformation, in each of its two major branches, proved itself hospitable to the new science. Lutheran men of learning played a prominent role in the publication of Copernicus's theories, and the principles of Reformed (or Calvinistic) theology were supposedly an important incentive to scientific research. On the other side, it is alleged that Protestant biblicism greeted the new astronomy with enraged opposition, and that by their obscurantism Luther and Calvin delayed acceptance of the heliocentric hypothesis. The Reformers, it is said, repudiated Copernicanism by quoting Scripture and initiated a campaign of suppression which was as vehement, but not as effective, as the Roman Church's silencing of Galileo. Bias, perhaps, has played its part in the debate, and even among the defenders of Protestantism interest may sometimes be divided along confessional lines. Be that as it may, the question has to be faced whether, in actual fact, Luther and Calvin really were biblical literalists in their attitudes toward natural science. The answer is that Luther in his so-called "doctrine of twofold truth" and Calvin in his "principle of accommodation" were operating with theories of theological language which made a conflict of biblical and Copernican science unnecessary. The relation between Reformation and science thus appears to be many-sided, and it is still perhaps an open question.[6]

I

Copernicus boldly dedicated his major treatise to Pope Paul III. But the dedicatory preface reveals the author's misgivings.[7] He is trying, in fact, to obtain the pope's protection against the expected slanderers; hence the judicious flattery of His Holiness as himself a learned mathematician. Diplomatically, Copernicus mentions the interest of Cardinal Nicholas Schönberg, of Capua, and Tiedeman Giese, bishop of Culm, together with "not a few other most eminent and learned men." Moreover, he represents his theory, not as an unprecedented novelty, but as a return to a neglected strand of antiquity, made necessary by difficulties in the accepted mathematics.[8] Copernicus anticipates that there will be those who oppose him on the basis of "some place of Scripture wickedly twisted to their purpose." But he hints, too, that his findings may be of practical utility to the church, since efforts under Leo X to reform the ecclesiastical calendar had failed for lack of accurate astronomical data. Copernicus did not live to witness either the religious controversy over his work or its ecclesiastical utility. The first copies of his *De revolutionibus orbium coelestium* (1543) reached him on his deathbed.

Among the "eminent and learned men" who showed interest in Copernicus's researches were certain Lutherans, whom he wisely neglected to name in his dedicatory letter. Although the *De revolutionibus* was not published until 1543, the manuscript was apparently completed much earlier (possibly by 1530), and the ideas it contained were not unknown in learned circles. A preliminary account had appeared in the *Commentariolus*, which Copernicus had written during the first decade of the century and distributed in manuscript among his friends.[9] In the spring of 1539, a young Wittenberg professor of mathematics, Georg Joachim Rheticus, was sufficiently intrigued by the rumors to pay a personal visit to Frauenburg in East Prussia (Ermland), where Copernicus was a prominent canon in the cathedral chapter. Rheticus became one of the keenest advocates of the new astronomy. The next year he published a preliminary report on Copernicus's findings;[10] and when he returned to Wittenberg (1541), he had been commissioned by Copernicus to publish the *De revolutionibus*.

The suggestion that Rheticus found himself persona non grata at Wittenberg has not been demonstrated from the sources.[11] The truth is that Copernicus's great work was published through the goodwill of the Lutherans, even—remarkably enough—the goodwill of those Lutherans who disapproved of Copernicus's thesis. Rheticus did not stand alone as the solitary Copernican among the associates of Luther. It was the Lutheran theologian Andreas Osiander who furnished *De revolutionibus* with an anonymous preface. One of Luther's closest friends and co-workers, Caspar Cruciger, professor of theology at Wittenberg, made no secret of his admiration for Copernicus. Erasmus Reinhold, a mathematician at the university, openly praised Copernicus and based a set of astronomical tables (the *Tabulae Prutenicae*) on his calculations. The evidence, then, seems perfectly plain: Copernicus won some of his keenest advocates among the Lutherans; and those Lutherans who remained unconvinced at least tolerated their more adventurous colleagues, even encouraged them.[12]

Reformed scholars were not so intimately involved in the early dissemination of Copernicanism. It is possible that at Geneva, as in Wittenberg, champions of the old and the new astronomy taught side by side during the sixteenth century.[13] But with regard to Calvinism the somewhat different claim is made that Reformed theology was in some degree a nursing mother to scientific research. Attention has been drawn to evidence that Protestants in general have predominated over Roman Catholics among the leading scientists of modern Europe, and that within Protestantism the Reformed churches (at least until the nineteenth century) played the larger role in nurturing men of science.[14] In this connection, the case of Calvinist Holland is particularly interesting. The telescope and the microscope are both claimed as Dutch inventions; the Reformed Christians of the Lowlands expressed their gratitude to God for deliverance from Roman Catholic powers by founding the University of Leyden; and many Dutch Calvinists distinguised themselves by their passion for the natural sciences.[15] Even when allowances are made for patriotic and confessional loyalties, the evidence may seem sufficient to catch the historian's attention, though not every historian is likely to be impressed.[16]

Various attempts have been made to explain the evidence by analysis of the Calvinist mentality. In fact, there is a parallel here to the attempts of Max Weber and others to establish a correlation between the Calvinist "ethic" and the "spirit" of modern capitalism.[17] It is noteworthy that S. F. Mason's attempt to explain the historical correlation of Protestantism and science echoes, in part, Weber's explanation of the connection between Protestantism and capitalism. The followers of Calvin, according to Mason, "experienced an imperative need to know whether they were predestined." They obtained this assurance through the performance of good works, including scientific activity, which was valued as beneficial to mankind. Hence the Calvinistic-Puritan mentality was not merely congruous with scientific activity but provided it with "a positive impulse," since it was able to use science for the attainment of religious ends.[18]

Other features of the Calvinist tradition have been highlighted as possible incentives to scientific activity: Mason finds a further "congruence between the early Protestant ethos and the scientific attitude" in Protestantism's antiauthoritarian appeal to religious experience and individual interpretation of the Scriptures.[19] W. F. Dankbaar maintains that the most significant feature of Calvin's Academy at Geneva was the way in which the entire pursuit of science was subsumed under the religious duties of glorifying God and christianizing society. Similarly, Prince William the Silent desired that at the University of Leyden science, in the service of God and for his glory, should dedicate its powers to the good of both church and society, religion and freedom. The scientific enterprise was given a certain religious dignity through its inclusion under the rubric of glorifying God.[20] Others have sought the clue in the Calvinistic doctrine of common grace, according to which truth in every domain comes from God, so that the quest for truth is an act of piety which honors him.[21] Finally, it is claimed that the doctrine of predestination, so boldly emphasized in the Reformed tradition, was "the strongest motive in those days for the cultivation of science." For God's decrees are the sure foundation of nature's laws, and scientific inquiry depends on confidence in the unity, stability, and order of nature.[22]

None of these attempts to explain the sympathy between Calvinism and the scientific temper amounts, I think, to a convincing demonstration, even if we

4

grant the historical correlation which they seek to explain. Both the explanations and the correlation itself need further research. Mason's thesis concerning the Calvinistic use of science in the quest for assurance is not substantiated.[23] Dankbaar's argument, though more persuasive, is qualified by the admission that the University of Leyden was modeled on humanistic and medieval patterns, so that one cannot speak of a distinctively Calvinistic style of scientific activity.[24] Further, it may be asked, what makes even the "Calvinistic" concept of glorifying God anything more than a Christian commonplace, a vision shared by medieval educators as well? Nevertheless, the glory of God, common grace, and predestination—though none of them individually is without its counterparts in other Christian traditions—do seem to me, when taken together and given a special prominence, to be indicative of a distinctively Calvinistic view of the world and a corresponding Calvinistic "ethic." The vocation of the scientist receives a religious dignity,[25] and it may even be that the mechanics of providential working in Calvinist theology furnished a kind of midway point between the unpredictable angel- (and demon-) filled world of the Middle Ages and the deterministic order of seventeenth-century science. This much could be maintained without claiming that science everywhere had to cross over this particular bridge.

II

If, then, some of Copernicus's key advocates were enlisted from Lutheran circles, and if there seems to have been a certain affinity between Calvinism and the scientific temper, why has it been repeatedly maintained that Protestantism arrested the advance of modern science? The answer is that a kind of sacred tradition has been faithfully transmitted in the literature, both English and foreign,[26] according to which the first generation of Reformers initiated a campaign to suppress the new astronomy. The origins and foundation of this tradition are seldom examined by those who pass it on. And it has to be conceded that some who write as the avowed champions of science have been strangely reluctant to transfer the scientific temper and method into the domain of history.

The five main features of the tradition can be readily enumerated, though they do not always appear together. First, Luther, Melanchthon, and Calvin rejected the heliocentric hypothesis.[27] Second, they refuted Copernicus by quoting Scripture.[28] The first point is correct, and the second, as we shall see, two-thirds correct: Luther and Melanchthon did reject Copernicanism on biblical grounds. But from this evidence it is assumed, third, that the Reformers were in principle opposed to scientific investigation[29] and, fourth, that they sought to suppress the Copernican viewpoint.[30] This, as far as I can judge, is an unwarranted inference from the first point and is already refuted by our previous discussion.

5

Finally, it is suggested that, if Copernicanism nevertheless flourished in Protestant lands, this was only because the Protestants were less effective than the Roman curia in silencing scientific heretics.[31] This, too, is a suggestion which seems unnecessary in the light of our previous conclusions, since no campaign of repression was in fact undertaken during the Reformers' lifetime.[32] It remains, then, to examine the actual sources in which Luther, Melanchthon, and (allegedly) Calvin expressed opposition to Copernicus on biblical grounds.

By 1539, even before the publication of his major work, Copernicus had become a topic for conversation in Wittenberg. It was in the spring that Rheticus left for Frauenburg, to obtain firsthand information from Copernicus himself. The same year, on 4 June, Copernicus and his theories came up for discussion in Luther's household, and the Reformer's admiring disciples jotted down notes on the master's astronomical opinions. Here is Lauterbach's version of the discussion:

> Mention was made of some new astrologer [*sic*] who would prove that the earth moves and not the heaven, sun, and moon, just as if someone moving in a vehicle or a ship were to think that he himself was at rest and that the earth and the trees were moving. But [Luther's response] this is the way it goes nowadays: anyone who wants to be clever should not be satisfied with the opinions of others [*der soll ihme nichts lassen gefallen, was andere achten*]. He has to produce something of his own, as this man does, who wants to turn the whole of astrology upside down. But even though astrology has been thrown into confusion, I, for my part, believe the sacred Scripture; for Joshua commanded the sun to stand still, not the earth.[33]

The parallel passage in Aurifaber's version of the *Table Talk* includes the remark greatly beloved and faithfully reproduced in the secondary literature: "The fool wants to turn the whole art of astronomy upside down."[34] In general, Lauterbach is to be considered the more reliable reporter, so that there must be some doubt about the authenticity of the notorious "fool" clause.[35] Nevertheless, even without it the passage seems to be plainly anti-Copernican.

To be sure, Wilhelm Norlind has read Lauterbach's version as complimentary to Copernicus. "Now it is very curious," he remarks, "that, according to Aurifaber, Luther may *first* seem to praise the man ('er muss ihm etwas Eigens machen') and *then* blames him as a 'Narr'!" Since the disparaging expression *der Narr* was not in the corresponding passage of "the more trustworthy Lauterbach," we are bound, so Norlind maintains, to "regard the 'famous' expression given by Aurifaber as an interpolation not consistent with the text." It could be replied that Luther is not commending Copernicus for his inventiveness, but disparaging him for wanting to be thought clever.[36] In any case, the main point is sufficiently clear: Luther thought he could refute Copernicus by quoting

6

Scripture, though he did not therefore try to prevent the spread of Copernican astronomy.[37]

Melanchthon, too, like Luther, adduced scriptural arguments against Copernicanism.[38] But Melanchthon was not simply a theologian. He was also a philosopher of the humanistic type, and he held astronomical opinions on non-theological grounds. For him, the study of nature rested upon the authority of the approved ancients—that is, Aristotle and Ptolemy. Hence the greater part of his case against Copernicus consisted of arguments drawn from antiquity.[39] In other words, Melanchthon believed himself to be taking up the debate against a misguided effort to revive outmoded science. Nonetheless, he did not permit his disagreements to intrude upon his friendships nor even to detract from his respect for Copernicus.[40] So far from initiating a campaign of repression, he somewhat mitigated his criticisms after 1549.[41] Still, it must be admitted that Melanchthon, like Luther, thought it legitimate to refute a scientific theory with scriptural arguments. Moreover, he repaired the fateful alliance of theology and Aristotelianism that Luther had shattered; and thereby he created for later Protestantism a problem that did not exist for Luther and Calvin.[42]

As notorious as the "fool" passage in Luther's *Table Talk* is the rhetorical question commonly attributed to Calvin: "Who will venture to place the authority of Copernicus above that of the Holy Spirit?" But although the question is faithfully transmitted in the English literature, the exact reference does not accompany it, and it has so far proved impossible to locate it in any of Calvin's known writings. I have seldom come across it (or its equivalent) in the foreign literature;[43] and I suspect that its currency in English and American studies is the most striking proof of the influence of A. D. White. In White's own words:

> Calvin took the lead, in his *Commentary on Genesis*, by condemning all who asserted that the earth is not at the centre of the universe. He clinched the matter by the usual reference to the first verse of the ninety-third Psalm, and asked, "Who will venture to place the authority of Copernicus above that of the Holy Spirit?"[44]

Where, then, did White himself find Calvin's question, since it cannot be found either in the *Commentary on Genesis* or in the exposition of Psalm 93?

In a splendid piece of detective-work Edward Rosen has tracked the citation back to F. W. Farrar, who likewise offered only the "quotation," not the reference.[45] Rosen explains this omission by giving a rather mischievous turn to a eulogy of Farrar by his son, who wrote: "Quotation with him [F. W. Farrar] was entirely spontaneous, almost involuntary, because his marvellous memory was stored, nay saturated with passages." The famous Calvin quotation seems, in fact, to be a fiction due to Farrar's overconfidence in his marvelous memory. Rosen concludes: "What, then, ... was Calvin's attitude toward Copernicus?

Never having heard of him, Calvin had no attitude toward Copernicus."[46] This, perhaps, says too much. It is hardly necessary to suppose that Calvin had never heard of Copernicus. What is plain, however, is that if he knew of Copernicus, he felt no compelling need to quarrel with him. It has not even been established that Calvin once mentioned Copernicus in all his voluminous writings.[47]

III

It remains true, however, that the Lutheran reformers, at any rate, did oppose Copernicanism with arguments drawn from Scripture. A. D. White and others were perfectly right in seeing here a phase in the warfare between science and theology, even though they constructed false inferences upon the evidence, some even magnifying rejection of the Copernican theory into an imaginary campaign of suppression. Luther and Melanchthon set the pattern for later Protestant biblicism, according to which the sacred Scriptures furnish inerrant information on scientific matters. The basis was already laid, by the first generation of Lutheran reformers, for what Draper called "the fatal maxim that the Bible contained the sum and substance of all knowledge useful or possible to man."[48] Luther and Melanchthon assumed that not only the meaning of the gospel, but also the scientific picture of nature could be read off from the pages of Scripture, literally interpreted. This much is clear enough in the sources used by White. It must now be pointed out, however, that gross injustice is done to Luther by the extraordinary procedure of isolating a solitary passage from the *Table Talk* and assuming that his entire attitude toward the natural sciences—and indeed the sacred Scriptures—is adequately presented in this stray, offhanded remark.

According to White, the Reformers "turned their faces away from scientific investigation."[49] Even in the narrow sense of modern English usage, which virtually identifies "science" with natural science, this statement is incorrect. Luther had a lively interest in scientific progress and explicitly raised the question of the relationship between science and theology.

It is true that a superficial reading of Luther could uncover further apparent evidence of hostility towards science. Part of the difficulty is resolved when one recalls that the natural sciences in the sixteenth century were entangled in sorcery, alchemy, and astrology. Some of Luther's judgments can only be understood as an attempt to disentangle science from quackery. What looks at first like an obscurantist assault on "natural philosophy" may turn out to be a protest against unwarranted procedures in science. "Those who lie about far-distant lands, lie with all their might, there being none with experience to contradict them." But science is tied to experience. For Luther, the two sources of knowledge were experience (*erfarung*) and revelation.[50] They correspond to

8

philosophy and theology respectively, or to reason and faith (the two modes of cognition).[51] And by "philosophy" Luther understood the sum total of the human "sciences." Hence he admired astronomy as an empirical science, but had no respect for astrology:[52] and he contrasted the astrologer's predictions with the physician's prognosis, which has "symptoms and experience" as its guide.[53]

Luther was not ignorant of the fact that he lived in an age of scientific progress. He greeted the new science with enthusiasm and liked to contrast himself in this respect with the humanist Erasmus. In the advance of scientific knowledge he saw the gradual recovery of Adam's dominion over the world of nature.[54] Reason was understood by Luther as the divinely given organ by which man was to move out into the world and have mastery over it.[55] Hence he did not need to become defensive when science and Scripture ran into apparent conflict. He was willing, for example, to accept the astronomers' conclusion that the moon was the smallest and lowest of the "stars": perhaps the Scriptures, in calling the sun and the moon two great lights, were simply describing the moon as it looks to us.[56] Luther recognized that religious and scientific interest in nature are two different things. The light of the moon was for him, religiously, a token of divine care; but he acknowledged that the astronomer's concern was to show how the moon's light was in fact reflected from the sun.[57] In other words, even when theology and science are directed to a common object, like the heavenly bodies, they talk about it in different, but not necessarily exclusive, ways. Faith penetrates beyond the visible object to the unseen God, whose gracious care the object attests.[58]

It is the attempt to distinguish the proper spheres of theological and philosophical language that lies behind Luther's interest in the so-called medieval "theory of double truth."[59] As usually formulated, the theory maintains that a proposition may be true in theology but false in philosophy, and vice versa. It seems to have been not so much a consciously formulated doctrine as an accusation leveled against theological opponents,[60] and it is commonly assumed that the accused were guilty of a dishonesty which tokened the bankruptcy of scholastic theology.[61]

In his important *Disputation on the Proposition, "The Word was made flesh"* (1539),[62] Luther states explicitly, though without using the expression "double truth," that the same thing is not true in different disciplines. And yet his intention is not to allow, but to exclude, the possibility of contradiction between two disciplines. It remains axiomatic that one truth agrees with another.[63] Luther begins by affirming that the proposition "The Word was made flesh" is true in theology, but simply impossible and absurd in philosophy (thesis 2). In the course of the disputation the objection is made that if the same thing is true in theology and false in philosophy, then philosophy and theology contradict each other. Luther's reply, in effect, is that there can only be contradiction *within* a particular language system, not *between* one system and another.[64] "God is

9

man" and "God is not man" would only be contradictory if both were asserted in the same discipline.[65] The fact is that the words "God is man" do not mean for the theologian what they mean for the philosopher. The philosophical sense of the word "man" is "self-subsistent person"; but when the theologian speaks of the Incarnation, he has in mind "a divine person bearing humanity."[66] Similarly, in the syllogism "Every man is a creature, Christ is a man, therefore Christ is a creature" there are really four terms, not the required three, since "man" has a different sense in the major premise than it has in the minor.[67]

In his distinction between the two uses of the word "man" Luther was borrowing from the Schoolmen. But he turns a scholastic distinction against the Paris Schoolmen themselves, and argues that if they find it necessary to invoke the notion of equivocalness, then they ought really to agree with him. That is, they should not attempt a reconciliation of theology and philosophy, but should concede his point that the same thing is not true in both theology and philosophy. A proposition could only be said to be true in both contexts if the terms of the proposition were used with the same significance.[68] In answer to a further objection, Luther insists that the propositions "God is man" and "Every man is a creature" are both "simple." He means, I take it, that they are unambiguous within *either* context, theology *or* philosophy.[69] But if you compare their meaning across disciplines, so to say, they are not strictly the same propositions, because (as Luther has already shown) the terms are differently used. We cannot admit ambiguity into our syllogisms *within* any discourse; we have to keep them unambiguous by distinguishing the disciplines.[70] When we observe the necessary distinction, then the fact that one discipline seems to affirm what another denies proves not to be a genuine contradiction.[71] The need to maintain the distinction of the diciplines is what Luther intends by thesis 14: Lady Reason must do as the Apostle says, and keep quiet in church.[72]

What Luther suggests, then, against the Sorbonne—that "mother of errors"— might properly be called a "theory of multiple discourse" rather than a "theory of double truth." Neither "double" nor "truth" expresses his position accurately. He is concerned with various disciplines, not just two (since "philosophy," in his parlance, is the sum of the departmental sciences); and with truth only indirectly, as a consequence of his theory of meaning. His thesis is that each of the various disciplines *(professiones)* operates with its own special discourse. Words and propositions do not have a fixed meaning in a universal language. Their meaning is relative to a particular discourse. A word transferred from one discourse to another may have a different meaning in its new context or even no meaning at all. Hence it is a mistake to ask how many lines there are in a pound, or how many feet there are in a pint; and in geometry you do not reckon up pounds and ounces.[73] If this principle holds true within philosophy—that is, among the various sciences *(artes)*—it is all the more true when we compare philosophy with theology, which works, from a wholly different kind of data.[74]

10

The conclusion is, then, that much more can be said about Luther and science than is contained in the notorious fool-passage. Not only did Luther take a lively interest in scientific progress, he also reflected about the relation of science and theology—that is, about the place of theology among the various university disciplines. And his overriding intent is plain: to give each discipline autonomy in its own "sphere." Admittedly, his reflections in the *Disputation* are not fully developed. But they are not out of harmony with his general theological position, in which theology and philosophy are related to the doctrine of the two realms. The thesis that the same word or proposition changes its meaning (and therefore its truth value) if transferred from one realm to the other is fundamental to Luther's thoughts on justification and ethics.[75] Words are like coins, which are acceptable currency only in the area where they are minted;[76] and the various disciplines are like the distinct spheres which God has placed in the heavens.[77] Clearly, it was Luther's intention to allow the various disciplines full autonomy within their own limits. But apparently he forgot at the dinner table on 4 June what he had argued in a public disputation on 11 January. Or, at least, he failed to draw the consequences. Even so, an obvious injustice is done to him if his dinner conversation is treated as the better source for his opinions on theology and science.

IV

The features of Calvinistic theology which may be viewed as inducements to a scientific interest in nature have already been noted. It hardly needs to be demonstrated that they have their source in Calvin's own thinking, even though later Calvinists may have developed the master's thoughts beyond the limits he himself imposed.[78] Calvin was intensely interested in the world of nature, on which he saw the manifest traces of God's handiwork. The world is a "mirror," in which God may be viewed.[79] It is the "theater" of God's glory, and men are placed in it as spectators.[80] True, since Adam's fall most people walk like blind men in this divine theater. But the Word of God is given to restore our eyesight— to furnish us, as Calvin puts it, with spectacles.[81] And although the evidences are open even to the unlearned, men of science are privileged to penetrate more deeply into the secrets of divine wisdom.[82] We should be guilty of base ingratitude if we failed to acknowledge the bountiful hand of God both in the works of nature[83] and in the human intelligence which comprehends them.[84] Of course, Calvin was not himself a "scientist" in our sense; that was not his special calling.[85] And only a faithful admirer could describe him as a *savant*, of prodigious erudition, who knew just about all there was to be known in his day.[86] But it is hardly true that Calvin "appears to have had no taste for the sciences."[87] On the contrary, he writes almost enviously of the astronomer, to whom the

11

intricate workings of providence were more openly displayed than to other men.[88] And, like Luther, he felt a corresponding disdain for the astrologers, who abused the study of the heavens.[89]

It still has to be asked, however, whether Calvin left the scientists free from theological interference. Did he recognize the autonomy of science as well as its religious utility? It seems that, unlike the Lutheran reformers, he did not oppose the new astronomy on biblical grounds. But this is not necessarily to his credit; it may indicate only that he was less well informed than they. The real question is whether or not he believed that there are theological criteria for statements about the natural order. He ought, in principle, to have been freed from the practice of using Scripture as a source of scientific information, since he could present the christological content of the Bible as, so to say, an intellectual limit. That is, he affirmed that the function of the Bible was to furnish knowledge of Jesus Christ, so that our minds, as we read the Scripture, should come to a halt when this goal is attained.[90] From which one must justly infer that the Bible does not furnish, in addition, revealed information about astronomy. But in actual fact Calvin was no more consistent than Luther in maintaining a "christocentric" view of the Bible.[91]

It has been suggested by Albert-Marie Schmidt that Calvin bequeathed to his disciples as a criterion of scientific truth, not the letter of Holy Scripture, but "the test of God's glory as Scripture reveals it generally."[92] To which it must be replied that such a criterion would end the autonomy of science just as effectively as the biblical literalism of Luther's notorious *Table Talk*. But not one shred of evidence is advanced to demonstrate that this was in fact Calvin's approach to questions of secular learning. It is one thing to believe that the pursuit of science will give access to the glory of God, quite another to use God's glory as a test for scientific truth. Further, although Schmidt treats the opinions of Lambert Daneau (Danaeus) under the rubric *rédaction de la doctrine,* he is obliged to begin by drawing attention to the differences between the author and the redactor. Calvin considered as true all the scientific information contained in the Bible, but he set no limits on the scientific activity of the human spirit by which the information was to be elucidated. Daneau, on the other hand, spoke as though there were no need to look beyond the letter of Scripture, and he expressly opposed "those who deny that a knowledge of physics can truly and properly be learned from sacred Scripture."[93] If, then, Calvin's disciple performed the useful service of gathering what Calvin himself had sown throughout his various writings, it remains true, as Schmidt concedes, that he ruined the crop *(il dénature la récolte).*

More important is the fact, not mentioned by Schmidt, that Daneau explicitly rejected, or at least qualified, the hermeneutic principle by which Calvin was able to maintain simultaneously the truth of biblical science and the autonomy of natural science. True, Daneau admitted that there were some particulars concerning nature on which it is necessary to consult physicians and natural historians, "since that *Salomons* Bookes whiche were written copiously of the Nature of all thynges, are, through the negligence of men, perished." Cosmological questions, however, are not of this kind, but are chiefly to be settled by appeal to Scripture, inasmuch as the Author of Nature is best qualified to discourse about it. The contrary view, Daneau points out, rests on two arguments: that natural philosophy and divinity are two distinct disciplines, and that because Mosaic science is "fitted to our capacitie," an exact knowledge of nature is "other whence to bee drawne." In rejecting these contrary arguments, Daneau claims that Moses wrote "barely [i.e., in a plain style], but rightly." Calvin, on the other hand, went further, as did Luther, and made the language of Mosaic astronomy relative to the viewpoint of an untutored observer.[94]

According to Calvin, the forms of revelation are adapted in various ways to the nature of man as the recipient. His general term for the several types of adaptation is "accommodation."[95] It is axiomatic for Calvin that God cannot be comprehended by the human mind. What is known of God is known by revelation; and God reveals himself, not as he is in himself, but in forms adapted to man's capacity.[96] Hence in preaching he commuicates himself through a man speaking to men,[97] and in the sacraments he adds a mode of communication adapted to man's physical nature.[98] Now, in speaking of the Bible, Calvin extends the idea of accommodation beyond the mode to the actual content of revelation, and argues that the very diction of biblical language is often adapted to the finitude of man's mind. God does not merely condescend to human frailty by revealing himself in the prophetic and apostolic word and by causing the Word to be written down in sacred books; he also makes his witnesses employ accommodated expressions. For example, God is represented anthropomorphically as raising his hand, changing his mind, deliberating, being angry, and so on.[99] Calvin admits that accommodated language has a certain impropriety about it.[100] It bears the same relation to divine truth as does the baby talk of a nurse or a mother to the world of adult realities.[101]

Calvin allows for yet another form of accommodation, which is a concession, not to the finitude or sensuousness of human nature as such, but to the special limitations of the people to whom the scriptural revelation was originally given. For example, under the old dispensation spiritual benefits were depicted as earthly goods, and this is no longer necessary since the manifestation of the gospel in Jesus Christ.[102] Again, because of the uncultured state of the ancient Israelites, not only language about God and salvation but also language about the created order had to be "accommodated." Just as anthropomorphisms represent God, not as he is in himself, but as he seems to us,[103] so biblical statements about nature may represent the heavenly bodies as they appear to a simpleminded observer, and not as the astronomer would describe them scientifically.[104]

The principle of accommodation in this sense—that is, in the sense of condescension to the unlearned—underlies Calvin's entire exposition of the "history of creation." He expressly points to a number of statements in Genesis 1-3 as accommodated to the mentality or the received opinions of a simple folk.[105] And he repeatedly affirms that throughout the entire narrative Moses spoke in a popular, not a scientific, manner.[106] The story has, in fact, a strictly religious purpose: to make the believer aware by *revelation* of what he would see, were it not for the dullness of his vision, simply by *observation*, namely that he is placed in the world as a spectator of God's glory.[107] Biblical affirmations about the heavens and the planets are not scientific statements but inducements to thankfulness, and they are therefore expressed in a homely style which even the simplest believer can understand. They are made from the standpoint of an unlettered man, who is simply using his eyes. For instance, the expression "great lights" in Genesis 1:16 does not refer to the actual size of the sun and the moon, but to the amount of light that an ordinary person observes coming from them. The expressions are relative to the observer. The moon simply *looks* bigger than the other planets, though in fact Saturn *is* bigger. Nor was it relevant to Moses' purpose to mention that the moon borrows light from the sun.[108]

If any are disdainful of this biblical simplicity, Calvin warns that they will "condemn the entire economy of God in ruling the church."[109] On the other hand, it would also be wrong to oppose the science of astronomy just because its conclusions are contrary to popular opinion. Astronomy is both enjoyable and useful, since it unfolds the marvelous wisdom of God. The astronomer is worthy of our praise, and those who have the leisure and the ability should not neglect "this sort of exercise."[110] The Bible, however, is the "book of the unlearned." Anyone who wants to learn about astronomy must therefore look elsewhere.[111]

Calvin's cosmology was, of course, geocentric. But it was geocentric because he accepted the established astronomical views of his day.[112] Had he been confronted—as nobody in fact was during Calvin's lifetime—with convincing evidence for the heliocentric hypothesis, there is no reason to assume that he would have found the evidence embarrassing. He considered it an act of accommodation when the Psalmist spoke of the sun as passing from one end of the sky to the other. The Psalmist's aim was to evoke thankfulness by pointing to what the eye sees; had he been talking among philosophers, he might have mentioned that the sun completes its revolution around the other hemisphere.[113] Would it have been so difficult, then, for Calvin to assimilate the new ideas and to admit that the Psalmist's language was rather differently accommodating than he had imagined? As Calvin remarks on another psalm, it was not the Holy Spirit's intention to teach astronomy; he preferred to use "baby talk" *(balbutire)* rather than close the door of learning against the uneducated.[114]

V

The relations between natural science and the Protestant Reformation prove to be much more complex and fascinating than the standard quotations (and pseudo-quotation) have allowed. A complete discussion would need to take account of the contrast between Reformation and later Protestant attitudes towards science.[115] Worthy of attention, too, are the opinions of other Reformers—of Andreas Osiander, for example, whose anonymous preface to the *De revolutionibus* presented the heliocentric theory as a method of calculation, not as a claim to objective truth. Osiander's account of an astronomical "hypothesis" was not just a piece of shrewd diplomacy, but deserves to be taken seriously as an interpretation of scientific language different from Copernicus's own.[116]

Further, the cosmologies of Luther and Calvin themselves are not fully considered until their use of such theological terms as "heaven" and "hell" has been examined. They recognized that the theological and the cosmological use of the terms are not to be confused. Hence Luther refused to think of Christ's Ascension as comparable to climbing up a ladder.[117] And Calvin could only understand the Descent into Hell as Christ's experiencing in his soul the torments of a man forsaken by God.[119] The theology of the Reformers was less closely tied to a particular cosmology than might be expected; "demythologization" had already set in. The doctine of twofold truth (to retain the usual designation) and the principle of accommodation by no means exhaust their reflections on the nature of religious language. It is true that neither of them had a comprehensive theory of religious language; Calvin's principle of accommodation, for instance, was used chiefly as a problem-solving device, to be rolled out only when needed. But it is also true that the problems of theological discourse had occurred to them, precisely in the context of scientific questions. Their tentative moves toward a solution are not without historical interest, whether or not they make a permanent contribution to the debate between religion and science.

But what impact, if any, did their theological ideas make upon the actual development of science? Our conclusions have been partly negative: Luther and Calvin did nothing to *hinder* scientific progress. And there was no theological reason why they should. The Reformers were not literalists in the sense that they took all biblical statements about nature as literal reports of the plain truth. They were literalists in the sense that they insisted on taking the Scriptures in the meaning intended by their authors (or Author). A. D. White himself gives a good example of the kind of nonliteral exegesis which the Reformers deplored. He tells us that a Dominican preacher countered the researches of Galileo and his disciples with a sermon on Acts 1:11: "Why do you Galileans stand gazing up into heaven?" A "wretched pun," as White justly remarks.[119] The "literalism" of Luther and Calvin was designed to rule out allegories and other forms of fancy exegesis, but it still left room for maintaining the autonomy of natural science. Where the reigning astronomical opinions seemed to conflict with Scripture, they knew how to make the necessary adjustments. But this meant that they had to make the adjustments to Ptolemaic, not Copernican, science, precisely because the scientific revolution remained incomplete during their lifetime.[120]

If Calvin himself did not apply the principle of accommodation to the problem posed by the new science, Kepler and Galileo did so apply it[121] —which raises intriguing historical questions about the origins and dissemination of the principle. Not only did scientific interest in nature find a congenial ally in Calvinistic theology, but the principle by which leaders of the new science sought to avert a conflict between science and religion was a key notion in Calvin's theology. The currency of this principle in some circles—in Puritan England, for example— may have owed something to John Calvin.[122] In any case, the principle of accommodation, whatever the means of its transmission, assumes a historical importance not shared by Luther's reflections on double truth.

But by the time the scientific revolution was complete—let us say by the time Newton's *Principia* was published (1687)—the problem of religion and science had moved to a deeper level. It was no longer a question of reconciling Scripture with the heliocentric hypothesis, but of finding a place for God in the cosmos. The Newtonian world was causally self-contained, needing God only to set the mechanism in motion and to solve (at least temporarily) one or two problems that continued to resist scientific explanation. Was it enough, then, to concede the methodological autonomy of science?[123] Or does the scientist also demand an actual autonomy of the physical universe?[124]

CALVIN'S ATTITUDE TOWARD COPERNICUS

By Edward Rosen

> There will be a time when false and unprofitable
> professors will be made manifest and discovered.[1]

Bertrand Russell, in a book which has achieved an extensive distribution, quoted Luther's well-known denunciation of Copernicus as a fool, and then added:

Calvin, similarly, demolished Copernicus with the text: " The world also is established, that it cannot be moved " (Ps. 93:1), and exclaimed: " Who will venture to place the authority of Copernicus above that of the Holy Spirit? "[2]

Russell put this exclamation in Calvin's mouth without indicating on what occasion the Genevan reformer expressed his attitude toward the founder of modern astronomy.[3] This absence of any reference to a source for Calvin's exclamation should not surprise us, since Russell's *History of Western Philosophy* was " originally designed and partly delivered as lectures at the Barnes Foundation in Pennsylvania,"[4] where the students' primary interest is focused on a topic somewhat removed from the development of speculative thought. Moreover, in his preface Russell acknowledged that he owed

a word of explanation and apology to specialists on any part of my enormous subject. It is obviously impossible to know as much about every philosopher as can be known about him by a man whose field is less wide; I have no doubt that every single philosopher whom I have mentioned, with the exception of Leibniz, is better known to many men than to me. If, however, this were considered a sufficient reason for respectful silence, it would follow that no man should undertake to treat of more than some narrow strip of history. . . . On such grounds I ask the indulgence of those readers who find my knowledge of this or that portion of my subject less adequate than it would have been if there had been no need to remember " time's winged chariot."[5]

To withhold our indulgence from Russell would surely be ungracious. Nevertheless it is difficult to repress the feeling of curiosity aroused by his tantalizing omission of documentary support for Calvin's anti-Copernican exclamation. I for one, as a student of early modern science, would be happy to learn exactly when and where Calvin exclaimed against Copernicus.

[1] John Owen, *An Exposition of the Epistle to the Hebrews* (2d ed., Edinburgh, 1812–1814), IV, 605; Observation VII on 5:12–14.

[2] Russell, *A History of Western Philosophy* (New York, 1945; London, 1946), 528; Italian tr. by Luca Pavolini, *Storia della filosofia occidentale* (Milan, 1948), 3 vols.

[3] This lack of documentation did not prevent an American Catholic philosopher from accepting Russell's remarks about Calvin at face value; see Pierre Conway, O.P., " Aristotle, Copernicus, Galileo," *New Scholasticism* XXIII (1949), 58.

[4] Russell, *Hist. West. Phil.*, xi.   [5] *Op. cit.*, x–xi.

This information was not furnished by Russell when, in an earlier work which has been re-issued five times, most recently in 1956, he ascribed the same anti-Copernican exclamation to Calvin.[6] Neither in his *Religion and Science* (1935) nor in his *History of Western Philosophy* (1945) did Russell evince any first-hand acquaintance with writings by Calvin, as distinguished from writings about Calvin. But more than once in his *Religion and Science* Russell quoted from A. D. White, *A History of the Warfare of Science with Theology in Christendom,* " to which," Russell admitted, " I am much indebted." [7]

Andrew Dickson White (1832–1918) was a historian who helped to found Cornell University and became its first president. When sectarian criticism of the new university intensified, White tells us,

having been invited to deliver a lecture in the great hall of the Cooper Institute at New York, [I] took as my subject " The Battle-fields of Science." In this my effort was to show how, in the supposed interest of religion, earnest and excellent men, for many ages and in many countries, had bitterly opposed various advances in science and in education, and that such opposition had resulted in most evil results, not only to science and education, but to religion. This lecture was published in full, next day, in the *New York Tribune;* extracts from it were widely copied; it was asked for by lecture associations in many parts of the country; grew first into two magazine articles, then into a little book which was widely circulated at home, reprinted in England with a preface by Tyndall, and circulated on the Continent in translations, was then expanded into a series of articles in the *Popular Science Monthly,* and finally wrought into my book on *The Warfare of Science with Theology.*[8]

In his " little book " (1876) White mentioned Calvin twice: once to recall that the Jesuits deemed Galileo's *Dialogue* " more pernicious for Holy Church than the writings of Luther and Calvin," [9] and once to praise Calvin for having drawn a distinction between lawful interest on a loan and oppressive usury.[10] Many years later, in the articles which White contributed to *Popular Science Monthly,* he introduced the following passage:

While Lutheranism was thus condemning the theory of the earth's movement, other branches of the Protestant Church did not remain behind. Calvin took the lead, in his *Commentary on Genesis,* by condemning all who asserted that the earth is not at the centre of the universe. " Who," he said, " will venture to place the authority of Copernicus above that of the Holy Spirit? " [11]

[6] Russell, *Religion and Science* (London, 1935), 23; (New York, 1935), 20.

[7] *Op. cit.* (London), 84; (New York), 86.

[8] *Autobiography of Andrew Dickson White* (New York, 1905), I, 425.

[9] *Le Opere di Galileo Galilei,* national ed. (Florence, 1890–1909; reprinted, 1929–1939), XV, 25; cf. XVI, 458.

[10] White, *The Warfare of Science* (New York, 1876; re-issued, New York, 1893), 36, 129.

[11] White, " New Chapters in the Warfare of Science," *Popular Science Monthly* XL (1891–1892), 587.

The latter part of this passage was then expanded by White in his *Warfare of Science with Theology* (1896) to read as follows:

Calvin took the lead, in his *Commentary on Genesis*, by condemning all who asserted that the earth is not at the centre of the universe. He clinched the matter by the usual reference to the first verse of the ninety-third Psalm, and asked, " Who will venture to place the authority of Copernicus above that of the Holy Spirit? " [12]

If we now compare this final version of White's comments about Calvin with our opening quotation from Russell, we shall feel fully justified in concluding that it was from White, not from Calvin, that Russell took the anti-Copernican exclamation which interests us.

Russell was of course not the only writer who borrowed from White. For instance, William Ralph Inge, Dean of St. Paul's in London, asserted that " Calvin asked, ' Who will venture to place the authority of Copernicus above that of Holy Scripture? ' " [13] Dean Inge's substitution of " Holy Scripture " for " the Holy Spirit " need not deter us from recognizing his dependence on White. The latter was quoted more faithfully by a director of the Lick Observatory,[14] by some American historians of science,[15] and also by a highly successful popularizer.[16] Lastly, in his recent volume on *The Reformation*, Will Durant rated Calvin " ahead of his time in doubting astrology, abreast of it in rejecting Copernicus." [17]

These nine diverse authors may serve to exemplify the strong, broad, and enduring influence exerted by White's *Warfare* which, since its first publication in 1896, has been frequently re-issued, most recently in 1955. But if we want to know the source of the anti-Copernican exclamation attributed to Calvin, we shall not find the answer to our question in White. He, unlike Russell, was a professional historian. In his effort to comprehend Calvin's mentality, White read not only books written about the Genevan reformer, but also treatises composed by Calvin himself, including his *Commentary*

[12] White, *A History of the Warfare of Science with Theology in Christendom* (New York, 1896), I, 127.

[13] *Science, Religion, and Reality*, ed. Joseph Needham (New York, 1925), 359.

[14] Edward Singleton Holden, " Copernicus," *Popular Science Monthly* LXV (1904), 120: " To Calvin the pronouncement of Copernicus was sheer blasphemy. It seemed to him to lie entirely within the sphere of religion. Judged by the accepted standards of that sphere it was audacious heresy " (reprinted in *Scientific American Supplement* LVIII [1904], 24068).

[15] Henry Smith Williams, *The Great Astronomers* (New York, 1930), 236; Benjamin Ginzburg, *The Adventure of Science* (New York, 1930), 95; Grant McColley, " The Ross-Wilkins Controversy," *Annals of Science* III (1938), 166, with the 1919 re-issue of White's *Warfare* cited on p. 154; Thomas S. Kuhn, *The Copernican Revolution* (Cambridge, Mass., 1957; reprinted, New York, 1959), 192, with White cited at p. 281.

[16] Hermann Kesten, *Copernicus and His World*, English tr. by E. B. Ashton and Norbert Guterman (New York, 1945; London, 1946), 315–316; French tr. by Eugène Bestaux, *Copernic et son temps* (Paris, 1951).

[17] Durant, *The Reformation* (New York, 1957; *The Story of Civilization*, VI), 477, with the 1929 re-issue of White's *Warfare* listed in the bibliography on p. 952.

on Genesis.[18]   Yet when White assigned the anti-Copernican exclamation to
Calvin, he did not specify as his source any of the reformer's writings.   Instead, he said: "On the teachings of Protestantism as regards the Copernican theory, see citations in Canon Farrar's *History of Interpretation,* preface, xviii." [19]

Frederic William Farrar (1831–1903), in his long and distinguished
church career, was at various times canon and archdeacon of Westminster,
dean of Canterbury, and chaplain of the House of Commons as well as of
Queen Victoria.   In recognition of his ecclesiastical attainments he was invited to deliver the Bampton Lectures in 1885.   More than a century before,
the Rev. John Bampton, canon of Salisbury, had bequeathed his estate to
Oxford University for the purpose of endowing annual lectures, the first of
which were delivered in 1780.   Choosing the development of Biblical exegesis as the subject of his Bampton Lectures in 1885, Farrar upheld the freedom of interpretation.   He zealously maintained the traditional Protestant
right of private judgment, aware of but not bound by received opinion.
Hence he delighted in cataloguing the errors of earlier theologians: Lactantius ridiculed the idea that the earth was round, Augustine denied that
there were antipodes, and "'Who,' asks Calvin, 'will venture to place the
authority of Copernicus above that of the Holy Spirit?'" [20]

This anti-Copernican exclamation was taken, as we observed above, by
Russell from White, and by White in turn from Farrar.   But here our trail
ends in a blind alley, Farrar having failed to say where he found the exclamation which he imputed to Calvin.

If we wish to understand the reason for this failure on Farrar's part, let
us listen to his son and biographer:

In judging Farrar's work, and this is true not only of the *Life of Christ,* but
of all his books, it must not be forgotten that there are two orders of
scholars, the "intensive" and the "extensive" school, both necessary to the
world—those whose function is original research, and those whose function
it is to interpret and make available the labors of the former class, whose
work would otherwise remain buried under its own weight. And it was to
this latter class that my father unquestionably belonged.[21]

Farrar's son further informs us that his father was "up to the eyes in pastoral and literary work, [and] burdened with a large correspondence." [22]
Not only was Farrar overworked, but

expression was easy to him; he poured out his ardent soul as the Spirit gave
him utterance, and without effort lavished from the rich treasures of his
memory garnered stores of poetic illustration and historic parallel. . . .
Quotation with him was entirely spontaneous, almost involuntary, because
his marvelous memory was stored, nay, saturated with passages.[23]

[18] *Warfare,* I, 10, 28.

[19] *Warfare,* I, 128; at I, 83–84, White lauded Farrar's behavior during the
controversy over Darwin's theory of evolution; for another eulogy of Farrar's cour-
age, see White, II, 206.

[20] Farrar, *History of Interpretation* (London, 1886; New York, 1886), xviii.

[21] Reginald Farrar, *The Life of Frederic William Farrar* (New York, 1904), 193.

[22] *Op. cit.,* 255.   [23] *Op. cit.,* 255–256.

Even if we make every allowance for filial devotion, this portrait of a non-intensive scholar, overburdened with work, facile in expression, and relying on a marvelous memory for his quotations, inevitably creates a certain doubt in our minds. Did Farrar perhaps read in some other author the anti-Copernican exclamation to which he attached the name of Calvin? Our doubt grows deeper when we recall that in his preface Farrar candidly declared:

In a work which covers such vast periods of time and which involves so many hundreds of references it would be absurd to suppose that I have escaped from errors. All that I can say is that in this, as in my other works, I have done—not perhaps the best that I might have done under more favorable conditions of leisure and opportunity—but the best that was possible to me under such circumstances as I could command . . . . I beg the indulgent consideration of all who believe that I am actuated solely by the desire to do nothing against the truth.[24]

Despite this forthright disclaimer of infallibility, Farrar's unsupported ascription of the anti-Copernican exclamation to Calvin was repeated without hesitation not only by White and those who followed him, but also by Miss Dorothy Stimson, former dean of Goucher College. After quoting the exclamation from Farrar, Miss Stimson asserted that " Luther, Melanchthon, Calvin, Turrettin, Owen, and Wesley are some of the notable opponents " [25] of Copernicanism. Her assertion was echoed by the foremost German historian of astronomy,[26] from whom it passed into a biographical dictionary of German history.[27] The grave danger that the German-speaking world may now in the twentieth century begin to look upon Calvin as an outspoken adversary of the Copernican theory was increased by the publication of the German version of Kesten's popular book.[28]

As we have just seen, Miss Stimson accepted without reservation Farrar's attribution of the anti-Copernican exclamation to Calvin. But she balked at the following statement by Farrar: " ' Newton's discoveries,' said the Puritan John Owen, ' are against evident testimonies of Scripture.' " [29] Reporting that she was " unable to verify this statement," Miss Stimson astutely added that " Owen died [in 1683, four years] before the *Principia* was published in 1687." [30]

---

[24] F. W. Farrar, *History of Interpretation*, xxix.

[25] Dorothy Stimson, *The Gradual Acceptance of the Copernican Theory of the Universe* (Hanover, New Hampshire, 1917; New York, 1917), 41, 99. Although Miss Stimson listed (p. 131) the 1898 re-issue of White in her bibliography, and at pp. 100–104 cited White's discussions of other writers, for Calvin she relied on Farrar. She in turn was followed by the popular biographer Phillips Russell, *Harvesters* (New York, 1932), 75, with Miss Stimson cited at p. 301.

[26] Ernst Zinner, *Geschichte und Bibliographie der astronomischen Literatur in Deutschland zur Zeit der Renaissance* (Leipzig, 1941), 33; at p. 86 Zinner listed Miss Stimson's *Gradual Acceptance* among the works which he utilized.

[27] Hellmuth Rössler and Günther Franz, *Biographisches Wörterbuch zur deutschen Geschichte* (Munich, 1952), 478.

[28] Kesten, *Copernicus und seine Welt* (Amsterdam, 1948), 381; cf. n. 16, above.

[29] Farrar, *Hist. of Interpretation*, xviii.   [30] Stimson, *Gradual Acceptance*, 89.

21

Miss Stimson somehow failed to notice that Farrar treated Owen and Calvin differently. On the one hand, Farrar offered no source whatever for Calvin's anti-Copernican exclamation. On the other hand, according to Farrar, "John Owen (*Works*, XIX, 320) said that Newton's discoveries were 'built on fallible phenomena, and advanced by many arbitrary presumptions against evident testimonies of Scripture.'" [31] The words enclosed within single quotation marks were indeed used by Owen. [32] But his target was "the late hypothesis, fixing the sun as in the centre of the world," in other words, pre-Newtonian Copernicanism. Owen was not talking about "Newton's discoveries," despite Farrar's two misstatements to that effect.

This, then, is the sort of broken reed on which White leaned when he repeated Farrar's attribution of the anti-Copernican exclamation to Calvin. As we have already seen, Farrar did not designate any of Calvin's writings as the source of this exclamation. On the other hand, as the attentive reader will doubtless recall, one of Calvin's numerous publications was singled out by White when he declared that

while Lutheranism was thus condemning the theory of the earth's movement, other branches of the Protestant Church did not remain behind. Calvin took the lead, in his *Commentary on Genesis*, by condemning all who asserted that the earth is not at the centre of the universe. [33]

As was pointed out above, White was personally familiar with Calvin's *Commentary on Genesis*. [34] Yet it was not this work which White cited in his discussion of Protestant opposition to Copernicanism. On the contrary, he referred his readers to "Rev. Dr. Shields, of Princeton, *The Final Philosophy*, pp. 60, 61." [35]

Charles Woodruff Shields (1825–1904), "professor of the harmony of science and revealed religion in Princeton University," [36] published *The Final Philosophy* in the firm conviction that science and religion could be reconciled. Like his British counterpart Farrar, Shields found fault with earlier theologians who had impeded the advancement of science. To illustrate this regrettable tendency, Shields stated that

Calvin introduced his *Commentary on Genesis* by stigmatizing as utter reprobates those who would deny that the circuit of the heavens is finite and the earth placed like a little globe at the centre. [37]

[31] Farrar, *Hist. of Interpr.*, 432.

[32] *Exercitations concerning the Name, Original, Nature, Use, and Continuance of a Day of Sacred Rest*, Exercitation II = *An Exposition of the Epistle to the Hebrews*, Exercitation XXXVI, section 16 (*Works*, London, 1850–1855; re-issued, Edinburgh, 1862, XIX, 310).

[33] White, *Warfare*, I, 127.   [34] See n. 18, above.

[35] White, *Warfare*, I, 128; cf. I, 148; at I, 234 White cited Shields' "very just characterization of various schemes" for reconciling Genesis with geology.

[36] Shields so described himself on the title page of his book, *The Scientific Evidences of Revealed Religion* (New York, 1900).

[37] Shields, *The Final Philosophy* (New York, 1877; 2d ed., New York, 1879), 60; *Philosophia ultima* (New York, 1888–1905), I, 61.

Evidently White's assertion that "Calvin . . . in his *Commentary on Genesis* . . . condemn[ed] all who asserted that the earth is not at the centre of the universe " was based on Shields.

In trusting Shields, was White leaning on a stouter reed than Farrar proved to be?[38] With a view to answering this question, let us look at the following sentence in the Argument with which "Calvin introduced his *Commentary on Genesis*": "We indeed are not ignorant that the circuit of the heavens is finite, and that the earth, like a little globe, is placed in the centre."[39] "That the circuit of the heavens is finite and the earth placed like a little globe at the centre " is Shields' unmistakable echo. But Shields spoke of Calvin "stigmatizing as utter reprobates those who would deny that . . . the earth [is] placed like a little globe at the centre." In this passage of the Argument introducing his *Commentary on Genesis* Calvin did indeed speak harshly about persons professing certain other ideas, but the notion that the earth was at the centre of the universe was confidently affirmed by Calvin without referring to those who would deny it. Despite Shields, in this passage Calvin was not "stigmatizing as utter reprobates those who would deny that . . . the earth [is] placed like a little globe at the centre." As a reed on which to lean, Shields turns out to have been no less broken than Farrar.[40]

It was from Farrar that White took the unsupported anti-Copernican exclamation attributed to Calvin. It was from Shields that White took the misstatement about the condemnation of Copernicanism in the Argument introducing Calvin's *Commentary on Genesis*. But we should now recall

[38] "Owen . . . declared the Copernican system a ' delusive and arbitrary hypothesis, contrary to Scripture,' " said White (*Warfare*, I, 128), echoing Shields (*Final Philosophy*, 60–61; *Philosophia ultima*, I, 61–62). "Owen declared that Newton's discoveries were ' built on fallible phenomena and advanced by many arbitrary presumptions against evident testimonies of Scripture,' " said White (*Warfare*, I, 148), echoing Farrar (432). This anti-Newtonianism ascribed to Owen by Farrar and White was correctly discarded by Miss Stimson on chronological grounds. But was Owen as singlemindedly anti-Copernican as is implied by the curtailed quotation in Shields (echoed by White and by Henry Smith Williams, *Great Astronomers*, 235)? Owen goes on at once to say that, apart from theological considerations, there are against Copernicanism "reasons as probable as any that are produced in its confirmation . . . for it is certain that all the world in former ages was otherwise minded; and our argument is not taken, in this matter, from what really *was true*, but from what was universally apprehended *so to be*." Do not Owen's italics indicate his awareness that "what really was true " was Copernicus' rearrangement of the planets around the sun?

[39] Calvin, *Commentaries on the First Book of Moses called Genesis*, tr. John King (Edinburgh, 1847–1850), I, 61; re-issued, Grand Rapids, 1948. Calvin's works were collected in *Corpus reformatorum*, XXIX–LXXXVII (Braunschweig and Berlin, 1863–1900) = *Ioannis Calvini opera quae supersunt omnia*, I–LIX; for this passage, see *Calvini opera*, XXIII, 10.

[40] Yet Shields' thorough knowledge of Calvin's life and teachings was amply demonstrated in two spirited defences of Calvin's character and conduct, "The Doctrine of Calvin Concerning Infant Salvation " and "The Trial of Servetus," *Presbyterian and Reformed Review*, I (1890), 634–651, IV (1893), 353–389, as well as in Shields' play, *The Reformer of Geneva* (New York and London, 1898).

that White included the following third element in his formulation of
Calvin's attitude toward Copernicus: " He clinched the matter by the usual
reference to the first verse of the ninety-third Psalm." [41] With deplorable
reticence White declines to tell us where Calvin cited Ps. 93:1 against
Copernicus.

In the absence of such guidance from White, let us look at Calvin's
commentary on Ps. 93:1, the relevant portion of which reads as follows:

The heavens revolve daily, and, immense as is their fabric and inconceivable the rapidity of their revolutions, we experience no concussion—no disturbance in the harmony of their motion. The sun, though varying its
course every diurnal revolution, returns annually to the same point. The
planets, in all their wanderings, maintain their respective positions. How
could the earth hang suspended in the air were it not upheld by God's hand?
By what means could it maintain itself unmoved, while the heavens above
are in constant rapid motion, did not its Divine Maker fix and establish
it? [42]

We see that in Calvin's cosmology " the heavens revolve daily " [43] and the
sun has a " diurnal revolution." These two phenomena were interpreted by
Copernicus as mere appearances caused by the real rotation of the earth
around its axis once every twenty-four hours. Furthermore, in Calvin's
conception, the sun had an annual motion, which likewise was transformed
by Copernicus into an optical illusion produced by the actual revolution
of the earth around the sun once a year. The annual revolution and the
daily rotation were assigned by Copernicus to the earth, whereas Calvin
believed the earth to " hang suspended in the air " and to " maintain itself
unmoved." Clearly, Calvin's cosmology was pre-Copernican. But was it
anti-Copernican? Although we are told that Calvin " quoted Psalm 93
against Copernicus," [44] we look in vain for any anti-Copernican utterance
in Calvin's commentary on Ps. 93.

Theological opponents of Copernicus usually quoted Ps. 104:5 (God
" laid the foundations of the earth, that it should not be removed for ever "),
on which Calvin's comment begins as follows:

Here the prophet celebrates the glory of God, as manifested in the stability
of the earth. Since it is suspended in the midst of the air, and is supported
only by pillars of water, how does it keep its place so stedfastly that it cannot be moved? This I indeed grant may be explained on natural principles;
for the earth, as it occupies the lowest place, being the centre of the world,
naturally settles down there. [45]

Here we are reminded that Calvin believed the earth to be " the centre of

[41] White, *Warfare*, I, 127.

[42] Calvin, *Commentary on the Book of Psalms*, tr. James Anderson (Edinburgh,
1845–1849), IV, 6–7; re-issued, Grand Rapids, 1949; *Calvini opera*, XXXII, 16–17.

[43] Commenting on Ps. 19:4, Calvin says: " the firmament, by its own revolution,
draws with it all the fixed stars " (*Commentary on . . . Psalms*, I, 315; *Calvini
opera*, XXXI, 198).

[44] James Gerald Crowther, *Six Great Scientists* (London, 1955), 36.

[45] Calvin, *Commentary on . . . Psalms*, IV, 148–149; *Calvini opera*, XXXII, S6.

the world," where Copernicus stationed the sun. For Calvin, the motionless earth in the centre of the world posed a problem which he discussed as follows in his comment on Ps. 75:3: " The earth occupies the lowest place in the celestial sphere, and yet instead of having foundations on which it is supported, is it not rather suspended in the midst of the air? " [46] This concept of a stationary earth at rest in the air was picturesquely elaborated by Calvin in his sermon on the alphabetical Ps. 119:90 (" Thou hast established the earth, and it abideth ") : [47]

I beseech you to tell me what the foundation of the earth is. It is founded both upon the water and also upon the air: behold its foundation. We cannot possibly build a house fifteen feet high on firm ground without having to lay a foundation. Behold the whole earth founded only in trembling, indeed poised above such bottomless depths that it might be turned upside down at any minute to become disordered. Hence there must be a wonderful power of God to keep it in the condition in which it is.[48]

The Aristotelians explained the steadiness of the earth in a naturalistic way that was familiar to Calvin who, however, found their explanation inadequate:

The philosophers indeed hold that the earth stands naturally in the middle of creation, as it is the heaviest element; and the reason they give that the earth is suspended in mid-air, is, because the centre of the world attracts what is most heavy; and these things indeed they wisely discuss. Yet we must go further; for the centre of the earth is not the main part of creation; it hence follows that the earth has been suspended in the air, because it has so pleased God.[49]

On another occasion Calvin invoked the idea of an orderly cosmos to account for the stability of the earth, and he also took advantage of this opportunity to paint a vivid picture of the universe as a huge sphere. Preaching on the text of Job 26:7 (" He stretcheth out the north over the empty place, and hangeth the earth upon nothing "), Calvin declared:

It is true that Job specifically says " the north," and yet he is speaking about the whole heaven. And that is because the sky turns around upon the pole that is there. For, just as in the wheels of a chariot there is an axle that runs through the middle of them, and the wheels turn around the axle by reason of the holes that are in the middle of them, even so is it in the skies. This is manifestly seen; that is to say, those who are well ac-

[46] Calvin, *Commentary on . . . Psalms*, III, 186; *Calvini opera*, XXXI, 702.

[47] In Calvin's *Commentary on . . . Psalms*, IV, 469 (*Calvini opera*, XXXII, 253), this verse evoked only the brief remark " that the earth continues stedfast, even as it was established by God at the beginning."

[48] Calvin, *Two and Twentie Sermons . . . [on] the Hundredth and Nineteenth Psalme*, tr. Thomas Stocker (London, 1580), fol. 99v (somewhat modernized); *Calvini opera*, XXXII, 620: sermon 12, preached on April 9, 1553.

[49] Calvin, *Commentaries on the Book of the Prophet Jeremiah and the Lamentations*, tr. John Owen (Edinburgh, 1850–1855), II, 34; re-issued, Grand Rapids, 1950; *Calvini opera*, XXXVIII, 75–76. This John Owen (†1867) should not be confused with the Puritan John Owen (1616–1683).

quainted with the course of the firmament see that the sky so turns. For
on the north side there is a star apparent to our eye, which is as it were
the axle that runs through the middle of a wheel, and the skies are seen to
turn about the middle. There is another star hidden under us, which we
cannot perceive, and which is called the antarctic pole. Why? Because
the sky turns about that also, as though there were an axle to which the
wheel was attached, as has already been said. When I speak of this motion
of the heavens, I do not mean the course of the sun that we see daily,
since the sun has its own special movement, whereas this is a universal
motion of the whole firmament of heaven. And the said two stars are as it
were fastened to those places, so that they do not move or stir. Thus you
see why Job says: He stretcheth out the north .... The following is the
reason why he says: He hangeth the earth upon nothing. On what does the
earth rest? On the air. Just as we see the air above us, so is it likewise
on the other side of the earth, so that the earth hangs in the middle. True,
the philosophers often discuss why the earth stays this way, since it is at
the very bottom of the world; and they say it is a wonder that the earth
does not sink down, since nothing holds it up. Nevertheless they are able
to give no other reason than is seen in the order of nature, which is so
wonderful a thing.[50]

This extended discussion shows us how well Calvin absorbed the astronomy taught in his youth. Lest anyone suppose that he thought further
research unnecessary, let us recall his comment on Genesis 1:16:

Astronomers . . . investigate with great labor whatever the keenness of
man's intellect is able to discover. Such study is certainly not to be disapproved, nor science condemned with the insolence of some fanatics who
habitually reject whatever is unknown to them. The study of astronomy
not only gives pleasure but is also extremely useful. And no one can deny
that it admirably reveals the wisdom of God. Therefore, clever men who
expend their labor upon it are to be praised and those who have ability and
leisure ought not to neglect work of that kind.[51]

Obviously it was not lack of interest in astronomy that kept Calvin from
attacking Copernicus. Nor would his exegetical principles have compelled
Calvin to contradict Copernicus. For, although the Genevan reformer
" despised the allegorical method of interpreting Scripture, which had provided Christians with their favorite means of twisting the Bible into a religious book of their own liking," [52] he himself did not advocate or practice a
narrow literalism. Thus, commenting on Ps. 136:7, Calvin asserted:

The Holy Spirit had no intention to teach astronomy; and, in proposing
instruction meant to be common to the simplest and most uneducated persons, he made use by Moses and the other prophets of popular language,
that none might shelter himself under the pretext of obscurity, as we will see
men sometimes very readily pretend an incapacity to understand, when anything deep or recondite is submitted to their notice. Accordingly . . . the

[50] Calvin, Sermons . . . upon the Booke of Job, tr. Arthur Golding (London,
1574), 490 (somewhat modernized); Calvini opera, XXXIV, 429–430.
[51] Calvin: Commentaries, edd. Joseph Haroutunian and Louise Pettibone Smith
(London, 1958; Library of Christian Classics, XXIII), 356; Calvini opera, XXIII,
22.
[52] Haroutunian and Smith, in Calvin: Commentaries, 23.

Holy Spirit would rather speak childishly than unintelligibly to the humble and unlearned.[53]

Since Calvin believed that Scripture is sometimes couched in popular language to make it intelligible to the uneducated, he need not have felt himself bound by the letter of the most explicitly anti-Copernican passage in the Bible, namely, the miracle reported in Joshua 10:12–14:

Then spake Joshua to the Lord in the day when the Lord delivered up the Amorites before the children of Israel, and he said in the sight of Israel, Sun, stand thou still upon Gibeon; and thou, Moon, in the valley of Ajalon.
And the sun stood still, and the moon stayed, until the people had avenged themselves upon their enemies. Is not this written in the book of Jasher? So the sun stood still in the midst of heaven, and hasted not to go down about a whole day.
And there was no day like that before it or after it, that the Lord hearkened unto the voice of a man.

Concerning this mightiest weapon in the Biblical armamentarium of the anti-Copernicans, Calvin might have reasoned, as he did with regard to Genesis 1:16, that the author of the Book of Joshua " described in popular style what all ordinary men without training and education perceive with their ordinary senses." [54]   But Calvin did not apply this method of interpretation to Joshua's miracle.   Instead, in his *Commentarius in librum Iosue*, composed during the agony of his last illness, Calvin commented:

As in kindness to the human race He divides the day from the night by the daily course of the sun, and constantly whirls the immense orb with indefatigable swiftness, so He was pleased that it should halt for a short time till the enemies of Israel were destroyed.[55]

So Calvin wrote toward the close of his life, more than two decades after the publication of Copernicus' *Revolutions*.   What Calvin said about Joshua's miracle induced a nineteenth-century editor and translator of his works to remark: " One might almost suspect from this concluding sentence that Calvin was a stranger to the Copernican system." [56]   This incipient suspicion will inevitably grow stronger in our minds when we recall Calvin's treatment of Ps. 19:4–6, 75:3, 93:1, 104:5, 119:90, Jeremiah 10:12, and Job 26:7. Surely this ample body of evidence authorizes us to conclude, despite Professor Shields, Canon Farrar, President White, Miss Stimson, Dean Inge, Lord Russell, Father Conway, and Dr. Will Durant, that Calvin never demolished, condemned, rejected, opposed, or stigmatized as an utter reprobate the quiet thinker who founded modern astronomy.

What, then, may we ask at the end of our inquiry, was Calvin's attitude toward Copernicus?   Never having heard of him, Calvin had no attitude toward Copernicus.

The City College, New York.

[53] Calvin, *Commentary on . . . Psalms*, V, 184; *Calvini opera*, XXXII, 364–365.
[54] *Calvin: Commentaries*, edd. Haroutunian and Smith, 356; *Calvini opera*, XXIII, 22.
[55] Calvin, *Commentaries on the Book of Joshua*, tr. Henry Beveridge (Edinburgh, 1854), 153; re-issued, Grand Rapids, 1949; *Calvini opera*, XXV, 500.
[56] Henry Beveridge (1800–1863) in Calvin, *Commentaries on . . . Joshua*, 153.

SOME COMMENTS ON ROSEN'S "CALVIN'S ATTITUDE TOWARD COPERNICUS"

By Joseph Ratner

There are a number of errors, major and minor, in Rosen's "Calvin's Attitude toward Copernicus." (Cf. this *Journal*, XXI, 3 [July 1960], 431–41.)

1. Rosen ends up with two conclusions, one credible and one incredible. It is credible that some author erroneously ascribed an anti-Copernican statement to Calvin and that this error became established as historical truth. It is incredible that Calvin "never heard" of Copernicus. Rosen supplies some evidence for his first conclusion; he supplies none for his second. He simply argues from Calvin's "silence" to Calvin's "ignorance" and this is to be guilty of an elementary fallacy well-known to scholars even less erudite than Rosen. It may be contended that Rosen could not, in the nature of the case, produce any evidence for his second conclusion and therefore, if he was to draw it, he had to draw it as he did. To be sure, no evidence could be found in Calvin's writings for Rosen's second conclusion; but it is not inconceivable that, if his conclusion is true, evidence for it could be found in the correspondence or other writings of some of Calvin's contemporaries. Rosen does not reveal whether he has or has not sleuthed his way through the latter material.

The conclusion that Calvin "never heard" of Copernicus is incredible for at least two reasons. (a) Luther heard of Copernicus's work some four years or so before it was published; and Calvin lived for some twenty years after it was published. That knowledge of this work should not have reached Geneva in this span of time is incredible. (b) Traffic between Wittenberg and Geneva was constant and heavy. Even if knowledge of Copernicus's work did not come to Geneva by an independent route, it is incredible that it did not come via Wittenberg. This incredibility swells to practically infinite or infallible proportions when we remember that for some years the Copernican system was taught at Wittenberg by Reinhold.

Rosen is so enraptured with the scholarly sleuthing he did for the sake of his first conclusion, he apparently fails to appreciate the tremendous socio-cultural significance (or enormity) of his second conclusion. He tosses it in at the end the way the oldtime baker used to toss in the thirteenth roll.

2. Since Rosen's first conclusion is not incredible, there is no reason why it shouldn't be accepted—if Rosen's reading of Calvin's extant writings was sufficiently extensive, careful and competent. There is nothing Rosen says which enables one to judge whether his reading was or was not sufficiently extensive. That it was not, in all relevant respects, sufficiently careful and competent his remarks on Calvin's "exegetical principles" prove beyond any shadow of doubt. After two quotations from Calvin, one which "shows us how well Calvin absorbed the astronomy taught in his youth," and the other which is alleged to show us that Calvin did not think "further [astronomical] research unnecessary," Rosen states: "Obviously it was not lack of interest in astronomy that kept Calvin from attacking Copernicus. Nor would his exegetical principles have compelled Calvin to contradict Copernicus. For, although the Genevan reformer 'despised the allegorical method

382

28

of interpreting Scripture . . .' he himself did not advocate or practice a narrow literalism."

Rosen has packed into this statement two different arguments; the first, to put it mildly, obscures the real issue; the second, however it be put, is plainly false. The decision to attack or not to attack Copernicus did not in any way depend upon "interest" or "lack of interest" in astronomy. The issue at stake was the authority of Scripture or, what was the same thing for Calvin and all other Reformers, the authority of the Holy Spirit. The person who originally ascribed to Calvin the statement (quoted by Rosen at the beginning of his piece) "Who will venture to place the authority of Copernicus above that of the Holy Spirit?" clearly knew what the issue was; if he put these words into Calvin's mouth, he at any rate put in the right words. Rosen also obscures the real issue when he alleges that one of his quotations shows that Calvin did not think "further [astronomical] research unnecessary." In what sense "not unnecessary"? To verify or correct the astronomical views of the Holy Spirit? This is the only sense relevant to Rosen's inquiry, namely, Calvin's attitude toward Copernicus, and there is nothing in the quotation to support this sense. Why Rosen should indulge in this twofold obscuration of the real issue is difficult to understand; not that it is easy to understand why he should think that his quotations show that Calvin did not lack interest in astronomy when his own conclusion is that Calvin "never heard" of Copernicus!

Rosen's second argument is that Calvin's "exegetical principles" would not have "compelled" Calvin to attack or contradict Copernicus. This is true, but the reason Rosen gives for this truth is false. Neither Calvin nor Luther nor any other Reformer (nor any Catholic for that matter) had "exegetical principles" which "compelled" them to do anything. To suggest or imply that they had is to suggest or imply that their "exegetical principles" were comparable to the "principles" which regulate the inquiries of scientists. Nothing could be further from the truth. Calvin, like all the Reformers, had a variety of "exegetical principles" and in any particular case he used the "exegetical principle" which would promote the doctrine he espoused. The necessities of his doctrines determined his selection and use of his "exegetical principles"; it was not his "exegetical principles" which determined (or "compelled") him to espouse and defend or to reject and attack any given doctrine. Among the "exegetical principles" which Calvin used was "a narrow literalism" which Rosen, in flat contradiction to his own citations, declares Calvin "did not advocate or practice." The following example from Rosen covers both points: by way of introducing his quotation from Calvin's commentary on Joshua, Rosen says: "Calvin might have reasoned, as he did with regard to Genesis 1:16, that the author of the Book of Joshua 'described in popular style what all ordinary men without training and education perceive with their ordinary senses.' But Calvin did not apply this method of interpretation to Joshua's miracle." With regard to Genesis 1:16 Calvin uses one "method of interpretation" and with regard to Joshua's miracle he uses another. I assume that Rosen takes the phrase "method of interpretation" to be identical with "exegetical principle." If this assumption is wrong, then what is Rosen talking about? Calvin, by

Rosen's own showing, has at least two "exegetical principles" and one of them—the one used for Joshua's miracle—is "a narrow literalism." I am of course assuming that by "a narrow literalism" Rosen means "a narrowly literalistic" interpretation. If this assumption is wrong, and all Rosen means by "a narrow literalism" is that Calvin did not interpret every Scriptural passage literalistically, then Rosen's statement is, to put it mildly again, another example of his obscuring the real issue. Who ever said that Calvin (or any other Reformer) had one sole "exegetical principle" which he faithfully applied to Scripture, always and everywhere?

3. Rosen says that Calvin "might" have applied to Joshua's miracle "the method of interpretation" he applied to Genesis 1:16. Though Rosen does not explicitly say so, this is one of the pillars of his second conclusion: Calvin did not do what Rosen says he "might" have done because Calvin had "never heard" of Copernicus and therefore had no reason to take Joshua's miracle in any other way than literalistically (or with "a narrow literalism"). This is quite conclusive evidence that Rosen has made no study—or adequate study—of Calvin's mind, theological doctrines, or "exegetical" methodology. Calvin's interpretation of Genesis 1:16 is no basis for determining (conjecturally or otherwise) how Calvin "might" have interpreted Joshua's miracle had he in fact "heard" of Copernicus. What is at stake in the Joshuan case is the authenticity of Biblical miracles (as well as the astronomical authority of the Holy Spirit) and Calvin's position on Biblical miracles is clearly stated in his chapter on "The Sacraments" among other places:

The term *sacrament* . . . comprehends generally all the signs which God has ever given to men, to certify and assure them of the truth of his promises. These he has been pleased to place in natural things, and sometimes to exhibit in miracles. Examples of the former kind are such as these: when he gave Adam and Eve the tree of life, as a pledge of immortality . . . and when he "set" his "bow in the cloud" as a token to Noah and his posterity, that there should "no more be a flood to destroy the earth." These Adam and Noah had as sacraments. . . . The tree and the rainbow both existed before, but when they were inscribed with the word of God, they were endued with a new form, so that they began to be something they were not before. And that no one may suppose this to be spoken in vain, the bow itself continues to be a witness to us in the present age, of that convenant which God made with Noah. . . . Therefore, if any smatterer in philosophy, with a view to ridicule the simplicity of our faith, contend that such a variety of colours is the natural result of the refraction of the solar rays on an opposite cloud, we must immediately acknowledge it, but we may smile at his stupidity in not acknowledging God as the Lord and Governor of nature, who uses all the elements according to his will for the promotion of his glory. . . . Examples of the second kind were exhibited when God . . . watered the fleece with dew while the earth remained dry, and afterwards bedewed the earth without wetting the fleece, to promise victory to Gideon; when "he brought the shadow ten degrees backward in the dial" to promise recovery to Hezekiah.[1]

[1] Calvin, *Institutes of the Christian Religion*, tr. John Allen (Philadelphia, 1936[7]), II, 573–574.

Calvin's comments on the rainbow show (to follow Rosen) how well Calvin absorbed the relevant knowledge of his day. And since Rosen shows how well Calvin absorbed the astronomy taught in his youth, we can surely feel safe in saying that Calvin must have fully appreciated the fact that the Hezekiah miracle was at least as great as the Joshuan, if not greater: it involved not the mere suspension of the sun's motion, but its retrogression. If "any smatterer in philosophy" had ventured to object to the Hezekiah miracle, Calvin, we may be sure, would have smiled his fatal smile "at (the) stupidity" of the objector.

4. Rosen vastly, indeed, unbelievably, exaggerates the importance of his first conclusion. He writes: "The grave danger that the German-speaking world may now in the twentieth century begin to look upon Calvin as an outspoken adversary of the Copernican theory was increased by the publication of the German version of Kesten's popular book." Just what is this "grave danger"? Does the ascription to Calvin of the statement: "Who will venture to place the authority of Copernicus above that of the Holy Spirit?" in any way misrepresent Calvin's essential doctrine concerning the Authorship of Scripture and the authority of the Holy Spirit? Does it in any way misrepresent Calvin's essential attitude (truculent and ruthless) toward those who ventured to hold views which were not in conformity with his own? The statement, at the very most, makes of Calvin "an outspoken adversary of the Copernican theory" when he may not have been an "outspoken" one at all. If Calvin did not make the statement ascribed to him, the historical record should be set straight; and if Rosen does indeed set it straight, he should receive the commendation such kind of scholarly achievement properly deserves. However, to suppose, even for one moment, that by this kind of straightening out of the historical record a "grave danger" is averted is sheer nonsense.

Rosen underscores his nonsensical overevaluation in the "motto" for his piece which he takes from John Owen: "There will be a time when false and unprofitable professors will be made manifest and discovered." This "motto" struck me as apocalyptic and Rosen has confirmed that it is. The "time" Owen refers to is the time of the Second Coming, and "the false and unprofitable professors" are the "professors" of the false religions, including, naturally, the "professors" of the false (i.e. non-Owenite) versions of the Christian religion. For Rosen to suggest, in this outlandish way, that Farrar, White, Inge, and Russell (to select from Rosen's list only those with whose work I am somewhat familiar) are "false and unprofitable professors" because of the indifferent historical error he believes he has caught them in is fantastic.

5. Since Rosen is such a stickler for minutiae, he will welcome, I feel sure, my pointing out that he allows himself to speak (p. 441) of "the most explicitly anti-Copernican passage in the Bible." By virtue of the distinction which he makes on behalf of Calvin (p. 438), the Biblical passage is not "anti-" but "pre-" Copernican.

New York City.

[The editors regret having space only for Dr. Rosen's reply.]

A REPLY TO DR. RATNER

By Edward Rosen

According to my good friend Dr. Ratner, I supplied "some evidence" for the conclusion "that some author erroneously ascribed an anti-Copernican statement to Calvin." Actually I supplied not merely "some evidence," but decisive evidence, not about "some author," but about the fabricator of the erroneous ascription.

According to Dr. Ratner, I supplied no evidence for the conclusion that Calvin never heard of Copernicus. Actually I supplied the best available evidence: the complete silence about Copernicus in every one of Calvin's numerous discussions of astronomical topics. How else would this silence be explained by Dr. Ratner, who characterizes Calvin's attitude as "truculent and ruthless toward those who ventured to hold views which were not in conformity with his own"?

Dr. Ratner finds it "incredible that Calvin 'never heard' of Copernicus. . . . This incredibility swells to practically infinite or infallible proportions when we remember that for some years the Copernican system was taught at Wittenberg by Reinhold." For the assertion that Reinhold taught Copernicanism at Wittenberg, Dr. Ratner adduces no evidence whatever. Is he in fact doing anything more than uncritically repeating an earlier, equally unsupported, pronouncement that "Rheinhold [sic] continued to teach the Copernican system at Wittenberg"?[1]

Regulations governing the curriculum of the University of Wittenberg were printed in 1545, two years after the publication of Copernicus' *Revolutions*. For all students of the liberal arts, attendance was prescribed at lectures "expounding the elements of astronomy as compiled by John Sacrobosco," the author of a rudimentary medieval textbook; candidates for the master's degree were in addition required to learn "planetary theory and Ptolemy's *Great Syntaxis*."[2] These 1545 regulations were in force until modified, seven years after Reinhold's death, in 1560. In that year Kaspar Peucer was added as an alternative to Sacrobosco for elementary students; for advanced students, Proclus was coupled with Peurbach's planetary theory and Ptolemy's *Syntaxis*.[3] In short, throughout the period when Reinhold taught at Wittenberg, the entire curriculum in astronomy was thoroughly Ptolemaic. The official record of public lectures delivered at Wittenberg from 1540 to 1561 contains no reference to Copernicanism, and the same blackout pervades Reinhold's ceremonial addresses as dean in 1549 and rector in 1550.[4]

During the seventeen years when Reinhold was professor of mathematics at Wittenberg, the university's thinking was dominated by Luther's chief lieutenant, Melanchthon, author of the 1545 curriculum regulations. In 1539 Luther called Copernicus a fool.[5] In 1541 Melanchthon denounced the

[1] Preserved Smith, *The Age of the Reformation* (New York, 1920), 622.
[2] Walter Friedensburg, ed., *Urkundenbuch der Universität Wittenberg* (Magdeburg, 1926), 257.   [3] *Op. cit.*, 303–304.
[4] Ernst Zinner, *Entstehung und Ausbreitung der coppernicanischen Lehre* (Erlangen, 1943), 264.
[5] *D. Martin Luthers Werke*, Weimar edition, *Tischreden*, I, 419.

"crazy thing" done by "that Polish astronomer, who makes the earth move and the sun stand still. Really, wise governments ought to repress the impudence of the intellectuals." [6] In the first edition of a textbook published in 1549 Melanchthon again declared, with reference to Copernicanism, that "public proclamation of absurd opinions is indecent and sets a harmful example." [7] Melanchthon's son-in-law, Kaspar Peucer, Reinhold's pupil and successor, repudiated Copernicanism as offensive and not fit to be taught in the schools.[8] Yet Dr. Ratner asks us to believe "that for some years the Copernican system was taught at Wittenberg by Reinhold" in this bellicosely anti-Copernican atmosphere.

How could such an egregious historical blunder ever get into print? In his 1542 edition of Peurbach's *New Theory of the Planets* Reinhold lauded Copernicus as an "outstanding technician, who has aroused in everybody great expectations for a revival of astronomy; . . . his godlike intellect will not undeservedly be admired by all posterity." In his *Prussian Tables* of 1551 Reinhold once more heaped huge gobs of praise on Copernicus, as a technical astronomer and geometer. Hasty readers leaped to the conclusion that these eulogies signified Reinhold's adherence to Copernicanism. However, Reinhold insisted that he had taken nothing from Copernicus but "the raw observations and the outlines of the proofs." And the unpublished manuscript of Reinhold's commentary on Copernicus' *Revolutions* discloses that Reinhold was an anti-Copernican: "where I put the earth, Copernicus put the sun" in the center of the universe.[9] Reinhold was not the only practical astronomer in the XVIth century who utilized Copernicus' observational data while rejecting his conception of the cosmos. The long accepted belief in Reinhold's Copernicanism should be discarded in the garbage can reserved for hoary myths about the history of ideas.

Dr. Ratner remarks that I made a statement "after two quotations from Calvin." I count eight, and then three more; each of these eleven quotations was selected from a much larger number to illustrate an aspect of my argument. Dr. Ratner suggests that my reading of Calvin may have been "not sufficiently extensive." What essential passage did I overlook?

Dr. Ratner says that my reading of Calvin was not "sufficiently careful." Let us see who is the careful reader. Calvin declared: "Astronomers . . . investigate with great labor whatever the keenness of man's intellect is able to discover. Such study is certainly not to be disapproved. . . . Therefore, clever men who expend their labor upon it are to be praised and those who have ability and leisure ought not to neglect work of that kind." Concerning this passage Dr. Ratner makes the comment that it "is alleged to show us that Calvin did not think 'further [astronomical] research unnecessary.' " Where is the element of doubt that would justify Dr. Ratner's use of the word "alleged" ?

Without any doubt this passage proves that Calvin favored the study of astronomy for the sake of "whatever the keenness of man's intellect is able

[6] *Corpus reformatorum*, IV, 679.   [7] *Corp. ref.*, XIII, 217.

[8] Peucer, *Hypotheses astronomicae* (Wittenberg, 1571), dedication.

[9] *La Science au seizième siècle* (Paris, 1960), 176.

to discover." By my saying so, Dr. Ratner charges, I obscure the "real issue" of the authority of Scripture. In Calvin's time the authority of Scripture was a dogma, not a real issue. It is not an issue, real or unreal, in my note, where the real issue was Calvin's attitude toward Copernicus. On that issue I have thrown sorely needed new light. I have obscured nothing.

Dr. Ratner contends that my citations from Calvin contradict my statement that Calvin "did not advocate or practice a narrow literalism." The latter is put by Dr. Ratner "among the exegetical principles which Calvin used." But narrow literalism cannot be among exegetical principles; by its very nature, narrow literalism is an exclusive principle of interpretation, which rejects all alternative principles. My citations from Calvin, far from contradicting, confirm my statement that Calvin was not a narrow literalist. By saying so, Dr. Ratner charges a second time, I obscured the "real issue." Is this the same "real issue" as before (the authority of Scripture), or is this a different "real issue"? Dr. Ratner is obscure about what real issue I obscured.

Dr. Ratner insists that "Calvin's interpretation of Genesis 1:16 is no basis for determining (conjecturally or otherwise) how Calvin 'might' have interpreted Joshua's miracle had he in fact 'heard' of Copernicus." But isn't Calvin's interpretation of one Biblical passage a proper basis for supposing (not "determining") how he might have interpreted another Biblical passage?

Genesis 1:16 classifies both the moon and the sun as "lights" or self-luminous bodies. But Calvin knew that, whereas the sun is self-luminous, the moon is not. In this conflict between science and Scripture, Calvin realized that Scripture is wrong. Hence, resorting to a non-literal interpretation of Genesis 1:16, he wrote that it "described in popular style what all ordinary men without training and education perceive with their ordinary senses." This device, used here to eliminate the moon's self-luminosity from Scripture, could likewise have been employed to get rid of the earth's motionlessness.

My reference to the "grave danger" of a further spread of a historical falsehood is deemed by Dr. Ratner to be a "nonsensical overevaluation." Will any historian of ideas agree with his judgment? If our discipline is to prosper, our facts must be right. The uncritical repetition of falsifications, however ingenious, is a grave disservice to the cause of truth.[10]

The City College, New York.

[10] Research students will be interested in the following remarks in an unsolicited letter of Professor B. S. Ridgely, sent to me Dec. 31, 1960, and quoted here with his permission. "Would that I had known of your study sooner, for I would have been saved considerable confusion and waste of time at the Bibliothèque Nationale! For I was working in France, as I have been for a number of years, on the general problem of the extent and nature of the influence of the 'new astronomy' on French literary imagination in the XVIth and XVIIth centuries, and spent a considerable amount of time trying to track down Calvin's alleged comments about Copernicus, with absolutely no success, as you can well imagine."

[In this *Journal*, XXI (1960), 436, line 4, read "*Works*, XIX, 310."]

R. *Hooykaas* (Holland)

CALVIN AND COPERNICUS

I. INTRODUCTION

"Who", asks Calvin, "will venture to place the authority of Copernicus above that of the Holy Spirit?". This quotation from F.W.Farrar's *"History of Interpretation"* [1] (1886) found its way into numerous scholarly and popular works through mediation of A.D.White (1896), who in his widely read book accused Calvin of having taken the lead in the campaign against Copernicanism. [2]

Many years ago I was the first to point out in several international periodicals concerned with the history of science, that the "quotation" from Calvin is spurious. [3] I became suspicious of its authenticity because it does not fit in with Calvin's exegetical principles and because a similar quotation, allegedly borrowed from the Independent divine John Owen, could immediately be proven to be spurious. According to Farrar, Owen wrote: "Newton's discoveries are against evident testimonies of Scripture". [4] In the same work Farrar tells us *where* Owen said so: [5] "When John Owen (*Works* XIX, p. 310) said that Newton's discoveries were "built on fallible phenomena, and advanced by many arbitrary presumptions against evident testimonies of Scripture, his sentences may stand as but one specimen ... of exegetical errors". In fact, however, Owen, after mentioning the order of the planets according to the ancient system, continued: "What alteration is made herein by the late hypothesis fixing

---

[1] F. W. Farrar, *History of Interpretation*, London, 1886, p. XVIII.
[2] A. D. White. *A History of the Warfare of Science with Theology in Christendom*, London, 1896, p. 127.
[3] R. Hooykaas, "Thomas Digges' Puritanism", *Arch. internat. hist. Sc.*, vol. 8, 1955, p. 151; idem, "Science and Reformation", *J. World History*, vol. 3, 1956, pp. 136–8 (several times reprinted, a.o. in S. N. Eisenstadt ed.: *The Protestant Ethic and Modernization*, New York, 1968, pp. 211–39); *Rev. Hist. Sc.*, vol. 8, 1955, p. 180; *Philosophia Libera*, London, 1957, pp. 12–14.
[4] F. W. Farrar, *op. cit.*, p. XVIII.
[5] *Ibid.*, p. 432, n. 2.

the sun as the centre of the world, built on fallible phenomena, and
advanced by many arbitrary presumptions, against evident testimonies
of Scripture and reasons as probable as any that are produced in its confirmation, is here of no consideration". [6] Newton is not at all mentioned
and it would indeed have been odd if he were, for Owen's work is
dated January 1671, whereas Newton's *Principia* was published in 1687,
that is, after Owen's death.

A. It was proved by my articles (1) that in Calvin's commentaries on
Bible texts with cosmological implications there was not the slightest
indication of hostility towards Copernicanism as (2) he just ignored that
issue.

B. A second claim I made in my earlier publications was that Calvin's
exegetical method furthered the acceptance of the Copernican system by
his co-religionists.

More recently, some American authors repeated the claim I made in
my first points A(1) and A(2), without reference to my earlier statements.
As they reached a wide audience, one may say that until quite recently
the informed reader had to believe that Calvin hardly knew, or at any
rate never mentioned, the Copernican system. It should be emphasized
that also widely recognized "calvinologists", like Auguste Lecerf [7] and
Pierre Marcel [8] had arrived at the conclusion that Calvin never condemned the theory of the motion of the earth.

A few weeks ago professor W. Voisé kindly sent me an article by
R. Stauffer, in which is given incontrovertible proof that Calvin did know
the Copernican system and that he was dead against it. [9] Stauffer found
in the 8th sermon on chapters 10 and 11 of Paul's first epistle to the
Corinthians a passage which, though, not mentioning Copernicus by name,
energetically rejects the central position of the sun and the motion of the
earth. [10] On the other hand, the secondary point at issue, *viz* the spurious-
ness of the Calvin quotation by Farrar and White, is fully recognized. [11]

R. Stauffer does not level his criticism at my own publications, and
this is quite understandable: being an outsider in the history of science,
he had no reason to suppose that earlier publications touching this subject did exist, as the specialists whose articles he read did not mention
them. But, having in the past also put forward the theses he combats,
I feel justified to reconsider the whole problem and to see in how far my
earlier conclusions (A1 and A2 and B) may stand in the light of this new
find.

---

[6] *The Works of John Owen D. D.* ed. *W. H. Goold*, Edinburgh-London, 1854,
vol. XIX, p. 310.
[7] A. Lecerf, *Etudes calvinistes*, Neuchâtel, 1949, p. 116.
[8] Cf. *Revue réformée*, vol. 69, 1966, p. 51.
[9] R. Stauffer, "Calvin et Copernic", *Ann. Musée Guinet., Rev. Hist. d. Religions*,
vol. 179, 1971, pp. 31–40.
[10] *Ibid.*, p. 31.
[11] *Ibid.*, p. 37.

II. CALVIN'S THEORY OF ACCOMMODATION

From the beginning of the christian era it had been held by theologians that the Holy Spirit, speaking to Man through prophets and apostles, accommodated himself to the human capacity of understanding by using anthropomorphic terms, e.g. when saying that God is angry, or that he repents. In order to prevent too free a use of such an exegetical principle, the Council of Trent demanded that biblical exegesis should be as literal as possible and that in no case should be deviated from the exegesis given by the Church Fathers and the acknowledged doctors of the Church. The question at issue between Galileo and the Inquisition mainly regarded these points. Galileo recognized that his cosmology should be conformable to the Bible, but he pretended that the exegesis of texts with a cosmological or astronomical implication should not be left to ancient or modern theologians alone, but that the help of better-informed professional scientists was indispensable. [12]

On the other hand, Calvin went much farther than other theologians when stressing the twofold character of the Bible, a divine revelation doubtless, but adapted to weak, human understanding, a heavenly message couched in inadequate human language. In his commentary on Psalm 58:45 ("They are like a deaf adder that stops her ear, which will not hear the voice of the charmers, charming never so wisely"), he has doubts about the possibility of charmers charming serpents and of adders stopping their ears. But, as the psalmist's intention is not to combat biological errors but rather to bring home to the reader an ethical message, the psalmist uses a striking metaphor borrowed from common popular belief: "David borrowed he similitude out of the common error, as if he had said, there is no wiliness to be found in serpents which reigns not in these men; yea, though it be so that adders be fenced by their own slyness against enchantments, yet are these men as crafty as they". [13]

In contrast to many of his contemporaries, Calvin did not expect the apostles and prophets to be supernaturally endowed with infallible scientific knowledge. Just as the "Word made flesh" (Christ) took on the form of a servant and voluntarily submitted to the limitations of humanity, so the Word that became Scripture had, in his opinion, its glory hidden and had assumed human frailty, sometimes even manifest in an uneloquent style of writing (at first sight, a serious shortcoming in the eyes of such an accomplished humanist as Calvin was). [14]

On the other hand, Calvin's doctrine of "common grace" prevented

---

[12] Cf. "Galileo on Scripture and the Motion of the Earth", in: R. Hooykaas, *Religion and the Rise of Modern Science*, Edinburgh–London, 1972, pp. 124–6 and 129.

[13] J. Calvin, *Commentaries on the Psalmes*, 1957, LVIII, 4–5.

[14] J. Calvin, *Commentary on Romans*, V, 15.

any wholesale disavowal of the scholarly heritage of the Greeks. Especially Greek astronomy and anatomy were highly praised by him, and he urged those "who have leisure and ability", not to neglect astronomical research. [15]

One might expect, then, that Calvin would follow the practice of the main Church Fathers and medieval doctors and that he would project Greek cosmology into Scripture. On the contrary, however, he recognized more clearly than his contemporaries that there was a discrepancy between the Aristotelian astronomy still prevalent in his own days and the world picture given in the Bible: whereas the Book of Genesis speaks of *one* expanse, the astronomers make a distinction between several spheres or heavens. Whereas Genesis calls the sun and moon the "great lights", the astronomers prove by conclusive reasoning that the little star of Saturn is greater than the moon. [16]

Calvin, being a layman in astronomy, could hardly be expected to do anything else than take for granted the system of the world that had been generally accepted since Antiquity and was still held by practically all contemporary astronomers and philosophers. But, having so keenly realized the incompatibility of this Aristotelian world picture with the naive world picture of the Bible, one might perhaps expect that he would reject the former, or at least correct it, in order to reconcile it with the words of the Bible. Calvin, however, has another explanation of the difference between Genesis and the astronomers: in his opinion Moses wrote in a popular way and described what all ordinary people are able to follow, whereas the astronomers investigate whatever the sagacity of the human mind can understand. [17]

According to Calvin, the Spirit of God has opened a common school for all; Moses was ordained a teacher of the unlearned as well as of the learned and therefore chose what is intelligible to all; had he spoken of things generally unknown, the uneducated might have pleaded in excuse that such subjects were beyond their capacity, and therefore Moses "rather adapted his writing to common usage". Calvin evidently wanted to base his exegesis on the Reformation doctrine which held that the message of the Bible is accessible to everybody and not to a select group of scholars only, and, moreover, that it does not purport to teach scientific truths but only religious and moral doctrine. The Bible, so he says, is "a book for laymen"; "he who would learn astronomy and other recondite arts, let him go elsewhere". [18]

In Calvin we meet with a leading biblical exegete who, while recog-

---

[15] J. Calvin, *Commentaries upon the First Book of Moses, Called Genesis,* transl. J. King, Edinburgh, 1874, I, 16.
[16] J. Calvin, *Commentary on Genesis,* I, 16.
[17] *Ibid.,* I, 6 and 16.
[18] *Ibid.,* I, 15, 16.

nizing the authority of Holy Scripture in religious and ethical matters, tries to demonstrate that it does not give information on scientific issues and that in cosmological matters it adapts itself to the conceptions of the common people. The Holy Ghost had not the purpose to teach us astronomy, but he "chose rather to stammer with us, than to shut up the way of learning from the vulgar and unlearned sort". [19]

His respect for the work of the astronomers made him accept the current Ptolemaic astronomy in spite of its being incompatible with the literalistic interpretation of the biblical text. If, then, one may accept the Aristotelian or the Ptolemaic geocentric system as objective truth, in spite of its being incompatible with the letter of the Bible, one is also free to admit that the Copernican heliocentric system might be true without its being in the Bible.

It is quite irrelevant whether Calvin himself was a Copernican or not; if one accepts his exegetical principles, one can no longer appeal to the authority of the Bible in order to combat the doctrine of the motion of the earth.

We should realize, however, that the Reformed Churches never were committed to Calvin's theology in the same way as the Lutheran churches were bound to Luther. They took rise with Zwingli (Zürich), Oecolampadius (Basel), Bucer (Strasburg) and others, *and* Calvin (Geneva), and the latter merely was the most influential and the greatest exegete of them all. But many of his followers in dogmatic theology and church discipline, felt free not to follow him in his bold way of interpretation. On the other hand, we might expect that astronomers who held the theory of the motion of the earth and who had read Calvin's commentaries, would reject "biblical" arguments against their theory, with a reference to *his* exegetical principles. [20]

We have elsewhere demonstrated that this took place indeed. [21] Edward Wright (1600), Philips van Lansbergen (1619 and 1629), Jacob van Lansbergen (1633) and John Wilkins (1638 and 1640) rejected attacks on the Copernican system that had been made with an appeal to biblical texts, by repeating Calvin's arguments for the non-scientific character of biblical "cosmology". Jacob van Lansbergen emphatically mentioned that he borrowed his arguments from "our Calvin" (Calvinus noster), though he fully realized that Calvin did "not intend to write on behalf of Copernicus". John Wilkins, too, repeatedly mentioned Calvin's name in corroboration of his view that Scripture does not use scientific language and,

---

[19] J. Calvin, *Comment on the Psalms*, CXXXVI, 7.
[20] R. Hooykaas, "Thomas Digges' Puritanism", *Arch. intern. hist. sc.*, vol. 8, 1955, p. 151.
[21] Cf. *J. World History*, vol. 3, 1956, pp. 135–7; *Philosophia Libera*, London, 1957, pp. 12–13; *Religion and the Rise of Modern Science*, Edinburgh–London, 1972, pp. 122–4, 126–35.

therefore, should not be adduced against Copernicanism. [22] Even Kepler's exposition of the relevant biblical texts, practically coincided with Calvin's ideas.

The Roman-Catholic priest L. Fromondus (1631), not without good reasons, called Lansbergen's expositions a "copernicano-calvinistic theology".

The protestant theologian Gisbertus Voetius (1635), who was a violent opponent of the doctrine of the motion of the earth, when advising beginners in theological studies about which commentaries on Genesis they should read, recommended (in spite of his anti-papalism) that of the Jesuit B. Pereira. This strict "calvinist" kept silence about Calvin's commentary, because he realized that, if he followed Calvin's way of interpretation, this would weaken his anti-Copernican position.

III. CALVIN'S REJECTION OF THE EARTH'S MOTION

R. Stauffer's find does not alter the fact that White's and Farrar's "quotation" from Calvin about the incompatibility of Copernicanism and the Biblical text is fruit of their imagination. But we cannot maintain any longer that Calvin never mentioned the doctrine of the earth's motion, and we should not rashly say that Copernicus' name was unknown to him. [23] Stauffer emphasizes that those who said so, only scanned Calvin's Bible commentaries and that they looked only for his interpretation of texts that mentioned cosmological topics, [24] whereas they neglected purely theological texts. The present author added Calvin's Institutes to his reading, but he did not find any anti-Copernican verdict in places where all anti-Copernicans would have found a ready occasion to launch attack against the new system. Evidently, 17th century scholars acted in the same way and with the same negative results. The pro-Copernicans Lansbergen and Wilkins quoted the well-known "cosmological" passages from Calvin's commentaries on Genesis, Joshua and the Psalms and they used them to demonstrate the neutrality of the Bible with respect to scientific theories and they did not take into account Calvin's Sermons. Even Voetius, who certainly would not have neglected the anti-Copernican verdict of the sermon on I Corinthians 10, did not quote it in support of his own anti-Copernican standpoint. Whether Calvin was a Copernican or an anti-Copernican did not play a role in the way he influenced his

---

[22] We hope to come back on this topic in our forthcoming work, *The Reception of Copernicanism in the Netherlands, 1550–1700*, to be published by the Royal Netherlands Academy of Science in commemoration of the 500th anniversary of Copernicus' birth.

[23] In historical statements of this kind it is always safest to add "as far as we know".

[24] R. Stauffer, *op. cit.*, p. 39.

followers, who all knew that he adhered to the *old* system in spite of its being incompatible with the biblical text when interpreted in a literal sense. The fact remains, then, that Calvin's exegetical method, when applied to "cosmological" texts, made it easy for *them* to accept the Copernican system. And, besides, that the same exegetical method made it impossible for *him* to use "cosmological" texts from the Bible to combat the Copernican system. Calvin's rejection of the Copernican system had nothing to do with biblical arguments. The question then becomes: what other reason could he have to reject it?

Dr Stauffer, who found the anti-Copernican quotation when editing Calvin's sermons, did not meet with any reference to the heliocentric system in Calvin's sermons on Genesis. He points out that this "only passage" in his sermons where the opponents of the geocentric system are mentioned, occurs in a purely theological and not at all in a cosmological context. [25] This explains why it escaped the attention of those who were interested in the Copernican controversy not only in modern times, but also when it still was a hot topic.

But it is precisely this circumstance (viz the non-cosmological and *ethical* character of the context), which makes it highly probable that even if they had known this quotation, this would not have prevented them from making an appeal to Calvin's accommodation theory on behalf of their cosmological standpoint.

It was a generally accepted tenet of christian theology that God does reveal himself in a *special* revelation through prophets and apostles in Holy Scripture, and in a *general* revelation to all people by an innate knowledge and by the work of his hands in the creatures. [26] Most christians held also that knowledge about Nature should be acquired from Nature and not from the Bible. Calvin, too, held that a small spark (scintilla) of innate, "natural" knowledge of truth remained in Man even after Adam's Fall. The result was the common sense [27] in which all people partake, the learned as well as the unlearned— and also the more sophisticated learning of the heathen philosophers, astronomers and physicians. Over against those protestant extremists who would only recognize the truth of biblical revelation and the inner light of the Holy Spirit in the souls of the faithful, and who despised all pagan science and learning as vain and useless, Calvin maintained that "if we hold the Spirit of God to be the only source of truth, we will neither reject nor

---

[25] R. Stauffer, *op. cit.*, p. 40, says that, as far as we know, Calvin did not come back on this subject, though perhaps there might be found something in his commentaries or his correspondence (*op. cit.*, p. 39). As, however, the commentaries were widely read in the 16th and 17th centuries, it seems improbable that an anti-copernican text there would have escaped notice.

[26] J. Calvin, *Institutes*, Book I, 1.

[27] "Common sense" is "the understanding of things acquired by vulgar exercise and daily use" (Antonius Brugmans, *Oratio inauguralis de sensu communi, matheseos et philosophiae matre, dicta publice ... X Martii 1756,* Franeker, 1761).

despise the truth, wherever it may reveal itself, lest we offend the Spirit of God". [28]

In particular, sound common sense was highly appreciated by him and it played an important role in his interpretation of the Bible. [29] This becomes evident when he interprets the "waters above the heaven" of Genesis I, neither as a real ocean (as the literalists thought), nor as angels (as the allegorical exegesis would have it), but as clouds: " For it appears opposed to common sense, and quite incredible, that there should be certain waters above the heaven." and, therefore, we should rather think of waters "such as the rude and unlearned also may perceive". [30]

In his Sermons on Paul's first epistle to the Corinthians Calvin emphasizes that the passage in I Cor. 10:19–24 teaches us not to disguise good and evil, but to call right what is right and wrong what is wrong. We should not resemble those who have such a spirit of contradiction that they "turn upside down the order of nature", those phrenetics "who will say that the sun does not move and that it is the earth which moves and that she revolves". When one says: this is warm, they will say it is cold and "when they are shown a black thing, they will say that it is white, or the contrary as one who says that snow is black". [31] These madmen would change the order of nature and they would blind people's eyes and dull their senses. [32]

Though Copernicus' name is not mentioned, this evidently is a rejection of his system. Calvin did not belong to those "mataiologoi", who, as Copernicus said, founded an astronomical opinion on "some place of Scripture, wrongly distorted in order to suit their end", [33] but he did belong to that multitude of people who rejected, as Copernicus expected, the motion of the earth "because of its absurdity". [34] After all, "mathematics is written for mathematicians" (or, more adequately: astronomy is written for astronomers), [35] but even the vast majority of the "math-

---

[28] J. Calvin, *Institutes*, II, 2, 15.

[29] See e.g. the examples adduced in my *Religion and the Rise of Modern Science*, p. 120 and p. 153, n. 21.

[30] J. Calvin, *Comment on Genesis*, I, 7. On another occasion (*Comment. on Ps.*, 148) he considers this text as a plain accommodation to a popular belief; those who "hence conclude that there is a sea in the heavens ... too servilely tie themselves to the letter of the text", as we know that Moses and the prophets, to accommodate themselves to the capacity of ruder people, often use a vulgar expression, and "therefore it would be a preposterous course, to reduce their phrases to the exact rules of philosophy".

[31] Probably an allusion to Anaxagoras' saying that "snow is black" (Cicero, *Academica*, II, 23 and II, 31).

[32] Calvin, *Opera quae supersunt omnia*, Braunschweig, 1892, vol. 49, col. 677. The 8th sermon on chapters 10 and 11 of I Corinth. 10: 19–24, 1556.

[33] N. Copernicus, *De revolutionibus orbium coelestium*, Norimbergae, 1543, Praefatio, p. IV vs.

[34] Ibid., p. III r.

[35] Ibid., p. IV vs.

ematicians" (astronomers) considered his theory, if conceived in a realistic sense, as an absurdity.

An appeal to common sense often is legitimate, but it is well-nigh impossible to decide when it ceases to be so. In general we have a tendency to consider ideas and facts to which we have been accustomed since our school days as quite rational and not absurd. [36] Initially our common sense would only observe one expanse, but indoctrination with Greek astronomy was to make acceptable that in reality there are many invisible planetary spheres around the earth. "Common sense" made the contemporaries of Moses and David accept the one expanse, but it did not *prevent* Calvin and his contemporaries to accept many heavens, as it did not prevent them from accepting that "the little star of Saturn is greater than the Moon". Yet it was extremely absurd to them that the Earth is in motion and the Sun is standing still. And, indeed, in this case "common sense" seemed to speak particularly strongly against it: with our own eyes we *see* the sun moving and "sound reason" tells us that, if the earth performed a full revolution within 24 hours, we would get dizzy and we would be thrown off into space. [37] Moreover, one of the principles of Aristotelian physics (which was so strongly inculcated into the minds of 16th century people that its tenets were identified with the "order of nature" itself) is that heavy bodies (like earth) have only one "natural" motion, viz that in a straight line towards the centre of the universe. Aristotelian physics, however sophisticated it might be, started as a rule from naive daily experience. Consequently it is quite understandable that saying that the earth moves and the sun is standing still, was considered a perversity of the same kind as saying that snow is black [38] or soot is white, sayings which stem from an evil spirit of contradiction.

That is to say, in the passage under discussion the theory of the motion of the earth was condemned by Calvin not because it is against Holy Scripture ("special revelation"), but because it is considered to be against "general revelation" as given in the testimony of the senses and reason which have been given to all people on earth.

It goes without saying that, as the Greek astronomical system was partly highly sophisticated (the invisible spheres and their circular movement) and partly conformable to naive, immediate observation (the daily rotation of the heaven), the *former* (sophisticated) part would not be found in the Bible, so that on that account only the accommodation

---

[36] Cf. R. Hooykaas, *The Principle of Uniformity*, 2nd. ed., Leiden, 1963, pp. 165–8.

[37] Of course, our 20th century "common" sense has some difficulty in appreciating these arguments of the learned and the unlearned of some centuries ago.

[38] "Anaxagoras said that snow is black: would you endure me if I said the same? Not you, pot even if I expressed myself as doubtful, and yet he was a man of high renown" (Cicero, *Academica*, II, 23).

principle must be resorted to when interpreting the texts. On the other
hand, as far as the sun's motion and the earth's standing still are
concerned, there was no need for "accommodation", for in these cases
the scientific and the naive conceptions were coinciding, and they were
true both for the learned and the unlearned. Therefore when Scripture
speaks of the motion of the Sun accommodation is not assumed because
there is no need of it.

Consequently, it is strange that R. Stauffer for once agrees with one
of the people he criticizes, when accusing Calvin of inconsistently aband-
oning his accommodation principle when (in his commentary on Joshua
10:13) taking the words "And the sun stood still, and the moon stayed",
as literally true. [39] What else should he have done, while thinking the
motion of *sun* as well as that of the moon to be objective truth. In that
case there is no question of "accommodation". And when it is said that
"the moon stayed", even a Copernican would not have considered this
an "accommodation to common speech" but objective truth. It is asking
too much from the interpreter that he should have considered the motion
of the sun as an accommodation to common speech and the motion of
the moon as an objective reality. To the naive observer as well as to the
philosopher of the 16th century both motions are reality.

SUMMARY

(1). A. D. White's quotation in which Calvin is said to condemn Copernicanism
as conflicting with the Bible, is spurious.
(2). Calvin's conception of the Bible leaves the problem of the true cosmological
system undecided and thus paved the way for the acceptance of Copernicanism.
(3). Several scholars of the early 17th century quoted Calvin's Bible commentaries to demonstrate that arguments borrowed from Scripture against Copernicanism have no value.
(4). Calvin rejected Copernicanism, not on Scriptural arguments but because
of its being against the "order of nature" as revealed through "common sense" and
the astronomical science of his days.

---

[39] R. Stauffer, *op. cit.*, p. 36.

CALVIN, COPERNICUS, AND CASTELLIO

by Christopher B. Kaiser

During the past three decades at least eight articles have been published on the subject of Calvin and Copernicus. In 1960, Edward Rosen showed that none of the supposed references of Calvin to Copernicus cited in the literature to that time had any textual basis in Calvin's own writings.[1] Then, in 1971, Richard Stauffer pointed out a passage in Calvin's *Eighth Sermon on 1 Corinthians 10-11* that clearly refers to the idea that the earth moves while the sun does not.[2]

Five of the eight articles on Calvin and Copernicus that I mentioned have appeared since the publication of Stauffer's article, but they suggest no consensus concerning whether or not Calvin was referring specifically to the heliocentric cosmology of Copernicus in the passage Stauffer pointed out.[3] It is my intent in this essay to show that his remark was directed against Castellio rather than Copernicus and that it is based on a well-known passage in Cicero's *Academica*.

Calvin's understanding of natural philosophy was based on the physics and cosmology of Aristotle, which was the standard science of his time. He made frequent references to the Aristotelian model of the universe as a system of homocentric spheres with the stars at the outer boundary and the earth at the center.[4] Moreover, he accepted the basic dynamics of Aristotle's model: God is the direct cause of the

EDITOR'S NOTE: This essay is a revised version of a paper presented at the Central Renaissance Conference at Southern Illinois University, Carbondale, Illinois, on 29 March 1985.

[1]Rosen, "Calvin's Attitude toward Copernicus," *Journal for the History of Ideas* 21 (1960) 431-41. See also Joseph Ratner, "Some Comments on Rosen's "Calvin's Attitude toward Copernicus,'" *Journal for the History of Ideas* 22 (1961) 382-88.

[2]Stauffer, "Calvin et Copernic," *Revue de l'histoire des religions* 179 (1971) 37ff.

[3]For an excellent review of the situation, see Robert White, "Calvin and Copernicus: The Problem Reconsidered," *Calvin Theological Journal* 15 (1980) 233-43.

[4]See, for example, his *Commentary on Genesis* 1:15-16 and *Commentary on Psalm* 19:4ff.

5

rotation of the outermost sphere (the *primum mobile*), and the force of motion is passed down through the planetary spheres, with diminishing strength, to the sun and moon.[5] Both Aristotle and ordinary sense perception argue that the earth itself is stationary.

Calvin held the stability of the earth in the midst of the swirling heavens to be a precious sign of God's care for his people even in a world of turmoil. He believed that the earth was stationary in space not as a result of Aristotelian physics but as an apparent exception to it—an exception that gave clear testimony to the particular providence of God.[6]

Calvin's training in natural philosophy took place primarily at Paris and Orleans during the 1520s, well before the new ideas of major Renaissance scientists such as Copernicus came into vogue. We must consider the possibility, however, that Calvin at some point became aware of the new speculations concerning the motion of the earth. Given the theological significance he attached to the earth's immobility, we can assume that any such awareness would have given rise to close scrutiny and serious questioning on Calvin's part. It surely would not have been a matter of indifference for one to whom the natural, civic, and ecclesiastical orders were so closely related.

I. IDEAS ABOUT THE MOTION OF THE EARTH IN THE MID-SIXTEENTH CENTURY

When we consider the issue of the motion of the earth, we naturally think of Copernicus's *De revolutionibus orbium coelestium*, which was published in 1543, just before his death. In an earlier version of the work written around 1511-12 and privately circulated, Copernicus argued that the sphere of the earth revolved around the sun, which itself remained stationary at the center of the cosmos.[7] In the final version he concluded that the best point of reference for the planetary system

[5]See the *Institutes*, 1.14.21 and 1.16.1, 3; *Commentary on Genesis* 3:17; and *Commentary on Psalm* 68:31ff. I treat the subject of Calvin's interpretation of Aristotelian physics and cosmology more fully in an as-yet-unpublished paper, "Calvin against the Background of Classical and Medieval Science."

[6]See the *Twelfth Sermon on Psalm 119* (*Calvini Opera* [henceforth abbreviated *CO*] 32:620); and *Commentary on Psalms* 93:1 and 119:90 (*CO* 32:16-17, 253-54). The dates these texts were published (1553-57) overlap that of the publication of the *Eighth Sermon on 1 Corinthians 10-11* (1556), so there is no evidence of a chronological development of his thinking on this point.

[7]See Rosen, *Three Copernican Treatises*, 3d ed. (New York: Octagon, 1971), pp. 58, 345.

is neither the earth nor the sun but the center of the earth's orbit, which, in turn, revolves around the sun. But in this system, too, the sun can be understood to be stationary.[8]

For the most part, Copernicus's work was known only to natural philosophers and mathematicians in the mid-sixteenth century. It is very unlikely that Calvin would have had first-hand knowledge of it.[9] A more accessible source of Copernicus's ideas would have been the *Narratio prima*, a brief preliminary account of the larger work composed by George Joachim Rheticus. The *Narratio prima* was written in 1539 and published in 1540 at Danzig; a second edition was printed in 1541 at Basel. According to Rheticus, Copernicus taught that the sun was at rest in the center of the universe with the earth and the other planets revolving around it.[10]

Neither Copernicus nor Rheticus is ever referred to by name, so far as we know, in the writings of Calvin. Rheticus was a student of Philip Melanchthon, however, and received some encouragement in his work from this mentor, who was himself greatly interested in the physical sciences.[11] Indeed, both Luther and Melanchthon are known to have commented on Copernicus's ideas. Let us review what is known about this Wittenberg circle very briefly, with an eye to detecting any influence it may have had on Calvin's natural philosophy.

[8]See Copernicus, *De revolutionibus orbium coelestium*, 1.9-10. See also A. C. Crombie, *Augustine to Galileo*, 2d ed., vol. 2 (Cambridge: Harvard University, 1961), pp. 178-79.

[9]Such is Rosen's contention in "Calvin's Attitude toward Copernicus," p. 441, and in "Calvin n'a pas lu Copernic," *Revue de l'histoire des religions* 182 (1972) 183ff. On Owen Gingerich's research concerning the circulation of *De revolutionibus* in the sixteenth century, see William J. Broad, "A Bibliophile's Quest for Copernicus," *Science* 218 (1982) 661-62. For a good overall review of the sixteenth-century awareness of Copernicus, see Marie Boas Hall, *The Scientific Renaissance: 1450-1630* (New York: Harper & Row, 1962), chap. 4. Omar Talon noted already in the 1550 edition of his commentary on Cicero's *Academica* that Copernicus had proved that the earth moves and the heavens are motionless (*terra mota et caelo quiescente*); Charles B. Schmitt, *Cicero Academicus* (The Hague: Martinus Nijhoff, 1972), p. 90n. We have no reason to suppose that Calvin had access to this work either.

[10]Rosen, *Three Copernican Treatises*, pp. 10, 138, 143-46, 150. See also Reijer Hooykaas, "Rheticus's Lost Treatise on Holy Scripture and the Motion of the Earth," *Journal for the History of Astronomy* 15 (1984) 77-80.

[11]See John Dillenberger, *Protestant Thought and Natural Science* (Garden City, NY: Doubleday, 1960), pp. 41, 47-48. See also Robert S. Westman, "The Melanchthon Circle, Rheticus and the Wittenberg Interpretation of the Copernican Theory," *Isis* 66 (1975) 169-70.

Luther's rather disparaging comment appears in two slightly different versions of the Table Talk (*Tischreden*) for 1539, the year before the publication of Rheticus's *Narratio prima*. In all likelihood, it was not known to Calvin. The earliest printed version was not published until 1566, and I have been able to find no references to such discussions by Luther in any of Calvin's correspondence.[12] In any case, the basis of Luther's criticism of Copernicus seems to have been the late medieval reaction to vain curiosity and speculation in matters that were inaccessible to human testing and of no evident practical value.[13] Calvin might well have concurred with Luther's judgment on this point if he had been aware of it. However, Calvin would have taken the idea of the earth's motion more seriously, whether in a negative or positive sense, than Luther did, because of his close association of the stability of the earth with the special providence of God.

Melanchthon knew of the work of Copernicus primarily through his former student Rheticus. In fact, Rheticus sent his mentor a copy of the *Narratio prima* early in 1540, as soon as it was available. So Melanchthon's comments would have been better informed than Luther's. Still, we find very little detail in them and, until about ten years later (1549-50), very little appreciation for Copernicus's work.[14] Only the two earliest references give any real indication of the content of Copernicus's theory, and so only these two are of interest to us as possible sources of information for Calvin. The first is a letter addressed to one Mithobius in which Melanchthon refers to Copernicus as a typical rebel of

[12]For Luther's comment, see Aurifaber's version of the *Weimarer Ausgabe* (henceforth abbreviated *WA*), *Tischreden* no. 855 (1: 419). In Lauterbach's version of the *WA*, which was not published before the twentieth century and is generally thought to be more reliable, the comment can be found in *Tischreden* no. 4638 (4: 412-13). The comment can be found in volume 54 of the English translation, *Luther's Works* (henceforth abbreviated *LW*), ed. Helmut T. Lehmann, trans. Theodore G. Tappert, Jr. (Philadelphia: Fortress, 1955-76), pp. 358-59. See also William Norlind, "Copernicus and Luther," *Isis* 44 (1953) 275-76; and Brian Gerrish, "The Reformation and the Rise of Modern Science," in *The Impact of the Church upon Its Culture*, ed. Jerald C. Brauer (Chicago: University of Chicago, 1968), pp. 243-44. The argument from silence on Calvin's part with respect to Luther's reported comment receives some support from source-critical grounds in notes 57, 58, and 60 herein.

[13]On this, see Heiko Oberman, "Reformation and Revolution: Copernicus' Discovery in an Era of Change," in *The Nature of Scientific Discovery*, ed. Owen Gingerich (Washington: Smithsonian, 1975), p. 139. See also *The Cultural Context of Medieval Learning*, ed. J. E. Murdoch and E. D. Sylla (Dordrecht: Reidel, 1975), p. 401.

[14]See Westman, "The Melanchthon Circle, Rheticus and the Wittenberg Interpretation of the Copernican Theory," pp. 172-73.

the time in that he "moves the earth and fixes the sun" (*qui movet terram et figit Solem*).[15] The second reference appears in Melanchthon's introductory lectures on Aristotelian physics *Initia doctrinae physicae*, presumably written soon after the curricular reform of 1545 and published in 1549. He cites Copernicus's contention that the earth moves (*moveri terram*) but that the stellar sphere and the sun do not only to dismiss it as an ingenious but unconvincing novelty. He presents five kinds of evidence to refute the Copernican hypothesis: (1) the evidence of the senses, particularly the eyes; (2) the testimony of Psalms 19 and 104; (3) various arguments based on Aristotelian precepts to the effect that the earth must be at the center of the cosmos; (4) the Aristotelian doctrine that a simple body such as the earth could have only one simple motion and not a combination of rotation on its axis and revolution around the sun as Copernicus held; and (5) the fact that Aristarchus of Samos, a heretic even to the Greeks, had taught the paradox that the sun was immobile and the earth revolved around the sun (*Solem stare immotum, et terram circumferri circa Solem*).[16]

We have no evidence that Calvin had read Melanchthon's lectures or was aware of their content. The known correspondence between the two men concentrates on other, more pressing issues, such as the eucharistic view of Westphal. Several points of reference should be kept in mind, however, by anyone pursuing the Copernican issue as a possible point of contact between the two: (1) the association of geodynamic ideas with rebelliousness and the repudiation of the senses in particular; (2) the use of Psalm 104; (3) a worldview rooted in Aristotelian natural philosophy and a clear association between the *via antiqua* and political stability; (4) particular consideration for the proposed multiplicity of the earth's motion; and, not least, (5) the association of geodynamic ideas with heretical philosophers of the ancient Greek world.

Closely associated with Melanchthon and Rheticus were two other members of the Wittenberg circle, Erasmus Reinhold and Caspar Peucer. Reinhold published a new set of astronomical tables in 1551 in which he used Copernicus's method of calculation, but he said nothing about the underlying heliocentric cosmology in his introductory state-

---

[15]Melanchthon, in *Corpus Reformatum* (henceforth abbreviated *CR*), 4: 679. And see Bruce T. Moran, "The Universe of Philip Melanchthon: Criticism and the Use of the Copernican Theory," *Comitatus* 4 (1973) 13.

[16]Melanchthon, in *CR*, 13: 216ff. And see Moran, "The Universe of Philip Melanchthon," pp. 13-14.

ment.[17] Peucer also published a work on the revolution of the heavens in 1551, and he also omitted any description of the Copernican hypothesis.[18] A later work that discussed various hypotheses refers to Copernicus's ideas as offensive and unfit to be taught in the schools.[19]

So far we have found very little material that might have been a source of information to Calvin concerning the idea of a moving earth. However, Copernicus and the Wittenberg circle were not the only possible sources of geodynamic ideas in the sixteenth century. There were at least two others: a treatise of Calcagnini and a new edition of Cicero's *Academica*. In order to be complete, we will have to consider these.

Celio Calcagnini, a native of Ferrara and professor at the university there, wrote a treatise entitled *Quod caelum stet, terra moveatur* sometime during the 1520s. It was not published until 1544, three years after the author's death and one year after the publication of the more substantial work of Copernicus. The place of publication, the same as that of the second edition of Rheticus's *Narratio prima* three years earlier, was Basel.[20] In Calcagnini's system the earth was at the center of the cosmos and rotated on its axis once every twenty-four hours, thus producing the apparent diurnal revolution of the heavens. He presents the rotation of the earth as a quite natural result of a tangential impulse delivered to it at the time of creation, while its center remained fixed. But then, in order to reconcile the concept of a fixed sun with its apparent annual motion from north in the summer to south in the winter, Calcagnini had to assign a second motion to the earth, which he described as an inclination, or tilting, of its axis, first toward the sun and then away from it. He tried to bolster this rather wobbly

[17]Reinhold, *Prutenicae tabulae orbium coelestium* (1551). And see Gingerich, "Heliocentrism as a Model and Reality," *Proceedings of the American Philosophical Society,* 117 (1973) 515; and "Reinhold, Erasmus," in the *Dictionary of Scientific Biography,* 11: 366a. Reinhold wrote *Eruditus Commentarius in totum opus Revolutionum Nicolai Copernici* around 1550, but it was not published; see Alexandre Birkenmajer, "Le commentaire inédit d'Erasme Reinhold sur le *De revolutionibus* de Nicolas Copernic," *La science au sezième siècle,* Union Internationale d'Histoire et de Philosophie des Sciences (Paris: Herman, 1960), pp. 171-75.

[18]Peucer, *Elementa doctrinae de circulis coelestibus et primo motu;* see Pierre Duhem, *To Save the Phenomena* (Chicago: University of Chicago, 1969), pp. 74ff.

[19]*Hypotheses astronomicae* (1571). See J. L. E. Dreyer, *A History of Astronomy from Thales to Kepler,* 2d ed. (New York: Dover, 1953); and Duhem, *To Save the Phenomena,* pp. 90-91.

[20]See Dreyer, *A History of Astronomy from Thales to Kepler,* pp. 292-93.

astronomy by citing a passage from Cicero's *Academica* that we will turn to shortly.[21] We have no evidence that Calvin was aware of Calcagnini's work, although he did visit Ferrara briefly in 1536.

A third possible source of geodynamic ideas for Calvin was well known in the mid-sixteenth century: Cicero's *Academica*, perhaps the most discussed of his works during this period. It was reprinted along with the rest of Cicero's works by A. Cratander of Basel in 1528.[22] Another edition was published by J. Hervagius, also of Basel, in 1540;[23] a copy was available in the library of Calvin's Academy in Geneva in 1572, when the holdings were catalogued.[24]

At this point, historical method becomes an important consideration. From our twentieth-century perspective, Cicero and the New Academy belong with the classics, not with the sciences. But in the sixteenth century much of the scientific discussion was based on or at least checked against classical references. The famous preface to Copernicus's *De revolutionibus* illustrates the point. The paradoxical character of the Renaissance mind—paradoxical to us, that is—at once looking forward and returning to the ancient sources, is a well-known fact of history, but it has not always been taken into account in our historiography. Among the lights and shadows on Calvin's horizon, Erasmus, Budé, Sadoleto, and Agrippa all cited the *Academica* in at least one of their works.[25] And Calvin cited it, too, in his *Seneca Commentary* (32.27), though not, as it happens, in connection with the

[21]See Dreyer, *A History of Astronomy from Thales to Kepler*, pp. 293-94. Dreyer also notes a reference to the idea that the earth revolves on its axis in Francesco Maurolico's *Cosmographia*, published in Venice in 1543 (see p. 295).

[22]See Peter G. Bietenholz, *Basle and France in the Sixteenth Century* (Geneva: Librairie Droz, 1971), p. 263 n. 127.

[23]Alexandre Ganoczy, *La bibliothèque de l'Académie de Calvin* (Geneva: Librairie Droz, 1969), p. 283. I wish to thank Mrs. Marion Battles of the Meeter Center for Calvin Studies in Grand Rapids for bringing this source, as well as those listed in notes 26, 33, and 87, to my attention.

[24]Charles B. Schmitt, *Cicero Scepticus: A Study of the Influence of the "Academica" in the Renaissance* (The Hague: Martinus Nijhoff, 1972); see also Panos Paul Morphos, *The Dialogues of Guy de Brues: A Critical Edition with a Study in Renaissance Scepticism and Relativism* (Baltimore: Johns Hopkins, 1953), and Richard H. Popkin, *The History of Skepticism from Erasmus to Spinoza* (Berkeley and Los Angeles: University of California, 1979), chap. 2: "The Revival of Greek Skepticism in the 16th Century."

[25]Schmitt, *Cicero Scepticus*, pp. 57ff., 105-6; Morphos, *The Dialogues of Guy De Brues*, pp. 35, 77-78; Popkin, *The History of Skepticism from Erasmus to Spinoza*, pp. 25-28.

topic we are investigating here.[26] The point is that whereas the possible sources of *Copernican* ideas about the motion of the earth were most likely not part of Calvin's reading, the *Academica* of Cicero, with its encyclopedia of bizarre ideas from the classical world, was very much in the background. In at least one instance, as we shall see, it came to the fore as well.

What specifically were the geodynamic ideas that Cicero could have presented to Calvin? And what evidence is there that Calvin might have considered these ideas in formulating his own view of nature?

The key passage concerns the views of a Pythagorean philosopher of the fourth century B.C. named Hicetas, as transmitted to Cicero by Theophrastus, a pupil of Aristotle.[27] The context is a discussion of various sayings of the Greek philosophers that members of the New Academy cited in support of their skepticism with regard to many conventional ideas, among which are Socrates's assertion that he knew nothing other than the fact of his own ignorance, Anaxagoras's famous inference that snow is really black, the claim of certain Stoics that things are quite different from what they appear to be according to the senses, and Aristotle's declaration that the world never had a beginning.[28] Just a few paragraphs after the passage we are concerned with, the topic shifts to a discussion of relativism in questions of good and evil.[29]

Here is the key passage dealing with the motion of the earth in Cicero's *Academica* (2.39.123):

[26]See *Calvin's Commentary on Seneca's "De Clementia,"* ed. and trans. Ford Lewis Battles and André Malan Hugo (Leiden: E. J. Brill, 1969), p. 93. The reference is to the *Academica,* 2.10.30, which deals with the relation of the mind and sensation. Three other classical authors cited in the *Seneca Commentary* who mention the possibility of the earth's motion are Diogenes Laertius, Seneca, and Plutarch (whose *De placitis philosophorum,* now attributed to Aetius, is cited along with Cicero's *Academica* in the preface to Copernicus's *De revolutionibus*). None of these three says anything about the motion of the earth in relation to the sun, however.

[27]Diogenes Laertius also mentions Hicetas briefly, in connection with Philolaus's view that the earth moved around a central fire. A Latin translation was published at Basel in 1524 (Ganoczy, *La bibliothèque de l'Académie de Calvin,* p. 287); the Greek text was published at Basel in 1533 (ET, *Diogenes Laertius,* trans. R. D. Hicks, Loeb Classical Library [Cambridge: Harvard University, 1933]).

[28]Cicero, *Academica,* 1.16; 2.72, 74, 100, 101, 119. For text and translation, see *Cicero: De Natura Decorum—Academica,* trans. H. Rackham, Loeb Classical Library (Cambridge: Harvard University, 1933).

[29]Cicero, *Academica,* 2.128.

The Syracusan Hicetas, as Theophrastus asserts, holds the view that the heaven, sun, moon, stars, and in short all of the things on high are stationary [*omnia stare*], and that nothing in the world is in motion [*moveri*] except the earth, which by revolving and twisting round its axis with extreme velocity [*quae cum circum axem se summa celeritate convertat et torqueat*] produces all the same results as would be produced if the earth were stationary [*stante*] and the heaven in motion [*moveretur*].[30]

The passage apparently assigns only a diurnal rotation to the earth. Even though two verbs are used to describe the motion of the earth, both are qualified by the stipulation of motion about the axis (*circum axem se*) and great speed (*summa celeritate*), so we can assume they are being used as synonyms.

Of all the sources of geodynamic cosmological ideas we have considered, Cicero's account is the one Calvin is most likely to have known from his reading. Not only was the *Academica* widely read in humanist circles of the early sixteenth century, but the passage dealing with Hicetas's ideas was cited by such controversialists as Sadoleto (*Phaedrus*, 1538) and Talon (*Academica posteriora*, 1550 edition), as well as by such less well-known natural philosophers as Copernicus and Calcagnini.[31] Moreover, as we have noted, there is at least one explicit reference to the *Academica* in Calvin's *Seneca Commentary* of 1532.[32] But before we proceed to draw any more firm conclusions, we should take a look at the one passage we know of in Calvin's writings in which he speaks of the idea of a moving earth.

II. CALVIN'S DEROGATORY COMMENT ON THE IDEA THAT THE EARTH IS IN MOTION

Almost all of the passages in Calvin's works that deal with cosmological matters are found in the commentaries on Genesis, Psalms, and Jeremiah and in the sermons on Job and Psalms. The intellectual background of these passages is essentially medieval, based on Aristotelian physics and cosmology. One of the key features of Calvin's thought connected with this medieval heritage is, as we have noted, his inter-

[30]*Academica*, Rackham translation, p. 627.

[31]Schmitt, *Cicero Scepticus*, pp. 57-58, 90; Popkin, *The History of Skepticism from Erasmus to Spinoza*, pp. 26-29. In his commentary on the *Academica* Talon also refers to Copernicus as having proved that the earth moves and the heavens remain still (*terra mota et caelo quiescenta*); Schmitt, *Cicero Scepticus*, p. 90n.

[32]See note 26 herein.

pretation of the apparent immobility of the earth as a sign of God's special providence in everyday affairs. Interpreting the cosmology of his day in this fashion was one way in which he attempted to resolve the deep-seated tension between the essential naturalism of Aristotelian science on the one hand and pietistic demands of his own views on the other hand for a world in which God could be understood to be immediately and continuously active in the normal course of events.

At the same time (i.e., the second quarter of the sixteenth century), ideas about the possible motion of the earth were abroad—not in everyday discussion, perhaps, but in a variety of loci going back to at least three distinct sources: Copernicus, Calcagnini, and Cicero. Are any of these ideas reflected in Calvin's writings? For the most part, no![33] To date we know of only one such passage, found in the *Eighth Sermon on 1 Corinthians 10-11*, generally presumed to have been written in 1556.[34] The passage was apparently overlooked by Calvin scholars until Richard Stauffer brought it to our attention in 1971.[35] Since then it has occasioned a fair amount of scholarly debate as to whether Calvin was criticizing the work of Copernicus as Luther and Melanchthon had done seven to seventeen years before.[36]

The text of the *Eighth Sermon* is 1 Corinthians 10:19-24, which deals with the misuse of Christian liberty by individuals in the Corinthian church who engaged in practices such as eating meat that had been offered to idols. Calvin uses the occasion to lash out at contemporary dissemblers, sometimes called Nicodemites, who claimed that their newly regained evangelical freedom allowed them to partake in such

[33]The *Commentary on Psalm* 119:90 refers to the world as revolving or turning about (*volvatur* [CO 32: 253]; *sujet à révolutions* [*Commentaires sur le Livre des Psaumes* (Paris: Librairie de Ch. Meyrueis, 1859), 2: 419a]). As the consideration of this possibility is ascribed to the psalmist in the context, I take it to refer to the general impermanence of terrestrial structures and not to the idea of rotation or revolution in the astronomical sense; cf. *Second Sermon on Job 38* (CO 35: 367-68).

[34]Calvin, "Huitieme sermon," in *Sermons sur le 10ᵉ et 11ᵉ chapitre de la première épistre aux Corinthiens* (Geneva: Badius, 1558); CO 49: 671-84.

[35]Stauffer, "Calvin et Copernic," pp. 37ff.

[36]See the excellent reviews of the debate by Robert White: "Calvin and Copernicus," pp. 233-43; Review of *Calvin et Copernic, la légende ou les faits?* by Pierre Marcel (Saint-Germain-en-Laye: Société Calviniste de France, 1980), *Calvin Theological Journal* 17 (1982) 270-74. A synopsis of Marcel's *Calvin et Copernic,* translated by Philip E. Hughes, tan be found in *Philosophia Reformata* 46 (1981) 14-36. I am personally indebted to Porfessor Marcel for my awareness and interest in this issue.

54

papal practices as the veneration of images and the mass.[37] This is hardly a context in which we might expect to encounter an opinion on geodynamic cosmology, but our suprise is only a measure of our distance from Calvin's own world of associations. A closer look at his medieval/Renaissance background and the immediate ecclesiastical and political issues that affected his ministry should make these associations easier to understand.

Calvin wrote a series of tracts against various Nicodemite groups between 1537 and 1544, over twenty years before he wrote the *Eighth Sermon*.[38] He touched on the problem of Nicodemism again in 1550 in *De scandalis*, concentrating more on the challenge of skepticism and libertinism represented, in his view, by Agrippa and Servetus.[39] The Libertines and Nicodemites were historically distinct groups,[40] but in Calvin's perspective there was a certain continuity between them as one replaced another on his horizon. During the 1550s the principal challenges to his authority came from various groups in Geneva, Berne, and Basel that he associated with skeptical and libertine tendencies.[41]

[37]*CO* 49: 674ff. See also Stauffer, *Dieu, la Création et la Providence dans la prédication de Calvin* (Berne: Peter Lang, 1978), p. 188; and Pierre Marcel, *Calvin et Copernic,* chaps. 2 and 3.

[38]See G. R. Williams, *The Radical Reformation* (Philadelphia: Westminster, 1962), pp. 602ff. On the variety of modern interpretations of Nicodemism, see Carlos M. N. Eire, "Calvin and Nicodemus: A Reappraisal," *Sixteenth Century Journal* 10 (1979) 45-69.

[39]See *John Calvin: Concerning Scandals,* trans. John W. Fraser (Grand Rapids: Eerdmans, 1978), pp. 59ff. According to Calvin, "skepticism" included the questioning of such established dogmas as the eternal deity of Christ, the immortality of the human soul, and eternal predestination. He closely associated the Genevan Libertines led by Perrin and Berthelier with antitrinitarians (e.g., Servetus), critics of the doctrine of predestination (e.g., Bolsec, Zebédée, and Curione), and advocates of religious liberty (e.g., Castellio). For more on this, see Benjamin Farley's introduction to his translation of *John Calvin's Sermons on the Ten Commandments* (Grand Rapids: Eerdmans, 1980), pp. 18-22.

[40]Eire, "Calvin and Nicodemus," pp. 50-51.

[41]Calvin describes his experience with these skeptics and libertines quite clearly in his preface to the *Commentary on Psalms* of 1557 (*CO* 31: 28ff.; ET, *Commentary on the Book of Psalms,* trans. James Anderson [Edinburgh: Calvin Translation Society, 1845-49], 1: xlv-xlvii). The association of Nicodemism with libertine tendencies is made explicit in his *Commentary on the Pentateuch* of 1563 (*CO* 24: 365ff.; ET, *Commentaries on the Four Last Books of Moses,* trans. Charles William Bingham [Edinburgh: Calvin Translation Society, 1852-55], 2: 90ff.). In the treatise *Contre la secte phantastique des Libertins* of 1545 he refers to an earlier group of French "libertines." Methodologically, one has to strike a balance between the need to differentiate be-

With this background in mind, it should be no surprise to find that Calvin subtly shifted the focus of his attack in the *Eighth Sermon* from Nicodemism in general to certain parties espousing skeptical and libertine views.[42] The unifying theme Calvin detects among the subjects of his attack is their contempt for God's ordinances: contempt for his ordinances concerning worship and the sacraments in the case of the Nicodemites and contempt for his ordinances concerning matters of morality and truth in the case of the libertines and skeptics. Accordingly, Calvin shifts from accusing his opponents of perverting religion to abolishing God's truth to gainsaying *everything*—not only religious matters but all matters, to the point of perverting the order of nature itself.[43] It is in this connection that Calvin alludes to certain geodynamic ideas in relation to the position he is attacking. I translate the key passage as follows:

> Let us not be like these madmen [*ces fantastiques*] who have a spirit of such venomous contradiction, contriving to gainsay everything and perverting the very order of nature. We shall find some who are so stark raving mad [*si frénétiques*], not only in matters of religion, but showing their montrous nature in all things, that they will even say that the sun does not budge [*ne se bouge*], and that it is the earth that bestirs itself and that turns around [*qui se remue et qu'elle tourne*]. When we come across such individuals we must really say that the devil has possessed them and that God placed them before us as mirrors in order to make us stay within the fold of those who fear him [*pour nous faire demeurer en sa crainte*]. So it is with those who debate with unquestionable malice and who think nothing of being contemptuous [*ausquels il ne chaut d'estre effrontez*]. When you tell them, "That is hot": "Not at all!" they will say, "It is obviously cold!" If you show them something black, they will say that

---

tween groups like these (Eire's emphasis—see "Calvin and Nicodemus," pp. 50-51) and the need to see the overlappings and continuities among them that a synthetic thinker such as Calvin would have perceived.

[42]So argues Marcel, *Calvin et Copernic*, pp. 24-27—a view White pronounces "undoubtedly correct" ("Calvin and Copernicus," pp. 272-73). The shift occurs at CO 49: 676-77.

[43]The phrases appear in the following sequence: *le nom de Dieu sera blasphemé; toute la religion pervertie; anéantir la verité de Dieu; son essence seroit anéantie; falsifier [la verité]; changeront l'ordre de la nature; toute religion soit mise bas; l'essence de Dieu [verité] soit foulée au pied; redire par tout; pervertir l'ordre de nature; non pas seulement en la religion, mais . . . par tout*. Other instances in which Calvin uses the phrase *l'ordre de nature* to describe the arrangement and driving mechanisms of the heavens can be found in *Contre la secte phantastique des Libertins* 14 (CO 7: 186), *De aeterna praedestinatione Dei* 10.1 (CO 8: 347-48), and the *First Sermon on Job 26* (CO 34: 430).

it is white! Or it could be the other way around, as in the case of the man who said that snow was black, for in spite of the fact that its whiteness is clearly visible, as everyone well knows, still he wished to dispute it openly. But that's the way it is. There are madmen around who would change the very order of nature and would even try to dazzle people's eyes and stupefy their senses.[44]

In the text immediately following this passage, Calvin castigates his opponents for challenging holy doctrines—whether from resentment of others or from personal ambition, he is not sure—and for arguing that bad is good and vice is virtue so as to suggest that God is no longer the final judge but rather that everything is a matter of private judgment.[45] He also charges them with evading appeals to the authority of Scripture with arguments that it is obscure and difficult to interpret (difficile à digére).[46]

Clearly Calvin's disparaging remark about the idea that the earth moves plays only a subsidiary role in his overall denunciation of libertine and skeptical views dating from the time of the sermon (1556).[47] Elsewhere in the sermon he does not hesitate to target certain individuals as if they were present in the congregation or at least close at hand. That he does not do so here constitutes further evidence his remarks about the idea of a moving earth are less likely a reflection of his reading of a contemporary natural philosopher such as Copernicus, Rheticus, or Calcagnini than it is a reductio ad absurdum of a general line of thinking that he wished to discredit in the minds of his listeners.

There are at least five compelling reasons to suppose that Cicero's Academica is the most likely of the three principal sources of geodynamic ideas to have been the source for Calvin's allusion. (1) As we have already noted, the issues presented in the Academica were widely discussed in humanist circles of the mid-sixteenth century, and Calvin was familiar with at least some parts of the text. (2) We have also noted

[44]CO 49: 677, ll. 25-49. The French can also be found in three works by Stauffer— "Calvin et Copernic," p. 38; "L'attitude de Réformateurs à l'egard de Copernic," in *La représentation de l'univers* (Paris: Albert Blanchard, 1975), p. 162; and *Dieu, la Création et la Providence dans la prédication de Calvin*, p. 188—and in Marcel's *Calvin et Copernic*, pp. 26-27. I have translated the passage in such a way as to bring out nuances of Calvin's debate with those who argue against established dogmas. For slightly different translations, see White, "Calvin and Copernicus," pp. 236-37; and Marcel, *Calvin et Copernic*, (Hughes translation), p. 18.

[45]CO 49: 677-78.

[46]CO 49: 678.

[47]So White, "Calvin and Copernicus," pp. 238-41.

that Cicero discusses skepticism in the context of both natural philosophy and morality in the *Academica*, the same context in which Calvin
presents the issue in his sermon. (3) Calvin's reference to "the man
who said that snow was black" would appear to be a clear reference
to the comments about Anaxagoras in the *Academica*.[48] (4) Calvin's
stylized expression of indignation concerning those who call black white,
dazzle people's eyes, and stupefy their senses is almost identical to a
passage in the *Academica* in which Lucullus repudiates skepticism as
"a system of philosophy that confounds the true with the false, robs
us of our judgment, despoils the power of approval, [and] deprives us
of our senses" (2.19.61).[49] And last, but not least, (5) Calvin's reference
to those who say that it is the earth rather than the sun that moves
matches the characterization of Hicetas's point of view in the *Academica:*

CICERO: Hicetas . . . holds the view that the heaven, sun, moon, stars, and
          in short all of the things on high are stationary, and that nothing
          in the world is in motion except the earth, which by revolving and
          twisting round its axis with extreme velocity . . .
CALVIN: They . . . say that the sun does not budge, and that it is the earth
          that bestirs itself and that it turns around.

The best way to account for Calvin's statement, in my judgment, is to
suppose that he was recalling the statement in the *Academica* and giving the gist of the passage for the benefit of some members of his
audience, whether actually present or addressed only rhetorically, who
were familiar with the views of the New Academy as recounted by
Cicero. We will return shortly to a consideration of why Calvin should
have alluded to Cicero and who it was he might have been addressing
in doing so.

There are two technical points about the passages we have looked
at that should be clarified. First, there is in Calvin's comment a striking
combination of noun clauses: "that it is the earth that bestirs itself and
that it turns around" (*que c'est la terre que se remue et qu'elle tourne*).
Richard Stauffer and Robert White have argued that he is speaking of
two different motions here—a motion through space, presumably
around the sun (*la terre . . . se remue*), and the rotation of the earth on

[48]See R. Hooykaas, "Calvin and Copernicus," *Organon* 10 (1974) 146n. See also
White, "Calvin and Copernicus," p. 274. Diogenes Laertius, another source of information about the New Academy for the sixteenth century, did not mention Anaxagoras's dictum about snow being black in his discussion of the philosopher (*Vitae*
2.6-15).

[49]*Academica*, Rackham translation, p. 545.

its axis (*elle tourne*).[50] Pierre Marcel, however, feels that the two clauses are parallel, the second repeating and emphasizing the idea of the first.[51] To some extent, the argument has been based on lexical considerations—the question of whether *se remue* specifies a motion from one place to another.[52] But it has also reflected different assumptions concerning the context in which Calvin was speaking at the time. Stauffer, Rosen, and White have assumed that Calvin is most likely referring to the ideas of Copernicus—partly because they did not consider other possible sources of geodynamic ideas to which Calvin had access. Marcel, on the other hand, makes reference to geodynamic ideas in the writings of Adelmann of Liège (Adelmann of Brescia), an eleventh-century critic of the rationalistic view of the eucharist espoused by Berengar of Tours.[53] The passage in question reads as follows:

> What is more absurd than stating that the sky and the stars are motionless [*omnia stare*], that the earth turns on itself [*in medio circumferri*] with a rapid rotary motion [*vewro rapida vertigine*], and that those who believe in the motion of the sky [*coelestia moveri*] are deceived in the same manner as sailors who see shores with their towers and trees recede from them?[54]

The parallel to Calvin's statement is striking, particularly in view of the fact that Adelmann also cited the opinions of those who say "the sun is not warm and that snow is black." Calvin referred to these counter-intuitive notions in exactly the same sequence. Marcel argues that Cal-

---

[50]Stauffer, "Calvin et Copernic," pp. 38-39; White, "Calvin and Copernicus," p. 273. Edward Rosen partly concurs with this view; see "Calvin n'a pas lu Copernic," p. 184.

[51]Marcel, *Calvin et Copernic*, p. 192; and "Calvin and Copernicus," p. 19.

[52]See White, "Calvin and Copernicus," p. 273. Marcel informed me in a letter dated 28 December 1984 of an exchange of correspondence he had with White in which they explicated and defended their respective positions. White argues that the antithesis in Calvin's passage between the motions of the sun and the earth implies that the motion normally assigned to the sun has been assigned to the earth instead. But since the motion of the sun in Aristotelian cosmology is simply the rotation of a sphere that carries the sun with it, the corresponding motion of the earth would be simple rotation around its axis, and not the twofold motion (motion through space and rotation) that White infers. See Seneca's *Quaestiones Naturalis* 7.2.3 for the alternatives in the case of the relative motions of the earth and the universe as a whole (Heath, *Aristarcus*, p. 308).

[53]Marcel, *Calvin et Copernic*, pp. 193-94; "Calvin and Copernicus," p. 20.

[54]Migne, *Patrologia Latina* 143: 1291; quoted by Émile Bréhier in *Histoire de la philosophie*, vol. 3 (Paris, 1931), pp. 553-54 (ET, *The History of Philosophy*, vol. 3, trans. Wade Baskin [Chicago: University of Chicago, 1965], p. 31).

vin was familiar with the controversy surrounding Berengar—it is mentioned a few times in his debates with Westphal about the mode of Christ's presence in the eucharist—and that he would therefore have known of the passage in Adelmann as well.[55]

On the basis of evidence he presents, it seems clear that Marcel's understanding of Calvin's antigeodynamic remark is more plausible than that of Stauffer and White. As the context shows, Calvin was arguing a point of ecclesiastical concern, not an issue of science. However, I can give at least five reasons why it is more likely still that Calvin was alluding directly to Cicero's *Academica*. (1) We have already noted that it is likely that Calvin and some of those to whom he was speaking were aware of Cicero's *Academica*, but we have no direct evidence so far that Calvin knew Adelmann's writings.[56] (2) The issue in Calvin's sermon is dissembling behavior and skeptical ideas, not the nature of the eucharist, as is the case in the Adelmann document. (3) The Adelmann text mentions only the heavens and the stars as being stationary, omitting any reference to the sun. Calvin, on the other hand, omits Cicero's reference to the heavens and the stars. It would appear that both passages are independent abbreviations of Cicero's list, which included the heavens, sun, moon, and stars.[57] (4) Adelmann's reference to the idea that the earth moves utilizes only one noun clause: "that the earth turns on itself with a rapid rotary motion." This is the equivalent of the second clause used by Calvin—"that it turns around"—but it does not account for the duplication of clauses in Calvin. Furthermore, Calvin does not follow Adelmann in men-

---

[55]The *Secunda defensio* of 5 January 1556 and the *Ultima admonitio* of 1557 contain Calvin's responses to Westphal's charges that he was reviving the heresy of Berengar; see *Tracts of John Calvin*, trans. Henry Beveridge (Edinburgh: Calvin Translation Society, 1844-51), 2: 260, 362-63. The dates of these tracts are very close to the date the *Eighth Sermon on 1 Corinthians 10-11* is presumed to have been written (1556). However, Westphal's charge would place him, not Calvin, on the side of Adelmann the critic of Berengar.

[56]In his letter to me of 28 December 1984, Marcel acknowledges that he has no proof that Calvin actually read Adelmann; he infers it from the discussion in the *Institutes*, 4.17.12ff. (see particularly sections 12 and 33 in the John T. McNeil edition of the *Institutes*, trans. Ford Lewis Battles [Philadelphia: Westminster, 1960], pp. 1372, 1405).

[57]Cf. Luther's anti-Copernican remark, in which he maintains that the heavens, the sun, and the moon are all at rest (references in note 12 herein). Notes 58 and 60 herein detail other features of Luther's supposedly off-the-cuff comment that suggest its literary dependence on Cicero's *Academica* in both the Aurifaber and Lauterbach versions.

tioning the rapidity of the earth's rotation. The best explanation again is that both Adelmann and Calvin were drawing on the passage about Hicetas in the *Academica*, rephrasing it in slightly different ways.[58] (5) Finally, there is further evidence that Adelmann was drawing on the *Academica* in the fact that he connects the apparent motion of the sky and stars as viewed from earth with the apparent motion of objects on land as viewed from a moving ship—since he would appear to have borrowed the latter illustration from Cicero as well, albeit from a different section of the *Academica* than the reference to geodynamic ideas.[59] The fact that Calvin does not pick up on the reference to the sailors watching objects on the shore tends to corroborate the assumption that he drew on the text of Cicero directly rather than drawing on Adelmann's citation of it.[60]

I agree with Marcel on the basic point of his argument, however—namely, that Calvin used a second noun clause in order to elaborate the first, not to describe a second type of motion. Both clauses refer to the rotation of the earth about its axis, just as they do in Cicero's citation of Hicetas. The intent of both Cicero and Calvin was to stress the shock value of the idea: none of the things that appear to move are in motion; only the earth, which appears to be at rest, is actually moving.

A second technical point that needs to be cleared up has to do with the use of terms such as "anti-Copernican" and phrases such as "hostility to heliocentrism" to describe Calvin's position.[61] We still have no evidence that Calvin was aware of any theory of heliocentrism, Cop-

[58]Cf. the duplication of verbs in Luther's anti-Copernican statement as reported by Aurifaber: *dass die Erde bewegt wurde und umginge . . . dass Erdreich . . . gingen um und bewegten sich.* Lauterbach has only the single verb *moveri*, which is also found in Cicero.

[59]*Academica*, 2.25.81. The illustration in this passage is not sailors at sea viewing objects on shore, as in the Adelmann document, but rather to individuals in a house on the shore (viz., the participants in the dialogue) viewing objects at sea.

[60]The connection was apparently also made in Luther's anti-Copernican statement in which the illustration was that of the land and its trees as viewed from a wagon or a ship. The connecting link between the two passages in Cicero was probably the proximity in both cases of a discussion about the relative size of the sun; *Academica*, 2.26.82, 2.39.123. I conclude that Adelmann, Luther (Aurifaber?), and Calvin have all three abbreviated Cicero's account independently.

[61]See Stauffer, "Calvin et Copernic," pp. 31, 38-39; and "L'attitude de Réformateurs à l'egard de Copernic," p. 162; and White, "Calvin and Copernicus," pp. 238, 240. Stauffer suggests that Calvin is both anti-Copernican and hostile to heliocentrism; White contends only the latter.

ernican or otherwise—hence my use of the term *geodynamic* to refer to the idea of the motion of the earth that he ridicules in the *Eighth Sermon*.[62]

Was Calvin "antigeodynamic," then, even if he was not anti-Copernican or antiheoliocentric? If the passage in the *Eighth Sermon* were the only evidence available to help us reach a conclusion regarding this larger issue, then even this matter would have to remain moot. But as we have already noted, there are at least three other passages, dating from 1553 to 1557, in which Calvin interprets the stability of the earth in the midst of celestial motion as a clear sign of God's continuous supervision of everyday events within the terrestrial sphere.[63] Against this background, stemming from the natural philosophy of Aristotle, Calvin would naturally have associated the notion that the earth spins with an outright challenge to the sovereignty of God. So we can assume that Calvin was in fact opposed to geodynamic ideas—not because he thought the earth was naturally motionless but because he attributed its otherwise inexplicable stability to the providence of God. Hence, it is no coincidence that he should have made an antigeodynamic statement in the midst of an attack on individuals who blaspheme God's name, destroy his truth, trample his essence, and presume to turn him out of his judgment seat.[64]

Having postulated that Calvin's antigeodynamic remark in the *Eighth Sermon* was based on Cicero's *Academica,* we might well wonder now why he would have drawn upon that classical document. Whom was he arguing against, and what was the real issue at stake?

III. Calvin and Castellio on the Socratic Suspension of Judgment

One of the reasons that the antigeodynamic passage in the *Eighth Sermon* was not recognized as such until Stauffer's article in 1971 is that no one expected to find such a seemingly technical point in one of Calvin's sermons. We have noted that the point of the passage was not quite so technical as supposed by those who interpret it in con-

[62]Rosen uses the terms *géocinématique* and *antigéocinématique* ("Calvin n'a pas lu Copernic," pp. 183-84). These terms are safe enough, but they do not convey the importance of the dynamical element in Calvin's argument, the sense of the stability of the earth in specific contradistinction to the motion all about it was a sign of God's special providence.

[63]See references in note 6 herein.

[64]CO 49: 676ff.

nection with the new astronomy of Copernicus and Rheticus. However, advocacy of such ideas would seem to presuppose a knowledge of the *Academica*, so the precise target of the comment can be narrowed down to those of Calvin's opponents who were fairly well known to his audience and who worked as he did with the classics. Moreover, Calvin must have perceived the targeted party as advocating at least some of the positions he was attacking in the passage: challenging established doctrine in religious matters, gainsaying not merely religious matters but also more general issues of good and evil, making personal judgment rather than divine judgment the final arbiter of truth in such issues, and holding that Scripture is obscure and open to various interpretations concerning some of the points of doctrine that Calvin taught.

When the evidence is formulated in this way, it all clearly points in the direction of Sebastian Castellio and his followers, called Bellianists. Castellio had been an understudy of Calvin at Strasbourg and Geneva from 1540 to 1544; he taught classical Latin at the Collège de Genève for three years before falling out with Calvin over the interpretation of the Song of Songs and the descent of Christ into hell. Upon leaving Geneva, he made his home in Basel, where, after years of poverty, he was appointed to the chair of Greek studies in 1553.[65]

Castellio's first written statements in favor of religious tolerance were published in the prefaces to his two translations of the Bible, the Latin in 1551 and the French in 1555. His basic argument is that God's will is clear in matters of civil crime such as murder, adultery, and theft but that in matters of religion and the interpretation of Scripture there are many unresolved problems. Tolerance in matters of faith is therefore a good thing, he argued, and persecution of supposed heretics is evil. Castellio lamented the fact that in his day good (i.e., tolerance) was often rewarded with evil (i.e., persecution). He maintained that we should all follow the advice of Gamaliel (Acts 5:34ff.) in order to avoid condemning the truth by mistake.[66]

It appears that Calvin had read Castellio's preface to the Latin Bible

[65]The standard reference on Castellio's life and writings is Ferdinand Buisson's *Sébastien Castellion: Sa vie et son oeuvre*, 2 vols. (1892; rpt., Nieuwkoop: B. de Graaf, 1964). On Calvin and Castellio, see Uwe Plath, *Calvin und Basel in den Jahren 1552-1556* (Basel: von Helbing & Lichtenhahn, 1974), especially chaps. 4, 6, 8, and 10-12. More accessible summaries can be found in Roland H. Bainton's *Studies on the Reformation* (Boston: Beacon, 1963), pp. 147-81; and Joseph Lecler's *Tolerance and the Reformation*, vol. 1 (New York: Association, 1960), pp. 336-64.

[66]Castellio, *Concerning Heretics*, trans. Roland Bainton (1935; rpt., New York: Octagon, 1965), pp. 212-16, 257-58.

(addressed to Edward VI) as early as 1552. In his *Commentary on Acts*, published in February of that year, he repudiates the policy of Gamaliel, whom he describes as "a gentle and moderate man" who was nonetheless lacking in prudence. If Gamaliel's advice were consistently followed, Calvin argues, "men must punish nobody, and, further, all crime must go uncorrected." Those few who regard his advice as an oracle from God are mistaken in their judgment, he asserts, for God has established magistrates to punish crime and has set elders over his church "to force the refractory to order." Gamaliel himself was in doubt about the matter at hand and did not dare make up his mind whether the punishment of religious dissenters (in this case, the apostles) was good or bad.[67]

The issue between Calvin and Castellio had been joined, therefore, even before the execution of Servetus, but the latter event in October 1553 was bound to have exacerbated their disagreement. In January 1554, Calvin published his *Defensio orthodoxae fidei* ("Defense of the Orthodox Faith"), which was a defense of the persecution of heretics as much as it was a refutation of the views of Servetus. In it he complains of "another fanatic" (*alter fanaticus*) who regards Servetus as his brother and denies that heretics should be punished on the ground that Scripture is unclear and is subject to different interpretations. But what will become of the true religion, he asks, if instruction in piety is uncertain and in doubt (*incerta as suspensa*)?[68] And if the sword is not to be used to counteract heresy, are theft, adultery, and murder to go unpunished as well? To the contrary, he argues, the divinely sanctioned calling of the magistrate requires "that impure and petulant tongues not be allowed to mutilate God's sacred name and trample upon his worship."[69] The critics of Servetus's execution cannot appeal to the authority of Gamaliel, he insists, because such advice would destroy both civil and ecclesiastical order. "Gamaliel was in doubt

[67]Calvin, *Commentary on Acts* (5:34), trans. John W. Fraser and W. J. G. McDonald, vol. 6 of *Calvin's New Testament Commentaries*, (henceforth abbreviated *CNTC*), ed. David W. Torrance and Thomas F. Torrance (Edinburgh: Oliver & Boyd, 1959-73), p. 152. Cf. Calvin's comments on the judgment of Ananias and Sapphira in Acts 5:1-9, especially such phrases as "contempt of God" and "perverse vanity and ambition," which he uses to describe the pair; he urges that in their punishment "there has been set before us, as in a mirror, the gravity of the spiritual judgment which is still hidden" (*CNTC*, 6: 132-33, 137).

[68]*CO* 8: 464 (*Concerning Heretics*, p. 267). The preceding two paragraphs (*CO* 8: 462-63) deal with the judgment of Ananias and Sapphira.

[69]*CO* 8: 468, 470 (*Concerning Heretics*, pp. 269, 271-72).

(*ambigens*) as to what was right and suspended judgment (*suspendit sententiam*) like a blind man in the dark."[70]

Before the end of March 1554, Castellio had published a massive defense of religious tolerance under the pseudonym Martin Bellius: *De haereticis, an sint persequendi* ("On Whether Heretics Should Be Persecuted"). This work was a collection of statements in favor of tolerance from various writers, including mainline churchmen such as Luther and Calvin on the one hand, and critics such as Agrippa and Castellio himself on the other hand. Calvin discerned Castellio's editorial hand in the arguments he presented in the introductory dedication (to Duke Christoph of Wurttemberg), which were almost identical to those of Castellio presented in his preface to the Latin Bible: issues of Christian doctrine such as the Trinity and predestination are not certain, yet those who hold dissenting views are hated even though they try to live good Christian lives; to hate the good, however, is the same as to love evil; in matters of conduct, God's will is clear, but in religion only a few things, such as the existence of the one true God, are beyond doubt.[71]

The general terms of the debate between Calvin and Castellio were thus well established by the summer of 1554, and they were exactly the same terms that appear in the context surrounding Calvin's antigeo-dynamic remark in the *Eighth Sermon*. However, the debate as of March 1554 did not yet make use of Cicero's *Academica* in any specific way, so far as I can tell.[72] It was more an issue of tolerance than of skepticism as such, but the latter issue came to the fore in the second half of 1554 and the first part of 1555. We turn now to this development.

[70]*CO* 8: 472-73 (*Concerning Heretics*, p. 279). Erasmus had already cited Cicero's *Academica* on Socrates in his *Antibarbari* of 1520 (*Erasmi Opera Omnia*, 1.1:88, 90-91).

[71]Castellio, *Concerning Heretics*, pp. 122-23, 131-32. Calvin attributed *De haereticus* to Castellio and his associates in his letter to Bullinger of 5 April 1554 (*CO* 15: 95-96; *Letters of John Calvin*, ed. Jules Bonnet [Philadelphia: Presbyterian Board of Publication, 1858], 3: 34-35).

[72]It is quite possible that Calvin had the New Academy in mind when he described Gamaliel (= Castellio?) as being uncertain and suspending judgment in the *Defensio* of early 1554. Already in 1550, Beza had referred to Claude d'Espence as an *Academicus* for his being undecided (*incertior*) on the issue of justification by faith (see *Correspondance de Théodore de Bèze* [Geneva: E. Droz, 1960], 1: 64). In 1525 Luther had charged Erasmus with taking refuge in the opinions of the Academics because of his reluctance to accept the doctrine of predestination (*WA*, 18: 603ff.; *LW*, 33: 19-24). All of this can be accounted for on the basis of a general acquaintance with the ideas of the New Academy rather than a specific reference to Cicero's *Academica*, however.

In August 1554 Calvin's *Commentary on Genesis* was published, and he took the opportunity to resume his attack on Castellio in the dedicatory epistle:

> In the meantime, audacious scribblers arise, as from our own bosom [*quasi e sinu nostro*], who not only obscure the light of sound doctrine with clouds of error, or infatuate the simple and the less experienced with their wicked ravings, but by profane license of scepticism [*dubitandi*], allow themselves to uproot the whole of religion. For, as if by their rank ironies and cavils, they could prove themselves genuine disciples of Socrates, they have no axiom more plausible than that faith must be free . . . so that it may be possible, by reducing everything to a matter of doubt [*quamvis de re ambigendo*] to render Scripture flexible (so to speak) as a nose of wax [*instar nosi cerei*]. Therefore, they who, being captivated by the allurements of this new school [*novae buius academiae*], now indulge in doubtful speculations, obtain at length such proficiency, that they are always learning, yet never come to the knowledge of truth [2 Tim. 3:7].[73]

The underlying issues of the perspicuity of Scripture and the certainty of Christian doctrine are the same here as in the earlier phase of the debate. The passing reference to "audacious scribblers . . . as from our own bosom" clearly points to Castellio and may be one of those rare passages in Calvin where a personal sense of betrayal and hurt comes to the surface. In addition, however, the descriptions of Castellio and his followers as "genuine disciples of Socrates" and members of the new school or academy (*nova academia*) probably refer to Cicero's *Academica*. Compare what the two have to say about Socrates on the suspension of judgment:

> CICERO: The method of discussion pursued by Socrates . . . is to affirm nothing himself but to refute others, to assert that he knows nothing except the fact of his own ignorance, and that he surpassed all other people in that . . . he himself thinks he knows nothing, and that he believed this to have been the reason why Apollo declared him to be the wisest of all men, because all wisdom consists solely in not thinking that you know what you do not know.
>
> . . . Socrates held that nothing can be known; he made only one exception, no more—he said that he knew that he knew nothing.[74]

---

[73]*CO* 15: 200 (*Commentaries on the First Book of Moses,* trans. John King [Edinburgh: Calvin Translation Society, 1847], 1: lii-liii).

[74]*Academica,* 1.16; 2.74 (Rackham translation, pp. 425ff., 561). The other major source of information about the New Academy, Diogenes Laertius, was much less impressive in his description of Socrates ("he knew nothing except just the fact of his ignorance"; 2.32). It must be kept in mind, however, as it was known in Calvin's

CALVIN: Genuine disciples of Socrates . . . have no axiom more plausible than that faith must be free.

Evidence for the general awareness of this debate comes from the fact that similar accusations were made by Calvin's associates. Beza's refutation of *De haereticis*, which came out in September 1554, uses the New Academy label to describe the Bellianists repeatedly throughout the text and even in the title: *De haereticis a civili Magistratu puniendis Libellus, adversus Martini Belli farraginem, & novorum Academicorum sectam* ("On the Punishment of Heretics by the Civil Magistrate: Against the Collection of Martin Bellius and the Sect of the New Academics"). Like Calvin, Beza used Cicero's account of the Socratic suspension of judgment as ammunition against Castellio (*Academicus quispiam*) though in a more sarcastic manner, as is evident in the following excerpt:

> Therefore, when you instruct him zealously, he begs that no force be brought to bear on his conscience. But, in the end, when you continue to press him and expose his impudence in distorting the testimony of Scripture, he will escape by saying that no one knows anything besides himself alone in spite of the resolution of the ancient academics who said that they knew only one thing, that they knew nothing.[75]

In spite of the difference in emphasis, Beza's tactic was the same as Calvin's: to discredit the classics teacher by implicating him in the paradoxical teachings of the ancient skeptics. Farel also described the Bellianists of Montbéliard as "Academics" in a letter of March 1555.[76]

The closest approximation I can find to the terms used in Calvin's *Eighth Sermon*, however, come in his epistle to the church of Poitiers of 20 February 1555. The purpose of this letter was to warn the church against the teachings of a disciple of Castellio's by the name of Jean Vertunien de Lavau, who was trying to spread the teachings of his master in the district of Poitiers.[77] As in the dedicatory epistle to his

circle: Beza cited Diogenes Laertius 2.38 on the accusation of impiety made against Socrates in his *De haereticis* (Geneva, 1554 edn., p. 214). Calvin cited other parts of the classic in his *Seneca Commentary* of 1552 and in the 1559 edition of the *Institutes* (3.10.1).

[75]Beza, *De haereticis a civili Magistratu puniende Libellus* (Geneva: Oliva Roberti Stephani, 1554), pp. 187-88. Cf. the French in Buisson's *Sébastien Castellion*, 2: 26-26.

[76]Farel, in a letter to Blaurer (*CO* 15: 509).

[77]See Bietenholz, *Basle and France*, p. 125n.; and *Concerning Heretics*, pp. 109-10. Calvin says that de Lavau became a disciple of Castellio and a doctor in his school of thought in only three days (*CO* 15: 445; *Letters of John Calvin*, 3: 149).

Commentary on Genesis, Calvin describes the Bellianists as this new school or academy (*ceste nouvelle escholle*) and ascribes to them

> their fine maxim that all contradictory discussions should be allowed, for this reason, that there is nothing certain or determined, and that the Scripture is but a nose of wax [*est ung nez de cire*], so that by their accounts, the faith held by all Christians respecting the Trinity, predestination, free grace, is quite indifferent, and about which people may dispute as much as they like.[78]

Beyond these now familiar references to the interpretation of Scripture and the certainty of doctrine, however, there were several new ideas in Calvin's argument that match the remaining features of the context of the antigeodynamic remark in the *Eighth Sermon* exactly. (1) Like the party attacked in the *Eighth Sermon,* Castellio is described as a "madman" (*ung fantastique nomme Sebastian Castallio*).[79] (2) Calvin likewise describes his opponents as those who "blaspheme the truth," "trample God under foot" (*le fouller aux piedz*), and "pervert all order."[80] (3) They are also said to be "actuated by the spirit of Satan."[81] (4) Calvin accuses De Lavau of tolerating "papal superstitions" and the "idolatries of popery."[82] (5) He also describes De Lavau as "one of those who call white black," apparently in reference to the ancient skeptics who cited the maxim of Anaxagoras.[83] (6) And in the same breath, he also describes De Lavau as one "whom God detests and curses by the mouth of his prophet Isaiah"—a reference to Isaiah 5:20, which he also applies to the adversary he attacks in the *Eighth Sermon.*[84]

I conclude that Calvin's antigeodynamic comment in the *Eighth Sermon* is best understood as the sequel to a series of attacks on Castellio and his followers that originated in Calvin's *Commentary on Acts,* the *Defensio orthodoxae fidei,* the dedicatory epistle in the *Commentary on Genesis,* and the epistle to the church of Poitiers. In his desire to refute Castellio's arguments for religious toleration, Calvin developed the notion that toleration was tantamount to skepticism and that tolerance in

[78]*CO* 15: 441-42 (*Letters of John Calvin,* 3: 144-45).

[79]*CO* 15: 440 (*Letters of John Calvin,* 3: 143). Calvin also used the term *fantastique* to describe Anabaptists and Libertines generally, of course.

[80]*CO* 15: 442, 445 (*Letters of John Calvin,* 3: 145-46, 148); cf. *CO* 49: 676-77.

[81]*CO* 15: 442, 445 (*Letters of John Calvin,* 3: 145-46).

[82]*CO* 15: 443-44 (*Letters of John Calvin,* 3: 147-48).

[83]*CO* 15: 444 (*Letters of John Calvin,* 3: 147).

[84]*CO* 15: 444 (*Letters of John Calvin,* 3: 147); cf. *CO* 49: 676.

matters of religion led to uncertainty in matters of natural philosophy and civil morality as well.[85] Already in the last two documents mentioned, Calvin had begun to mine Cicero's *Academica* for incriminating ideas that he felt Castellio would have to accept as corollaries of his own position in favor of tolerance. In the *Commentary on Genesis* he charged Castellio with advocating Socrates's maxim, as reported by Cicero, that nothing could be known for sure. In describing Castellio's disciple De Lavau in his letter to the church of Poitiers, Calvin added the paradoxical notion, attributed by Cicero to Anaxagoras, that white could be called black. Finally, in the *Eighth Sermon*, he spoke of the blasphemous notion that the sun stands still and the earth turns. Calvin's implicit ridicule of these notions is not antiheliocentric but anti-geodynamic, not anti-Copernican but anti-Castellian.

Thus far we have only considered Castellio's advocacy of tolerance and the rejoinders of Calvin, Beza, and Farel. We have evidence of a response in kind that Castellio formulated sometime during the period from the mid-1550s to the early 1560s. It appears in the *Contra libellum Calvini* ("Against the Book of Calvin"), written under the pseudonym Vaticanus in 1554 (though not published until 1612). The response did not add substantially to the argument with which we are concerned here, however; it merely took up the points of Calvin's *De orthodoxae fidei* one by one and reaffirmed the basic position Castellio had outlined in earlier writings, particularly stressing the fact that it was only in religion that matters are uncertain, not in matters of morality such as homicide and adultery.[86]

Of greater significance to us is Castellio's *De haereticis non puniendis* ("That Heretics Ought Not Be Punished"), written under the pseudonym Basil Montfort in the winter of 1554-55—that is, just about the same time as Calvin wrote his epistle to the church of Poitiers. It was translated into French soon thereafter, but neither the Latin nor the French was published until 1971.[87] Castellio vehemently denied Calvin's and Beza's charges that the Bellianists were Academics in any real

---

[85]Calvin took up these themes again in his *Commentary on Psalms*, both in the preface to the work (dated 22 July 1557) and in the treatment of Psalm 119:90-91 (*CO* 31: 29-32; 32: 254 [Anderson translation, xlv-xlvii; 4: 470]). The latter in particular shows the connection in Calvin's mind between the authority of God's commands in matters of faith and the stability of the order of nature.

[86]See *Concerning Heretics*, pp. 267-70, 281-82.

[87]*Sébastien Castellion: De l'impunité de hérétiques*, ed. Bruno Becker and M. Valkhoff (Geneva: Librairie Droz, 1971). The Latin manuscript is dated 11 March 1555 (p. 4).

sense inasmuch as they did affirm many things about God and Scripture.[88] But, since the matter had been raised, he asserted that the New Academy was in fact the best of the sects of the ancient philosophers and that no one of good sense would fault their basic policy of not being dogmatic on matters that were uncertain. He then cited two example from Cicero's *Academica*. First there was Socrates, the first of the skeptics, who knew that he really knew nothing and was rightly regarded as the wisest of the pagans for this bit of wisdom.[89] On the other hand, there was the archdogmatist Aristotle, who denied that the world was created and who advocated such crimes as abortion and infanticide.[90] Such is the fruit of dogmatism!

It was not until he wrote *De arte dubitandi et confidendi* ("On the Method of Doubting and Believing") in 1563, however, that Castellio took up any of the matters of natural philosophy mentioned in the *Academica*. There are two kinds of controversial statements, he explained. Some are controversial because they are contrary to the senses—for example, assertions that the eucharistic bread is Christ's body or that snow is black. Others are controversial because they are beyond the competence of the senses to determine—for example, propositions about the nature of God and the state of the soul after death or assertions about the nature of the stars and whether there is anything at the center of the earth (to fix it in place?)[91] The argument makes perfect sense as a surrejoinder to Calvin's earlier charge that uncertainty in matters such as the nature of God would lead to absurd consequences in other matters, such as the proposition that snow is black. Castellio points out that even Calvin was not dogmatic about undecidable issues in natural philosophy. And if Calvin could discriminate between the certain and the uncertain in natural philosophy, why couldn't he do the same in theology?

IV. Conclusions

We may sum up our conclusions as follows: Calvin and his associates tried their best to pin the label of the New Academy on Castellio

---

[88]*Sébastien Castellion*, pp. 22, 25 (Latin); 224, 227 (French).

[89]*Sébastien Castellion*, pp. 22, 224-25. Castellio adds to the French manuscript, "il est moins degereus de n'affirmer choses certaines que d'affermer choses incertaines" (p. 225); cf. *Academica*, 2.125.

[90]*Sébastien Castellion*, pp. 22-23, 225. Aristotle's dogmatism on the eternity of the world is ridiculed in the *Academica*, 2.119-20.

[91]See *Concerning Heretics*, pp. 294ff.; cf. the *Academica*, 2.72, 100, 122 concerning the issues of natural philosophy cited. Further citations of Cicero can be found in *Concerning Heretics*, p. 299; cf. the *Academica*, 2.19, 79, 81-82, 123.

and his followers in an effort to discredit them; this much is well known. It is less well known that after 1554 Calvin made specific references to Cicero's *Academica* and the skeptical views of ancient philosophers discussed in that work (e.g., Socrates and Anaxagoras) as an integral part of his attack on the Bellianists. This is confirmed by the fact that Castellio drew on other passages from the *Academica* in his attempts to refute Calvin's charge that he was an Academic in the strict sense.

Calvin's antigeodynamic remark in the *Eighth Sermon*, then, should be understood at three levels.

1. In the strictly literary sense, the remark is an allusion to the opinion of the ancient Pythagorean Hicetas as reported in Cicero's *Academica*. It was made, therefore, in reference to the notion that the earth rotates on its axis, not in reference to Copernicus's hypothesis that the earth revolves about a center located somewhere near the sun. It is antigeodynamic, not antiheliocentric.

2. In the context of Calvin's theological and political struggles of the time (around 1556), we can assume that the allusion to the *Academica* was aimed at Castellio and his followers and was intended to substantiate Calvin's claim that tolerance in matters of religion would lead to skepticism in natural philosophy as well as anarchy in civil affairs. Calvin's antigeodynamic remark was anti-Castellian (or anti-Bellianist), not anti-Copernican.

3. Calvin's choice of the notion that the earth turns as a sign of blasphemy makes sense in the context of his understanding of cosmology. Aristotelian physics could explain the dynamics of the heavens on purely naturalistic principles, but it could not account, in Calvin's view, for the stability of the earth against rotation forces. The everyday sense of the earth's stability was to his mind a clear indication of God's immediate and continuous control of events even in the terrestrial sphere. Conversely, anyone who challenged the absolute authority of God's will in everyday matters might be expected to doubt the very immobility of the earth, as Hicetas and the Academics had done

None of the evidence we have surveyed in this essay excludes the possibility that Calvin had some knowledge of the work of Copernicus or even that he may have been critical of it as Luther and Melanchthon had been. It is possible that the new cosmology was discussed while Castellio was working with Calvin in the early 1540s, but there is no evidence of such discussions comparable to Luther's Table Talk of 1539. Hence, we are back to the situation Edward Rosen described in 1960: we have no clear evidence that Calvin ever commented on or even knew of the work of Copernicus.

71

CALVIN AND COPERNICUS*

by

PIERRE CH. MARCEL

'If Calvin had opened the *Treatise on the World* he would have repudiated and condemned Copernicus, just as his successors condemned Galileo.' 'Who, Calvin asks, would be so rash as to place Copernicus above the Holy Spirit?' These affirmations are both without proof: the one concerning what Calvin *would have done* if he had known Copernicus, the other concerning what he *would have said* had he known him; and both are expressions of disrespect and slander.

Two other approaches to the thought of Calvin have been proposed: (a) Calvin was unfamiliar both with Copernicus and with the content of the first book of the *De Revolutionibus*, published in 1543, and consequently remained *pre*-Copernican. (b) The silence of Calvin does not prove that he had no knowledge of Copernicus; it is impossible for him not to have known of him. But, on the basis of knowing him, he is asserted to be *anti*-Copernican. Several fragmentary quotations have been advanced from different places in this connection, but the same texts are claimed in support of two divergent and doctrinaire *a priori* positions. This, specifically, is the unresolved debate which took place in 1960-1961 between Edward Rosen and Joseph Ratner.

In 1966 I had already — without developing the thesis — suggested that Calvin had certainly read Copernicus and knew his system, but that, respecting the limits of his vocation, he had the competence neither to approve nor to criticize him.

More recently (1971-1978) Richard Stauffer, professor in the faculty of Protestant Theology in Paris and director of studies at the Ecole des Hautes-Etudes, has claimed, thanks to the 'discovery' of a 'decisive text', which 'clearly constitutes an unequivocal condemnation of the supporters of heliocentrism', whose theories were plainly 'hateful' to Calvin, that he was a fierce *anti*copernican. '*Calvin continued to be the prisoner of geocentrism*'. Further discussion is henceforth quite impermissible: the question is settled, final! Calvin not only remained 'a man of his time' but, aware of the 'discoveries' of Copernicus through

---

* This article has been translated by Philip E. Hughes, Th.D., D.Litt., professor of New Testament, at Westminster Theological Seminary, Philadelphia, U.S.A.

It is a summary of Pierre Marcel's work, *Calvin & Copernic, La Légende ou les Faits? La Science et l'Astronomie chez Calvin*, published in *La Revue Réformée*, Tome XXXI, 1980/1, 210 pp.; 10 rue de Villars, F.78100 Saint-Germain-en-Laye, France. For the 'quotations, references, and texts of Calvin, and the bibliography, the reader is requested to turn to this volume.

14

his 'disciples', he declared himself fiercely hostile to the 'copernican revolution'.[1]

I was aware, well before this affirmation, of a historical error: in no way was there a 'copernican revolution' in the 1550s. No historian of astronomy would think of holding it against even a specialist because, in that epoch, he did not embrace the ideas of Copernicus, which in any case were neither systematic nor proven. If several generations of mathematicians and astronomers — without counting the philosophers — consistently questioned or opposed them, not only in the sixteenth but throughout the seventeenth century, how can one complain against a theologian who was not a mathematician? A reproach of this kind can only be an anachronism, a projection into the past of a post-newtonian situation! Accordingly, the force of the objection made against Calvin vanishes. The proof of this seems to me to be firmly established on the evidence of incontestable authorities.[2] This issue of chronology continues to be of capital importance in the appraisal of Calvin's thought and his place in history; all the same, it is not dependent on it. Therefore, once refuted, it is unnecessary to devote much space to it here. The debate lies elsewhere.

Richard Stauffer proposes to prove that the visceral anti-copernicanism he detects in Calvin is an integral part of what he believes to be '*his* cosmology'. This aversion happens to be, in an inconsistent and contradictory manner, in conflict with certain fundamental rules for the interpretation of the Holy Scriptures postulated by Calvin himself, without which he would never have succeeded — such spiritual incompetence! — in formulating an acceptable synthesis or in remaining faithful to his own principles.

The prejudice imported into the representation offered of Calvin's thought and its credibility far surpasses this verdict. '*Calvin condemned, slaughtered the disciples of Copernicus*' — '*Calvin continued to be the prisoner of geocentrism*' — '*Calvin had wind of the discoveries of Copernicus and rejected them without appeal*' . . . When such assertions, made by authors of repute, come to the attention of a reader at the end of the twentieth century, how can he not feel that he is intended to think that Calvin — if not historic calvinism — did not have due respect for the inventive capabilities of human reason, that he despised science and men of learning, and, as has been said, rejected 'a discovery of direct observation and calculation'. What good can be expected from a vehement and narrow-minded person who denies the reality of facts?

---

[1] Richard Stauffer, *Calvin et Copernic*, in *Revue de l'Histoire des Religions*, Jan.-March 1971, 31-40, and Oct. 1972, 185-186. *L'attitude des Réformateurs à l'égard de Copernic*, in 'Avant, avec, après Copernic', XXXIème Semaine de Sythèse, Librairie Scientifique et Technique Albert Blanchard, 9, rue de Médicis, 75006 Paris, 1975. *Dieu, la création et la Providence dans la prédication de Calvin*, ed. Peter Lang, Berne, 1978.

[2] Cf. the second part of my study, pp. 139-180: 'Copernicus and the Order of the World': I. The Inspirers; II. The Book of Revolutions; III. Copernicus did not demonstrate the immobility of the Sun; IV. The battle of the Hypotheses; V. The Order of the World; VI. The diffusion of Copernicanism; VII. Opponents and sceptics; VIII. The Disciples . . . and the proofs.

15

This is how the band of those who have not read Calvin will think. And if the Bible leads to this sort of confrontation with science, what is one to think of the theology of the Reformation,what is one to expect from the Bible today?

Certainly if, after serious study, this judgment brought against Calvin should appear to be accurate, we would readily receive this verdict and in accepting it submit ourselves to it. There can be no question of denying evidence for the sake of 'building up' Calvin today. But this is absolutely not the case!

It has thus been my aim to read and understand Calvin *according to himself*, following the line of his own thought — like the analogy of faith in the Scriptures — and thereby to discover, *for it is there*, the third solution. Calvin knew Copernicus; he read the Prefaces and the first book of the *De Revolutionibus*. Not only did he not criticize the hypotheses, but he regarded them as legitimate for the advancement of science. In doing so Calvin remained consistent with himself, for he always honoured the sciences, praised men of learning, encouraged research. Most particularly, he loved *astronomy*. He never placed faith and 'honest' and true science, Scripture and nature, in opposition to each other. He magnified each as 'one of the hands of God' to lead us to him and to draw out our admiration, our love. Accordingly, Calvin, expounder of the *order of nature*, and Copernicus, 'poet' and defender of the *order of the world*, were destined to be in harmony without the facts of nature ever being in conflict with the revelations of Scripture and the convictions of the Faith. That is what we intend to show, without there being any necessity to develop a proof of what is plain.[3] Our subject is therefore broader — and by a great deal — than would have been implied by the mere consideration of the too fragile hypothesis of Professor Stauffer, to the examination of which we here accord the first place before dealing with the fundamental themes of the thought of our Reformer.

I

Dr. Stauffer claims to have unearthed a text which hitherto has escaped the attention of investigators. It involves a short passage of twenty words which Calvin uttered, apparently in 1556, in the course of his eighth sermon on 1 Corinthians 10 (verses 19-22):[4]

They will say that the sun does not change position and that it is the earth that moves and turns.

Taken by itself, this short clause seems alluring, so much so that in the eyes of Dr. Stauffer it 'clearly constitutes and unequivocal condemnation of the supporters of heliocentrism'. The affirmation here cited proves this; the evidence is found in it alone. It is plain, however, that the sense of this passage should be based on that of the sermon of which it is a part. It is not beside the point to find out the spirit in which the matters preceding and following this passage were treated.

[3] What is of interest is to reproduce what Calvin says. That is why more than 300 quotations from all parts of his work are given here.

[4] Sermons on chapters 10 and 11 of the First Epistle to the Corinthians *Calvini Opera*, Vol. 49, p. 677.

16

What is the central theme of 1 Corinthians 10:14-22? The supper of the Lord Jesus Christ has nothing in common with pagan sacrifices which are offered to demons and not to God. Christians should flee idolatry: the communion of the body and blood of Christ,with the bread and wine, excludes all communication with demons. Every reasonable person, with the Bible in hand, judges the accuracy of this statement without difficulty. The situation was that certain Corinthians, pleading the vanity of idols and their non-being, considered that it was possible to associate themselves with 'the table of demons' with a good conscience. A sacrament, however, establishes participation by communication: the Lord's supper enables us to participate in communion with God himself, the sacraments of pagans with Satan. This is quite obvious! It is evidence which no Christian can deny.

But, it is asked, if the heart is not involved, does the external act still have any significance and does it deserve to be censured? Indeed it does, for every act has an *objective* aspect which necessarily implies the adherence of the heart: there is no middle term between God and the devil! No one should *give the appearance* of approving abominations which God condemns. *It is not possible to change the truth of God into a lie, light into darkness, good into evil, vision into blindness*: such is the *leitmotiv* of this sermon.

The importance of this theme was connected with a question of immediate relevance: *Today*, Calvin says, some members of reformed churches are prepared to associate themselves with the ceremonies of the Roman Church: the mass, baptism, burial, etc., under the pretext of courtesy and friendship towards one's neighbours or relations, in order to avoid unpleasantness. 'Our heart is not involved when we go', they say by way of excuse. Calvin, however, retorts that since idolatry cannot be committed without the heart being engaged their going cannot be without deceit, for they are ignorant neither of the teaching of Scripture nor of *the spiritual worship of the body*.

It is sufficient for the preacher to recall the malediction of the prophet (Isaiah 5:20): *'Woe to those who call evil good and good evil, who put darkness for light and light for darkness!'* Woe, therefore, to those who seek frivolous excuses for *'disguising'* their sins! In doing this they surpass the greatest of offences, for they attempt to nullify the truth of God. Then, suddenly, with dramatic intensity, we find ourselves confronted with the central biblical theme of the fall: 'Has God truly said?' (Genesis 3:1). For the deep inner cause of sin is precisely to doubt a word of God in order to welcome a lie of Satan, to change the truth of God into a lie and a lie into truth, to call God a liar and Satan truthful! Here is the focal point of this sermon. We are at the very depth of wickedness and abomination! It is an attitude which Calvin describes with the key-word, *disguise*, a term he uses on each occasion. Disguise? That means, through dissimulation, to manipulate something so that it cannot be recognized, to present it as being something other than it is, *to pervert the order of things* as it is apprehended by the naive experience of ordinary people *from what is seen in nature and from what is read in Scripture*. 'To walk in candour and in truth' — an expression dear to Calvin — is to acknowledge, simply and sincerely, what one sees as being nothing other than what one sees.

17

Here the act of 'disguising' is fundamental; it is associated with refusal to distinguish white from black and to see things as they present themselves to our eyes. What is tragic (and horrible!) is that men, knowing that the divine doctrine is pure and holy, 'attempt not only to permit themselves every kind of evil, but wish evil to be reckoned good, that vice should be virtue, that God should be dragged from his throne and should no longer be judge; in short, that we should no longer distinguish between good and evil'. This would be the height of hypocrisy, and we would then be encouraged 'to disguise everything and no longer to discern anything', to *falsify* the truth!

Now if one compares the teaching of the Apostles with the traditions attributed to them by the papists, 'one will find an antithesis as great as between light and darkness or between white and black'. Hypocrisy, adulteration, disguising, falsification, quite intolerable! Throughout these sermons, and especially in the one we are considering, we are in the presense of a systematic 'balancing' between biblical thought and profane thought, which our Reformer describes and depicts with a great wealth of opposites: truth and falsehood, good and evil, light and darkness, clarity and obscurity, vision and blindness, white and black, sweet and bitter, fire and water, virtue and vice, wisdom and folly, loyalty and deceit, openness and dissimulation, sincerity and hypocrisy, will and deed, genuineness and counterfeit, sensory perception and its disguise, God and Satan . . .

Very well! The thought which Calvin develops in a lively manner in the passage to which Dr. Stauffer refers is no different from this. What does he in fact say? (The emphases are mine.)

'We see what lesson we are to learn from this passage: it is *to disguise neither good nor evil but to walk in candour and in truth*. When we see something good and commendable we should acknowledge that *it is so*; and we should not imitate those fantastic persons who have a spirit of bitterness and contradiction, always trying to find fault and to *pervert the order of nature*. We will see none so frenetic, not only in matters of religion, but for the purpose of showing that they have a monstrous nature, so that *they will say that the sun does not change position and that it is the earth that moves and turns*. When we see such persons, it can only be that the devil has possessed them and that God presents them to us as mirrors in order to cause us to continue in his fear. This is the case with all who are maliciously critical and think nothing of being shameless. When one says to them: 'This is hot', 'Oh no', they will say, *'it is obviously cold'*. When one shows them something black, they will say that *it is white*. Otherwise, it is like someone saying that *snow is black*, despite the fact that *one perceives* its whiteness, which is something *acknowledged by all*; none the less he wishes to contradict it openly. But that is how it is with frenzied individuals who wish to *change the order of nature*, to *dazzle the eyes of* men, and to *stupefy their senses*.'

Is this not a faithful summary of the principal teaching of these sermons, that of this day as well as those which precede and follow? 'The lesson which we have to learn', says Calvin, 'is to *disguise neither good nor evil*'. To say that this snow *is* black, although everybody sees what it really *is*, namely, *white*; to assert that this *is* cold, although everybody perceives and knows that it *is* hot, this is to 'disguise', to *change the order* of nature, to *blind the eyes* of men, to *stupefy their senses*. To affirm, finally, that 'the sun does not change position and that it is the earth that moves and turns', although day after day everyone *sees* exactly the opposite, that is to give proof of effrontery and of a spirit of bitterness and contrariness, for the sake of contradicting always and everywhere and perverting true religion.

Do we find here a denial of what could be a scientific truth? But is it not solely a question of *denying what is seen* by 'disguising' it, of *falsifying what is obvious*, the very basis and certification of our experience, the direct and immediate knowledge which we have of things as they are perceived by us, of the texts of Scripture as we read them? The various examples given (cold, black, white, the earth) are placed in the same perspective with relation to what such persons *deny*, the experience of what *is*. Here Calvin does not oppose any scientific fact from the viewpoint of naive experience: he never did this! For the purpose of maintaining the purity of religion he simply demands that the judgment of what is seen should be in conformity with the criteria of sight, that what one feels should conform to the norms of touch, and that one should not pretend to see and cause others to see, to feel and cause others to feel things otherwise than we see and touch them. This is a theme fundamental to the thought of Calvin. The last section of this passage is formal: Calvin took up his position and remained on the theological plane; he remains in direct relation with the biblical text and does not venture into any pseudo-scientific digression.

If Calvin — and this observation is pertinent — keeps the terms he uses here to designate his most redoubtable adversaries, this is not because they were supposedly followers of Copernicus, but, as we have seen, the bitterest enemies of God, who were 'slaughtered' by Calvin, not just here in a few paragraphs but throughout the length of his sermons. More than fifty epithets, repeatedly directed against God's sworn enemies, adorn the two hundred and fifty pages of these sermons, before as well as after this passage. Moreover, does not Calvin favour, when appropriate, those who oppose science and scientific research with equally vigorous terms? Them also he calls 'fantastics', for example, when referring to the star of the magi.

Can the 'little passage', taken quite literally, really bear the meaning which Dr. Stauffer assigns it? The rotation of the earth on its axis is not a characteristic of the thought of Copernicus: it was a concept advanced in antiquity and it was almost a commonplace for a number of scholars in the 1500s. For these few words to have an authentic Copernican ring about hem, they should also signify the rotation of the earth *around the sun*. Who when hearing them would understand them in this way? 'Moves' and 'turns' are synonymous here and reinforce each other. If Calvin had intended to sigmatize the rotating and orbital movements of the earth would he have found it sufficient to say, 'the earth moves', in order to make us think, 'each year the earth makes a complete orbit around the sun'? . . . an affirmation his hearers were then incapable of conceiving!

Does not this little sentence, then, merely confront us with a simple matter of style designed to deride the unreasonable denial of the

19

evidence of the senses? One is reminded of the assertion of Paschasius Radbertus (786-865) that in the eucharist 'the substance of the bread and wine become the body and blood of Christ by virtue of the Spirit'; to which Berengar of Tours (c. 1000-1088) replied that it is impossible simultaneously to affirm and deny two contradictory things, namely, that the bread and wine subsist as such on the altar *after* the consecration. No affirmation, in fact, can be sustained in its entirety if one part of it is suppressed: we do not have the right to contradict ourselves when formulating dogmas, as the realists do quite shamelessly. It is an absurdity which Adelmann of Liège, Berengar's fellow disciple, derided by means of three images: 'What could be more absurd than to assert that the heavens and the stars are motionless, and that the earth turns on itself with a rapid movement of rotation, and that those who believe in the movement of the heavens are decieved like the sailors who see the towers and trees on the shoreline disappearing from their sight?' An absurdity just as absurd, he says, as the opinion of those who believe 'that the sun is not hot and that snow is black'. The structure of Calvin's logic is identical. There is no doubt that he read these texts. Did he recover the corresponding notions from his memory? Possibly; but it is enough that they could have been derived from places common to the eleventh century, so that there is no need for us to attribute to them in the sixteenth century the least copernican tinge.

We see with what prudence it befits us to elaborate our hypotheses when they are supported only by feeble evidence! The author himself, as we shall see, has noticed the unaccustomed tenor of his hypothesis. Unaccustomed? Yes, in that it is radically contrary to the constant and authentic thought of Calvin, and it is he himself who is going to tell us why.

II

Whatever may be the *a priori* of the one: 'Calvin remained *pre*-copernican', or the other: 'Calvin was *anti*-copernican', the same texts, as we have said, are invoked in both cases, because they both make reference to a unique 'fact', the supposed 'geocentrism' of Calvin. The biblical texts favoured here are those where the inspired psalmist, indeed God himself, declares that the earth is 'established', established by God, the consequence of the divine action being that the earth 'will not be moved': Psalms 93:1; 75:4; 104:5; 119:89-91; and Job 26:7.

Objection is taken to Calvin's comments on these passages: it is said that he does not question the *reality* of the biblical terms and offers no answer to the 'how?' of the fact that the earth hangs over a void, upon nothing, except that this is caused by the wonderful power of God.

The texts of the Psalms contain prayers, requests for help, hymns to the glory of God the Creator. The believer suffers and struggles; he seeks his strength in the faithfulness of God and wishes to make concrete proof of it. By what conception could he more effectively illustrate the certitudes of his faith, or could God confirm them, than by appealing to his own naive *experience*, which he has from the 'stability' of our earth and the immediate and certain knowledge that we all have of *what is seen*? Let us not be content here with fragment-

20

ary examples proposed as evidence. Let us refer to the commentaries of Calvin in their entirety. For every passage that is critized we find that it explains precisely and at length *the experience* of the believer who is battling for his faith and his God by drawing attention to the stability of *the order of nature*, as a visible sign which — better than any other — attests the immutability of God and his truth. His faithfulness in relation to our salvation also finds expression in the permanence of the order of nature which we experience. The prophet finds support in what *is* and *is seen*; there are a hundred places where he turns to astronomy! Calvin comments on the texts according to their intention and places himself on the same level as the inspired prophet or as God who condescends to give pledges of his presence — the pledges, namely, of the *immediate perception of the senses*, of the constancy we observe in the order of nature. Calvin speaks only of that which *is seen*, of that which every person, even if uncivilized, observes and experiences concretely (cf. pp. 11-14, 32-35).

It is difficult to understand the criticisms made against him in this connection. In writing his commentaries should he have condemned the biblical terminology of sensory experience? Should he have transposed his language to the scientific level? But then the criticism made against his vocabulary would fall back on to that of Scripture! This would no longer have been the Reformer but a precopernican mentality experiencing 'an unbroken geocentrism'. Would not that then be, and very precisely, to place Copernicus above the Holy Spirit?

To attribute to Calvin the attitude for which we see him criticized it is necessary to leave out of account his celebrated principle of interpretation which is concerned with the *intention* of the biblical authors relative to the order of nature. This *principle of accomodation*, the origin of which we shall attempt to define, holds that, in the passages of Scripture where the order of nature, the constellations, the stars, and the heavens are mentioned, the biblical authors speak of them solely *with reference to their visible appearance*, such as is commonly known to us through ordinary sensory experience. Thus God entrusted to Moses the office of 'pedagogue'. Moses, accordingly, 'frequently drew our attention to the stars in a manner befitting a theologian'. Within the community of the Church the Holy Spirit opens a school common to all. He wishes to instruct all kinds of people together and without exception, so that no one should ever be able to make the excuse that the teachings of the Bible are beyond his powers of comprehension. This is a point of view that Calvin propounded from the 1550s onwards. This intuition of genius is one of the pillars of the reformed hermeneutic. Scripture speaks the subjectively true language of sensory appearance. Without ever being inconsistent with himself, as he is charged with being, Calvin will always remain faithful to this principle.

If the 'principle of accomodation' makes it possible to honour *Scripture* as it really is, it enables us also to render to *science* the honour that is its due. To despise science is to disfigure man, to denature creation, to caricature God. Calvin expresses this point of view in the *Institutes* from the 1540s onwards. Among the 'natural graces' he includes the gifts necessary for the promotion of the arts and sciences found in the learned *pagans* of antiquity, whose works afford us an 'admirable light

21

of truth'. Accordingly, even though the nature of man is fallen and perverted, it does not cease to be adorned with many of God's gifts which we should honour wherever they are found if we do not wish to despise the Holy Spirit. The example of the arts and inventions within the family of Cain is significant here. It was God's will that the wicked and the faithless should minister to Christians in the understanding of the liberal arts and sciences: astronomy, medicine, physics, dialectic, politics, and other disciplines. No one should be indifferent to their researches and discoveries; everyone is obliged to interest himself in them according to his own level of culture. The contemplation of nature and its order, even by the least educated, offers to naive experience so many things worthy of admiration that each person is invited to recognize this and to glorify the wisdom of the Creator.

The calling — and the privilege — of learned persons is to discover and, as far as possible, to explain the 'secrets' of nature and, at the same time, to come to an ever better understanding of 'the secrets of God', not merely for their own sakes but for the benefit of all people as they too are invited by way of the paths of knowledge to admire the wonders of their God. Both pedagogue and theologian, Calvin rejoiced over the advances of his time: *today*, he says, 'God has revived and restored the arts and sciences in their entirety . . . to lead us to himself and to introduce us to his high and wonderful secrets'. All honour then to sicience, to each particular science in the field of research and thought assigned to it by God!

In a number of texts, too little known, the modernity of which is astonishing, Calvin sets out the conditions of scientific research and the mental attitude of the scholars. Science should be aware of its objective and its limits; it should remain humble; it cannot be independent of the wisdom of the Spirit. In the closing section of his *Treatise against Astrology* he writes: 'No science is contrary to the fear of God or to the doctrine he gives us to lead us to eternal life, provided we do not put the cart before the horse, that is to say, provided we have the good sense to make use of both the liberal and the mechanical arts as we pass through this world always for the purpose of leading us towards the heavenly kingdom'. There is no break between the life of nature and the life of grace. The redemption of Christ, as it is realized and proclaimed in Scripture, has in view not only the inauguration of a spiritual kingdom for gathering together those who are saved but also the rehabilitation of the entire cosmos as the new heaven and the new earth, when God will be all in all.

In this we have a fundamental principle of the thought of Calvin and of the calvinistic viewpoint of all times: *constantly to proceed from the Cross to Creation*, from saving grace to common grace which opens up to science the universe in its immensity and makes it its legitimate realm, without excluding anything from its calling: the study of heaven and earth, under the authority of Christ, to whom all glory redounds. The practice of science should never be separated from love: 'Science becomes insipid and unsavoury when it is divorced from love, because it is like the sauce of love', Calvin writes. Likewise the scholar should be humble and modest about his knowledge. 'Where there is pride, there ignorance and lack of the knowledge of God reign', for 'there is

22

nothing more arrogant than ignorance'. It is important also for science to operate in accordance with an adequate method, as Calvin explains in precise terms.

In the study of each aspect of nature no one can forget that God is the Creator of all. By the preservation of creation and his providence he establishes precise and indestructible relationships with each creature, being mysteriously and secretly present in the depth of each. He is and remains the prime cause of all. God can never be separated from his works. Secondary causes are the effects of the first cause. The discovery and study of secondary causes should turn the spirit of the researchers *towards* the Creator as worthy to receive the homage of our admiration.

Yet scholars imagine that they can posit a separation between God and his works: the *works alone* are taken into consideration under the pretext of studying them 'objectively', without any *a priori*. Nature becomes the common denominator of all phenomena. Science is then diverted from its calling and its objective: the 'work' alone receives attention; it is then only a question of "middle causes". But to turn nature back on itself is to cheapen it, to depreciate it, and it introduces the category of the 'supernatural'. One contents oneself with a superficial view of things which are not comprehended as 'acts of God'. Research, however, is not only exploration, it is also contemplation.

Combining Romans 10:13 and Psalm 19:2-5, Calvin shows how the Word of God makes itself understood by all men in two complementary ways, through two 'scriptures': the preaching of the Gospel of grace and the voice of the things of nature, a voice which should convince 'the whole world', and each man in particular, of the invisible perfections, the eternal power, and the divinity of the Lord of heaven. This is 'a common school open to all', especially to the heathen to whom God reveals himself 'by the voice of the heavens' — a preparation and *pledge* that the heathen will also be led, at the right moment, to the true knowledge of God through the Gospel. It is not natural reason but Holy Scripture that gives us spectacles which restore our ability to decipher the divine thoughts written by the same hand of God in the book of nature. God speaks to the members of his covenant: he also speaks to the heathen. God reveals himself to ordinary people: he also reveals himself to scholars. No one is excluded; the summons is universal: shepherds and scholars meet together at the cradle of the new-born Babe. Naive experience on the one hand, learned science on the other. There is no 'supernatural'. All must be evangelized. Science is 'an opening God has made to attract the heathen into his Church'.

God is not inactive in scientific research. He directs it, he animates the spirit of the researchers and causes their work to progress towards the expected results. 'It is God's office to show us what we ought to consider in his works for our own benefit'. And it is for us 'to know how to discern between what God reveals to us and what he keeps to himself'. Accordingly, far from being — as some think — restricted or paralysed by God's presence in his works and the development of research, the consideration that 'in the order of nature *we see what God discloses to us*' is a powerful stimulus always to remain on the alert. Our calling as man and as scholar is to attempt unremittingly to unveil or 'unmask' (the opposite of to 'disguise') this extra dimension of

23

refinement and distinctiveness, this enlargement of meaning, to the utmost limit of each 'moment', the message with which God impregnates even the humblest constituents of nature. Every creature carries the mark, the seal, the signature, the armorial insignia of its God. It is this which cuts short not only the sloth which says, 'Let us be content with what we already know', but also human pride and all aberration in the impasses where research comes up against antinomy. Calvin neither fears nor mistrusts any new discovery. The Gospel does not abolish science, it leads to it; it is understanding and not ignorance that is the mother of piety (cf. pp. 51-58).

Astronomy, more than any other science, has a fascination for Calvin. He heaps the highest praise on the labour and the discoveries of the pagan astronomers who, by observing what was *hidden*, '*unfolded* the great treasures of the wisdom of God' in the order of the heavens. It was thanks to God's grace that they *surveyed* the heavens and measured them as one measures an acre of land and established the distances between the planets and between the stars. 'True astronomy is the knowledge of the natural order and disposition which God has assigned to the stars and planets, so as to be able to form a judgment as to their function, property, and power, and to reduce everything to its proper end and use'. Not only does it describe the effects, but it should also' show the *hidden causes*, and explain *how* and *why* things are *what we see them to be*. Astronomy is truly excellent and admirable: the knowledge already acquired is simply stupendous; it is scarcely possible to believe that men have arrived at the end to which God is leading them! By it God is drawing them to himself. Astronomy is not merely praiseworthy, it is also useful and profitable. 'It affords not just a consideration and contemplation which gives great pleasure and satisfaction to the spirit of man, but beyond that it serves to kindle and arouse a true fear and reverence of God in his heart.'

Preaching on·Job 37:14, Calvin enumerates the regulations which true astronomers should respect. Every work of God is a bearer of excellence and majesty; it is not a matter of casual gleaning, but there must be intense application to the task and unremitting perseverence. Reason alone is not sufficient for forming right judgments; modesty and patience are necessary, for no one is so clever as 'to know everything in a moment'. Even when the professional astronomer reckons that he has reached the limit of the possibilities of his understanding, he should not relax his effort or cease from his research: it is never right for him to rest. And if, at certain stages or at a particular level of his research, the scholar thinks that he can go no further, that is no reason for him 'to take it easy and wander about aimlessly'. Does the study of the works of God justify taking a break? Its purpose is to seek for new weapons, to formulate other *hypotheses*, and to make fresh advances. 'Even those who pause to think upon the work of God withdraw (as the proverb says) in order the better to press forward, for it is not intended that we should wander about aimlessly.'

The astronomer has a double vocation: to explain the reason for things such as they are *seen* and to disclose them such as they *are*, but when there is need for him to formulate *hypotheses* it is not necessary for them to depict reality exactly as it is, because there are intermediate

24

stages in the approach to the truth. Here are two quotations whose importance could hardly be exaggerated:

(1) With reference to the biblical teaching about heavenly phenomena: *'God speaks to us about these things according to what we perceive them to be, not according to what they are'*.

(2) With reference to the researches and the intuition of scholars: *'It is true that they* (astronomers) *conceive of things that are not in heaven; but it is not without reason that they conceive of them; their purpose is by means of certain calculations and measurements to point to things which could be too high and profound to be comprehended'* (sermon 34 on Job 9:7, 1554).

Astronomy is not the preserve of scholars. It is, by definition, the science in which everybody should take an interest according to his level of culture. Man was created 'facing upwards' in order to contemplate the heavens and the stars, and in doing so to discern their Lord and admire the majesty of God. Since it is for us to know God in his works: *God wishes that we should all be astronomers.* Calvin was the very first to apply himself to this discipline of which he acquired a profound knowledge and to which, whenever possible, he attracted hearers and readers. As a pedagogue and a theologian he makes use of a vocabulary which is precise while remaining simple; but he frequently leaves the impression that he knows much more than he says. Calvin read widely. The older he became the more the study of the heavens and their mysteries fascinated him. One year before his death, when commenting on Jeremiah 10:1-2 before the pastors assembled for Bible study, he exclaims: 'What is the observation of the stars if it is not a consideration of that marvellous working in which the power and the wisdom and the goodness of God shine forth? *Indeed, astronomy may justly be called the ABC of theology.*[5] For whoever comes to consider this work of heaven with sincerity and singleness of purpose finds it impossible not to be totally enraptured with admiration of the wisdom, the goodness, and the power of God' (cf. pp. 59-66).

Calvin rejoices in the 'revival' of (scientific) astronomy in his day (cf. pp. 67-69), but he deplores the prevalence of astrology by which every level of society is corrupted (cf. pp. 74-83). In his *Warning against Astrology*, published in 1549, he categorically rejects it. Astrologers and their imitators seek to violate the secrets of God. Astrology survives only at the expense of Scripture and God: his graces are refused, his love is mocked, and men are rendered irresponsible by it. The stars are venerated like images of God, whereas God has placed them entirely for our service; it perverts the order of nature: most of the names given to the stars and constellations defile the mirror in which God wishes to be known, contemplated, and loved!

Here Calvin makes a distinction which will be surprising to some people between astrology (as we understand it today) and *natural astronomy*. On numerous occasions he alludes to the practical 'usefulness' of astronomy, which should not be regarded as merely the theoretical study of the heavens. Indeed, *'earthly bodies and in general all inferior creatures are subject to the order of the heavens for the*

---

[5] *Et certe astrologia potest merito vocari alphabetum theologiae.*

25

derivation of certain qualities'. It is therefore appropriate also to discover the *causes* of those things which have their origin in the dependence of our earth on the order of the heavens. In fact, there is a sort of 'affinity' between earthly bodies and the heavens: one can notice in the stars *something* of what happens here below; for 'there is a kind of mutual harmony between the heavens and the earth'. Natural astronomy is responsible for meteorology and all its applications, and for the statistics necessary for the forecasting of weather, in accordance with the *ordinary* course of nature. Calvin does not deny that one can seek in the stars the origin of occurrences observed in the world: 'I do not mean the primary and principal origin', he says, 'but a sort of means inferior to the will of God, such as serves even as a preparation for the accomplishment of his work as it has been determined in his eternal counsel'. There is nothing here, however, that is on the level of the sovereignty of God. The sequence of events, together with their probability, is hidden in the secret counsel of God. History does not belong to the order of nature and is not dependent on it, any more than evil, impiety, and ungodliness, wherever they are found, are linked to the stars. Our moral and spiritual life is independent of all necessity (cf. pp. 84-90).

If this is so with our souls, it is not the same with our bodies. Our human bodies, as God has made them, belong entirely to this order of nature. 'I readily admit', Calvin writes, 'that so far as the temperament of men and especially the emotions which participate in the qualities of their bodies are concerned they are *in part* dependent on the stars, or that there is at least *some correspondence*, as when we say that a man is more inclined to be choleric than phlegmatic, or the contrary . . . I admit that the stars do have a *certain concurrence* for the forming of temperaments, and especially those which are related to the body, but I deny that this is the principal cause . . . It must, then, be admitted that there is a *certain accord* between the stars or planets and the disposition of human bodies. All this . . . is comprehended under natural astronomy.'

After having demanded that science should not 'enlarge' its domain beyond the limits assigned to it, Calvin (with fine balance!) enjoins that it should not be 'restricted' within these limits. Science should occupy *only* its space, but also *all* its space! And now this thesis, after having been rejected as a superstition 'of his time', is found to be ultra-modern. The proof of this is seen in innumerable facts. Researches in these 'accords', 'correspondences', and 'concurrences' of all nature, astronomical and terrestrial rhythms, daily, monthly, or annual, etc., between the creatures of this earth and the universe, have a place today in the front rank of scientific preoccupations and the research programmes of numerous laboratories and institutes, both western and eastern, which legitimate the creation of several new sciences (cf. pp. 92-97). What is remarkable about this is that Calvin formulated his thesis on foundations that are more solid than the simple experience or the statistics of which we have spoken, for he based them on a foundation which is both theological and christological.

Theological, because faith that the world was created by God inevitably postulates that our universe forms a unity-totality like that

26

of God who created it. No single part is independent of the whole. No creature, whatever its rank, exists in isolation: all forms a Whole, a harmony designed to attain *in a solidary manner* the total fulness of its meaning in its dependence on the Origin of its existence and in its dynamic movement towards that Origin.

Christological, because all things were created in Christ, who is as it were the substance or the ground of all. John the Evangelist does not speak of what Christ is in himself, 'but of what he does in others'. In Christ there is an interdependence and a complementarity between all things, both sustained from the beginning of the second and new creation of the incarnate Son until their restoration in the resurrection. The order of nature remains firm and stable because Christ sustains all things by the word or the will of his power. And when we say 'all things', this expression extends also to the *life* of things without souls, which live in their own proper fashion. It is not that where faith exists in the organic interconnection of the totality of the universe there science has the possibility of passing from the empirical investigation of particular phenomena to the general, from the general to the laws which govern this universe, and, finally, from these laws to the principle which rules them all. Our whole life is placed under the power of the unity, the solidarity, and the order which has been established by God himself (cf. pp. 84-98).[6]

The facts that demonstrate the malefic influence on man of the whole of nature are innumerable and well known. But we must go further: we have asserted the existence of these bonds which, *from above downwards*, unite the heavens to the earth and to men. We must also ask whether, in this same order of nature, there are not certain connections which, *from below upwards*, may link men and the earth to the stars. This is actually the kind of relationship which Scripture presents as a reality! The order of nature, in fact, is neither independent nor autonomous: it is the reflection of a thought, the echo of a will that is expressed in it; it receives existence and meaning from the creative Word uttered at each instant of time with respect to it. In other words, this order is endowed, on the one hand, with a certain flexibility, a malleability, which enables it to present itself in a living and expressive manner; and, on the other hand, with a capacity of receptivity that is sensitive to the most delicate nuances of human behaviour.

Both sin and piety have an influence on the universal order, especially by the rebounding action of God (continuous creation and providence), which sanctions it. 'The earth will be cursed because of you' (Gen. 3:17). 'The death of all created beings has been determined by me' (Gen. 6:13). 'All these blessings will come upon you . . . All these curses will overtake you . . .' (Dt. 28:2,15). It is the fault of man that the whole order of nature has been overturned. The human *cause* is amplified by the divine power, that of the Judge and the Healer. The heavens, the earth, and all creatures bear the mark of the condemnation of the human race stamped upon themselves. Through our sins we disturb the heavens and the earth and the sea and all that exists. Extra-ordinary though it may be, it is a fact that we are admonished by heavenly signs appearing in

---

[6] According to Abraham Kuyper, *Calvinism*, pp. 151f.

27

the stars. Calvin gives a remarkable and dramatic picture of the solidarity of man with the universe: 'It should not seem strange that the pain of man's sin reacts on the earth, even though the earth is innocent; for just as the great heaven, which is called the *primum mobile*, causes all the other heavens to turn with it, so the ruin of man has cast down *all the creatures* which had been made for his sake and placed in subjection to him' (Commentary on Gen. 3:17).

That the order of the world is disturbed by our vices is a fact; but despite this effect the universe remains in position and nature keeps its course. If the earth has been cursed and garbed with mourning, 'I say', Calvin affirms, 'that it is the same earth which was originally created'. When God announces: 'I am going to create new heavens and a new earth' (Is. 65:17), this is the language of *metaphor* and *hyperbole* which befits the greatness of the blessing manifested since the first coming of Christ and right up to his return; for this restoration achieved in Christ extends beyond the Church to the world in its entirety. It is starting from the Church that the universe will be 're-established'. All creatures will be renewed and their function will be to cause the glory of God to shine forth! But will it really be *all*? Yes, all, for savage beasts and trees and even metals will be involved in this. But here it is desirable to control all curiosity and remain sensible.

Yes, Christ himself will accomplish all this by his power at the time of his return and of the final resurrection. Meanwhile we can but 'wait'. When the author of Hebrews 2:5 speaks of *the world to come*, it is plain, says Calvin, that it is not simply a question of 'the state of things as we expect it to be after the resurrection, but as it has begun to be since the beginning of Christ's reign leading up to its consummation in the ultimate redemption'. How, then, will the heavens and the earth be restored? By the doctrine of salvation! The Church is at the centre of the new heavens and the new earth established by God (Is. 51:16). The Church, with its preachers and teachers, its evangelists and witnesses: these are the ones who, since the first coming of Christ, are renewing the world, as though God were, *through them*, reforming the heavens and the earth. Is there any loftier calling than to be associated, here and now, with this reformation? Is there any greater honour and glory conferred by Christ on such unworthy servants as we are? (Cf. pp. 99-105).

It is interesting, finally, to notice the symbolical interpretation given by Calvin to the texts that speak of upheavals in the heavens. With his exceptional good sense he regards them as *pictures* or *hyperboles*; for example, the oracles against Babylon, the universal upheaval or the coming of the Kingdom, death, the glorious advent of Christ, and the last judgment, the third heaven of the apostle Paul, the blessedness of the Church and those who belong to it. What is striking here is the firmness with which Calvin refuses to allow that the astronomical and cosmic 'order of nature' could ever — during the present economy — be even partially modified. The stars never act 'capriciously' and do not function as free agents (cf. pp. 117-121).

In bringing this section to a conclusion, and in order that we may have a precise idea of Calvin's cosmological thought, an idea which is not without influence on our opinion of his appreciation of Copernicus, it is necessary to demolish a number of persistent legendary affirm-

28

ations. Among these, I adduce some which Dr. Richard Stauffer has not been afraid to advance in his recent book and which Calvin himself actually refutes in numerous places, that are clear as crystal (I have given these in my study, cf. pp. 106-116). The world of Calvin is *open*, not closed; he never proposes any 'conception' which could have been 'that of the Hebrews'. He never thought that the heavens 'form a solid vault": he insists that they are 'an empty space', and is strongly critical of the translators of the Septuagint for their rendering 'firmament'. When mentioned in Scripture, the 'opening of the heavens' never poses any 'problem of physics' for Calvin, as his comments on Acts 7:56 and 10:11, John 1:51, Matthew 3:16 and parallels, Ezekiel 1:1, and Luke 3:21 prove without exception — the last of these being the sole text Dr. Stauffer adduces in support of his view, while quoting, wrongly, only seven lines from some forty that Calvin devotes to the discussion. Six times, in the texts spread between 1552 and 1564, Calvin refuses to envisage the possibility of a 'physical opening of the heavens', which, even if it could be imagined, would not have served any purpose. In this economy the order of the cosmos cannot be and is never changed.

But what about Joshua's request? someone will ask. This is one of Calvin's most fascinating commentaries, for it is dated 1564, three months before his death in May. While seeking, he says, to be as brief as possible, he emphatically confirms his earlier affirmations and persistently refuses to inquire about the 'how?' of the *experience* of Joshua and his army. He dismisses as impertinent those who advance a particular hypothesis to explain what took place: the solution they offer is as inept as the question they propose. Calvin sternly repudiates the temptation to objectivize the occurrence. He declares that the order of nature was in no way changed, and this gives the account a universal and permanent significance, enabling Joshua to serve as an example to all generations of believers, since what is involved here is only an experience of real life. With brilliant acuity Calvin avoids stumbling-blocks and blind alleys.

But let the modern reader pay careful attention! Calvin's commenting is not conceived in conformity with the letter (literalistically), as it is reproached with being, but in conformity with Scripture. Here, as in numerous other places, he repeats, 'When we *read* . . ..', and he never speaks otherwise than with regard to what he *reads*. Calvin never fails to apply to himself and to the language of his commentaries the principle of scriptural accomodation, what he *says* follows on what he has *read*. There is nothing more than this, either alongside or outside of the account. If the reader should forget that Calvin, as a psychologist and as a theologian, accomodates what he says *to what is said in Scripture and is seen in nature*, he will inevitably attribute a pre- or anti-copernican tonality to certain of his pages, of which I give a number of examples. And this will be an unpardonable misconception (cf. pp. 123-136).

III

The preceding pages lead to several conclusions which we go on to outline (cf. pp. 183-204).

Calvin's *Treatise against Astrology* must be accorded its true import-

29

ance which is considerable. If he denounces astrology (with which astronomy was previously most often associated under the common denominator of mathematics) it is for the purpose of rendering all honour to the astronomy that is genuine. *'This present treatise'*, he writes, *'will be mainly for simple and unlettered persons, who would easily be misled by their inability to distinguish between the genuine astronomy and this superstition of magicians and sorcerers'*. Simple and unlettered individuals ought to have full access to the benefits and fruits of the genuine astronomy, which combines being of service to men with glorifying God.

When Calvin asserts that God has revived the human sciences, of which astronomy is among the foremost, he forms this judgment on the basis of an excellent knowledge of the subject. In 1549 Calvin was sufficiently interested in astronomy to be able to recognize and appreciate 'what is new'. It would not suffice to say that, *before* writing, Calvin was informed to the extent that he was not caught in the flagrant crime of ignorance by the scholars among his readers, but the fact is that in composing this *warning* with a pastoral purpose he was already well informed and had first hand knowledge. It seems chimerical, therefore, to suggest that Calvin had not read Copernicus and that he was unacquainted with the prefaces and the first book of the *De Revolutionibus*, which was published in 1543, still less the *Narratio Prima* which, in 1540, Rheticus had sent to Melanchthon who, at that time, was closely associated with Calvin. No doubt a non-mathematician could have received these writings in a quite different spirit than the specialists who found in them so much to criticize for mathematical and technical reasons. History confirms this (cf. pp. 158-180). Thus we are well able to reconstruct the 'meeting' of Calvin and Copernicus.

The one has a passionate interest in *the order of nature*, an order which arises from the foreordination of God and his decrees in general, and which is the foundation of the possibility and the rationality of science. *The other* is equally an enthusiast for *the order of the world*, an order which he posits in principle, which must be simple, and which, likewise, has no place for exceptions or particular cases, an order in which everything is connected and interrelated and which can and must be mathematically proved, an order which arises from immutable laws and admits neither disharmonies nor dissentions, because everything is 'symmetrical'.

The one considers that one of the principal tasks of genuine astronomy is to explain the course of the planets, 'their direct, oblique, or quasi-contrary movements'; any appearance of disorder is from the point of view of him who can perceive only what he *sees* and who delegates to astronomy the responsibility of determining the *why* and the *how* of this. *The other* affirms, in a *Letter to Pope Paul III* and in the first chapter of his natural philosophy, that everything is explained by the daily and orbital movement of the earth, which as soon as it is acknowledged makes it possible to understand the reason for these direct, oblique, and quasi-contrary movements and reveals an ensemble in which, in perfect harmony, all the stars are found to be so intimately linked that no modification could be made within it without over-

30

turning the whole universe: '*In the heavens themselves*', Copernicus writes, '*one finds such a relationship that it is impossible to make any sort of change in any of its parts without causing a confusion of all the other parts and of the universe in its entirety*'. In this 'the astonishing order of the world' is displayed: the earth and the heavens form an interdependent solidarity under the same law, *the Law of Order*.

Does the affirmation of this Order of the World really appear so 'odious' to Calvin? Is this apparent in 1556 when he is preaching on 1 Corinthians 10? Surely there would be some semblance of verisimilitude here for such a charge? What basis could there be then for postulating such petulant ill-humour? We find no trace whatever of it up to 1556; what we do see is an enthusiastic eulogy of the sciences. Calvin seeks, without any reserve, to communicate to both hearers and readers his admiration and his love for an astronomy which he regards as one of the most precious aids to the pastoral ministry.

From 1545 on, we encounter the expression the *Order of Nature*. The exegetical principle of accomodation was propounded in 1552, with reference to Acts 7:22. Two years later there appears the duly formulated axiom fundamental to the biblical teaching relating to the stars and the heavens:

'*God speaks to us concerning these things in accordance with how we perceive them and not in accordance with what they are.*'

and he propounds the principles and rules summarized above. There is no word of warning as he preaches: he encourages all the faithful to be well informed and cultured, since each Christian should — according to Job — be an astronomer 'to the extent that his ability permits'. Yet it is wished to persuade us that in 1556 Calvin 'cut down' the disciples of Copernicus and would have 'rejected without appeal' the findings of direct observation and of calculation? To fail to see that *to make such a 'rejection' would obviously have placed Calvin in flagrant contradiction with himself* one must be woefully deficient in perception and discernment. Everything that he previously wrote and said testifies to this. Preaching on Job 9:7 in 1554, he acknowledges the right of astronomers to formulate hypotheses — hypotheses that are always imperfect, for they do not succeed in describing reality as *it is*, but which only approach reality, 'in a certain measure', progressively 'by degrees'. He requires that they should never halt this research, but 'always press on further' and devise new hypotheses better than those that have preceded. This right to form hypotheses and this duty to elaborate new ones is of the greatest interest. If we miss this understanding, it will be more difficult for us to penetrate the profound thought of Calvin.

Our deep conviction is this: Calvin did not join battle with Copernicus over the ligitimacy of his hypotheses. The passionate champion of the Order of Nature found common ground with the no less enthusiastic champion of the Order of the World, recognizing that his hypotheses made it possible to assign order to the inexplicable disorder of the capricious family of the planets and their apparent movements: a rational explanation worthy of the Creator.

Four languages can therefore be used simultaneously: the language of the naive experience of the general public; the ordinary and technical language of scholars; the language of legitimate hypotheses which,

31

however, will never succeed in circumscribing the inmost being of things, which is 'too high and too profound for us to comprehend'; and, finally, the language of faith, which interferes with none of the other three.

There is another of Copernicus's statements which doubtless fascinated the biblical commentator. The astronomer wrote to Paul III: *'This mathematical knowledge of the world is developed in contradiction to its image as constructed from the direct experiences of man . . . Science concerns itself with the reality which is not that of our subjective experiences, but it represents the truth concerning the world, causing us to know how it exists in reality.'* If Calvin remains reticent over this last clause, would it be impermissible to think that, by a rapid flash of his understanding, he seized hold here of the support which this statement afforded him in his capacity as a biblical expositor, by simply rearranging the order of the terms? Does not his own principle: *'God speaks to us concerning these things in accordance with how we perceive them and not in accordance with what they are'*, correspond exactly with Copernicus's little clause when its terms are inverted? Calvin could not have failed to see at once the advantages it offered! If the task of the astronomers was to *save the phenomena*, by ridding them of the interferences of naive experience, and thereby to ensure the autonomy of science, was it not the task of the theologians to *save Holy Scripture*, by delivering it from the encroachments of scientific thought, and thus to ensure, *vis-à-vis* science, the autonomy of theology?

When these two 'little clauses' are put side by side it is practically impossible not to regard them as two sisters. The priority belongs to Copernicus in the announcement of his. Does Calvin's clause derive from it? This question cannot be posed without establishing at once that the first mention of the principle of accomodation seems to have been made by Calvin only in his commentary on Acts 7:22, which was published in 1552. It was scientific rather than theological reasons which governed the announcement of this principle: the apprehension of actual astronomical facts. At that juncture Calvin seems to have been the only one to have adopted this position, as difficult to grasp as to hold. In doing so he distanced himself from Roman Catholic theology, from virtually all Lutherans, and from innumerable others who were then uninterested in the ideas of Copernicus. But if there resulted a cleavage among men, Calvin, by a stroke of genius, liberated theology from every scientific judgment external to itself and science from any enslavement to theology: thereby he reconciled theologians and astronomers, with the proviso that the latter should practise their art with respect for true scientific method.

Is there not a striking connection between the publication of the *Treatise against Astrology* and the announcement of the principle of accomodation? Think of the time needed for drafting, composing, correcting, printing, and distributing this work! Better still, Calvin informs us, in a letter to Farel dated 10 November 1550, that he is working on his commentary — already at an advanced stage — on the book of Acts, having *interrupted* his work on the commentary on Genesis, which would be published in 1554, but which, in its earliest

32

chapters, abounds with references to the principle of accomodation. It seems clear that Calvin conceived his principle at the time when he was working on his *Treatise against Astrology*, with its important documentation ready to hand or committed to memory. And once this principle was formulated Calvin applies it first of all to Scripture in a manner appropriate to the teacher and the theologian; but, as we have seen, he applies it also to himself in all his pronouncements and in a manner so automatic and rigorous that at times it seems shocking.

Why, then, should Calvin suddenly, in 1556, have taken up a position 'against the disciples of Copernicus'? We look in vain for an answer! We have established as a fact that the little comment on 1 Corinthians 10 cannot have the meaning that Dr. Stauffer gives to his 'discovery'. The disciples of Copernicus? But which ones? Another question without an answer! Whichever way we turn, there is nothing that affords the least credibility to this thesis: everything is absolutely contrary to it: the historical facts in the first place, since in those years there was no 'Copernican revolution'. But again, to impose on the 'little sentence' an anticopernican character and with misleading obstinacy to restrict it to this meaning makes it necessary to suppose that Calvin's comments have no relationship to the biblical text which he is expounding and to the subject of these sermons. It becomes necessary also to detach this expression from all the preceding thought of Calvin, including the sermons on Job (1554-1555), in the course of which the preacher would have had the opportunity to say everything, if he had wished to express any reservation concerning Copernicus, his disciples (?), or his ideas. At the same time the *Treatise against Astrology* must be ignored — as though it did not exist! — as well as his laudatory commendations of astronomy and astronomers, together with their spirit, their task, their method, their researches . . . It is, in truth, a case here of the violent introduction into the 'thought' of Calvin of an idea which is as foreign to him as that of the 'firmament' which it is still wished to force on him!

But if it was only in 1556 that Calvin got wind of the ideas of Copernicus's disciples, would not their 'odious' character then have required Calvin to take the trouble to renounce the fifteen years of profound reflection to which his works bear witness? If this had been the situation, would not Calvin have disengaged the last years of his life to combat so scandalous a heresy? But the fact of the matter is that Calvin did nothing. Dr. Stauffer should admit, not without keen mortification, that, as he well knows, his 'discovery' constitutes only a criticism unique 'in the preaching and even in the work of Calvin'. This consideration alone should have been sufficient to dissuade Professor Stauffer from formulating a hypothesis so obviously contrary to all that Calvin thought and wrote, not only up until 1556 but right up to his death. After 1556, in fact, the *sermons* on Isaiah, Genesis, and Daniel, and the *commentaries* on Isaiah, the Psalms, the twelve Minor Prophets, Jeremiah, Ezekiel, Daniel, and Joshua were published, and also the monumental revision of the *Institutes*: each one of these volumes afforded Calvin many opportunities for opposing Copernicus or his disciples or their ideas and for condemning in express terms a hateful heliocentrism as antibiblical and pernicious. How is it that not once did

33

he honour this pastoral duty? How is it that he continued to praise astronomy and faithfully to apply his principle of accomodation? How could he have uttered this solemn affirmation which is also a confession: *Astronomy can with every justification be called the alphabet of theology*? No! Calvin himself replies to the injustice that has been done to him.

Should we then count Calvin among the 'disciples' of Copernicus? Not at all! He lacked the competence to appraise the mathematical 'proofs' of Copernicus and it was not possible for him to involve himself in or commit himself to a scientific battle. His silence convinces us: he is one of the very first not to have opposed, but on the contrary to have accepted the central idea, specifically as a hypothesis, as not inimical to Holy Scripture. As theologian and preacher, he could fight neither for a man nor for a theory. But if we are indebted to Copernicus's Order of the World for the origin or the force of Calvin's immortal pedagogical principle of the accomodation of revelation, then yes! in this respect *theology has certainly learned from astronomy*.

By his silence Calvin leaves science to its own proper vocation; he embodies a model of impartiality; he displays respect for its techniques and its legitimate hypotheses. He keeps theology and the Church far from partisan squabbles and demonstrates the peaceful relationships that science and the Christian faith have in common if each remains on its own territory.

Calvin maintains a lively interest in all things. With evident pleasure he seizes every opportunity to pose the right questions concerning the 'mysteries of God': what are the heavens and their order? what is the support of the sun? why does the earth not fall? what is the light? why does it travel so fast? In physics, in biology, and other branches of science Calvin is well aware of other matters which puzzle the scholars, but he does not speak of them, 'in order to avoid collecting rare and unaccustomed examples' (cf. pp. 196-199).

One often hears it said that 'geocentrism' was a characteristic of human pride. Certain classes of mentality, it is true, had founded their hopes on the intrinsic importance of our globe and the dignity and autonomy of the human person. Such hopes were destroyed by the progress of heliocentrism and astronomy! Let us not forget, however, that for others, and from antiquity, the universe was organized in accordance with a *hierarchical* system, with the earth placed at the lowest level, miserable in its situation and in the precarious conditions assigned to humanity. It is regrettable that this model had been adopted and maintained for a period of centuries in the history of 'Christian' theology. For Augustine in particular 'the terrestrial part is at the bottom, it is our inferior world, that part of the world filled with mortal and corruptible things . . . and with vile and abject particles'.

One has to wait until the fifteenth century for some dignity to be restored to our earth. Nicolas of Cusa (1401-1464), a precursor of Copernicus, seems to have been the first to deny all 'hierarchical structure' and 'the humble situation of the earth in the chain of entities', and to contest the notion that 'mutability was an evil confined within the sublunary sphere'. 'The earth is a noble star', he triumphantly affirmed; 'it is not possible for human knowledge to decide whether the terrestrial region is by one degree more or less perfect by comparison with the regions of the other stars'. Thus, contrary to what many imagine, the promotion of the earth to the rank of a planet, its projection in the heavens apart from every hierarchy and every 'centre', has, since the sixteenth century, been for many a deliverance from servitude and corruption, an emancipation from a 'dualism' which certain so-called 'Christian' traditions had, unfortunately, inherited from paganism. Calvin actually himself becomes involved in the rehabilitation of our earth. He denies any hierarchy of dignity in space. It is necessary, he says, to go *further* than the astronomers, *'for the centre of the world is not the principle of creation*. It follows that the earth is suspended in space because it pleased God for it to be so'. The earth has its importance from God alone and from his free decree.

Many imagine that Copernicus was the man of a period of transition, the last sage of the Middle Ages and the first sage of the modern epoch. Others see him as neither ancient nor modern, but a man in whose work two traditions are mingled. Does the unique turning-point of a highway belong to the section which precedes it or to that which follows on from it? From this point of view, the *De Revolutionibus* would have been the point of departure for a new astronomical and cosmological tradition as well as the culminating point of the ancient tradition.

The same questions may be posed concerning Calvin. Some see him only as 'a man of his time'. On the contrary, and within the limits of this study, we are astonished at the assurance of the way traced and determinedly followed by our Reformer, and at the number of the obstacles he wisely avoided, to the point that he appears as the greatest theologian of modern times. From the scientific point of view, reason and experience are the companions of faith, acknowledged in their own proper activity. God and Nature, the Creator and the Creation, faith and reason cannot be and are not separated or opposed. Observation and reflection play their part simultaneously and without alternation in time.

In astronomy Calvin carefully avoids any 'scale of entities'. Whatever their source, he rejects the fantasies of those who imagine the stars to be furnished with sense and intelligence. He does not think that either in time or in space there were solid frontiers between the different parts of the heavens. He believes neither in the ninth sphere nor in the empyrean realm. He seems to retain the idea of a 'sphere' as that only of a 'circle'. The stars possess no divinity: God has no companion. He never considered making the world an image of the Trinity. The stars are only creatures placed by God 'at our service' and not tyrannical entities presiding over our destinies. His criticism of astrology, however timely, has lost nothing of its relevance and can be taken up point by point today. Far from having become antiquated, his conception of natural astronomy stimulates fascinating inquiries, for science has made up its mind, at last! to occupy the whole of its field of research.

Calvin gives the impression that he aligned himself with what was best in the work of Copernicus as cosmologian, thanks to a sort of instinct that all which God created he made according to a particular order, and that this order is in harmony with the revelations of Scripture. Where this principle of accomodation is not honoured today exegesis loses

35

itself in insoluble antinomies or in false harmonization. If the Renaissance gives man an increased confidence in his cognitive faculties, it implants at the same time, through the destruction of the ancient image of the world, a cruel feeling of anguish, uncertainty, solitude, insignificance. A mathematical order of the universe prevails independently of the existence of man and is unconnected with his experiences and the feelings of his daily personal life. But thanks to the biblical message, which he delivers with integrity, Calvin has the answer to the feeling of solitude and anguish of the Renaissance, as well as to that of man today. Better than before, the world is truly the *Cosmos* which God created *for man* and which he put at man's service so that he could be loved and glorified thereby. Man is *enhanced* by the activity which God generously promotes in his favour by virtue of his providence and love, and man is invigorated in consequence: for *God's is the power to love*. And it is not man who has arrogantly made this position for himself: it is *offered* to him by God, the Creator and Preserver, the Redeemer and the Saviour through the Cross of Christ planted in the very centre of this earth. To receive this gift with modesty and sobriety, that is humility, and that is the wisdom which enables this man, today as then, to be moved and to exclaim:

'*O God, thy Name is present among us!*'

36

CALVIN'S DOCTRINE OF CREATION

John Murray

IN historical theology there are two dangers of which we need to be aware. One is that we impose upon a theologian of a particular period the thought-forms and distinctions which really belong to later developments of theological discussion. When we do this we place the theologian in question in a perspective which is not true to his position. The other danger is in the opposite direction, namely, the failure properly to take account of the continuity and even identity of thought between a particular theologian and his successors. Calvin has suffered from both of these tendencies on the part of his interpreters.

The subject of creation is one of basic interest to Christian theology. As is our concept of creation so will be the character of our theism. It may contribute a little to the better understanding of what is involved in the doctrine of creation and particularly to a better understanding of the concepts entertained by the protestant theologians of the sixteenth and seventeenth centuries if we study Calvin's utterances on this question in relation to the formulations which became current among the protestant theologians who succeeded Calvin.

IMMEDIATE AND MEDIATE CREATION

In formulating the doctrine of creation both Lutheran and Reformed theologians, particularly those of the seventeenth century, distinguished between immediate or primary creation, on the one hand, and mediate or secondary creation, on the other. The former they conceived of as that action of God by which he brought things into being *ex nihilo* by the mere fiat of his will, the latter they conceived of as the creative action of God superinduced upon the material brought into existence by the antecedent *ex nihilo* fiat. Immediate creation

21

is primary because prior to this action of God there was no preexisting or prejacent material through which the effect was wrought or upon which the action supervened: the whole effect embraced within the action designated as immediate creation is due to a completely originative action of God. Mediate creation, on the other hand, is secondary because there is presupposed the material antecedently brought into existence by the primary and originative fiat: the effect of the action designated as mediate creation draws within its scope previously existing material and comprises the use of that material. This is the distinction between *ex nihilo* and *ex materia*. In immediate creation the *terminus a quo* is *nihil*, in mediate creation it is *materia*.

A few quotations will illustrate this construction. John Wollebius, for example, says: "Creation is that by which God produced the world and the things that are in it, partly *ex nihilo* and partly *ex materia naturaliter inhabili*, for the manifestation of the glory of his power, wisdom, and goodness. To create is not only to make something out of nothing but also to produce something out of unapt material beyond the powers of nature."[1] The Leyden Synopsis expresses the distinction more fully when it says: "By the creation of the world we understand its production out of nothing solely by the omnipotent power of God .... This omnipotence of his God demonstrated in the things created by him in a twofold manner: either immediately, insofar as he produced the nature of certain things immediately out of nothing, such as the earth, the water, the angels, and the souls of our first parents; or mediately, insofar as he formed some things out of unformed preexisting material, such as the plants of the earth, the body of Adam, and the brute beasts. Hence we define the creation of the world as the external action of God omnipotent, incommunicable to creatures, by which of himself and his most free will, moved by no other, he created heaven and earth out of nothing at the beginning of time, and fashioned

---

[1] *Compendium Christianae Theologiae*, Lib. I, Cap. V (Amsterdam, 1638, p. 27). The phrase "ex materia inhabili" I have rendered "out of unapt material". The Latin word "inhabilis" is a difficult word to translate in this connection. It might be translated by words such as "inert" or "unfit".

certain things which he willed to form out of that primary material, by his arrangement, in the space of six days, in order that he might make known to his creatures, especially to rational beings, the glory of his great wisdom, power, and goodness, and invite them to the celebration of his name."[2]

While this type of definition and formulation was characteristic and widely current among Protestant theologians, there are two qualifications that must be made. (1) There was not complete unanimity as to the propriety of the distinction between immediate and mediate creation. Cocceius, for example, says that it is not necessary to distinguish between mediate and immediate creation since creation signifies nothing else than the bringing into being from non-being by the call of God.[3] (2) It is not quite certain that all who used the distinction between immediate and mediate creation meant

[2] *Synopsis Purioris Theologiae*, Disputatio X, Theses III, IV, V. *Cf.* also Melchior Leydecker: *Synopsis Theologiae Christianae*, Lib. II, Cap. III, §XVIII; Francis Junius: *Theses Theologicae*, Cap. XIV, Theses II and IV; Cap. XV, §3; Cap. XVI, Thes. 2 (*Opuscula Theologica Selecta*, Amsterdam, 1882, pp. 149 ff.); William Amesius: *Medulla Theologica*, Cap. VIII, §10; Mark Frederick Wendelinus: *Christiana Theologia*, Lib. I, Cap. V, Thes. VII; John Maccovius: *Loci Communes Theologici*, Cap. XXXVII (Amsterdam, 1658, p. 344); J. A. Quenstedt: *Theologia Didactico-Polemica*, Cap. X, Sect. I, Theses XIII, XIV, XV (Leipsic, 1715, p. 594); Benedict Pictet: *La Theologie Chrétienne*, Liv. V, Chap. I (Amsterdam, 1702, p. 230); Heinrich Heppe: *Die Dogmatik der evangelisch-reformierten Kirche* (Neukirchen, 1935), pp. 157 f. (English Translation, London, 1950, pp. 197 f.); Francis Turretine: *Institutio Theologiae Elencticae*, Loc. V, Quaest. I, §VI; Heinrich Schmid: *The Doctrinal Theology of the Evangelical Lutheran Church* (Philadelphia, 1899), pp. 160 f.; Charles Hodge: *Systematic Theology*, Vol. I, pp. 556 ff.; A. A. Hodge: *Outlines of Theology* (New York, 1908), pp. 238 f.

Roman Catholic theologians also use this distinction between first and second creation; *cf.* Joseph Pohle: *God the Author of Nature and the Supernatural* (ed. Arthur Preuss, St. Louis and London, 1934), pp. 3 ff., pp. 98 ff.; Sylvester J. Hunter: *Outlines of Dogmatic Theology* (New York, 1896), Vol. II, pp. 224 ff.

[3] "Ideo non est necesse distinguere inter creationem mediatam et immediatam; quasi in omni creatione sit indigitatio nihili: quum nihil significet nisi adductionem a non esse ad esse per vocationem sive *momentum voluntatis*, aut *imperii*" (*Summa Theologiae*, Loc. VI, Cap. XV, §5; *Opera Omnia* (Amsterdam, 1701), Tom. VII, p. 189). It is possible that P. Van Mastricht exercises similar reserve (*cf. Theoretico-Practica Theologia*, Lib. III, Cap. V, §IX).

by the latter precisely the same thing. At least it may be said that the terms in which mediate creation is defined do not follow a pattern so rigidly uniform as to assure us that the conception entertained was always in all its elements identical.

This does not mean, however, that we may not derive from the definitions given a rather well-defined notion of what mediate creation was conceived to be. It would appear that the following distinctions and observations are borne out by a study of the more classic expressions of the concept in question.

1. In distinguishing mediate and immediate creation it is not to be supposed that the *immediate action* of God was conceived of as excluded from that which is called mediate creation.[4] The contrast is not between mediate action and immediate: the contrasting epithets respect creation, not action.

2. The contrast respects the distinction between the action of God involved in bringing something into being when there was no antecedent or preexisting material out of which that being could be fashioned or formed and the action of God in bringing into being something in connection with which preexisting matter was wrought upon and used by God. The former is bringing into being *ex nihilo*; the latter is bringing into being *ex materia*.

3. Immediate creation is not restricted to the first creative fiat. The theologians in question included the soul of man in

---

[4] William Amesius (*Medulla Theologica*, Cap. VIII, §10) says: "Quaedam revera dicuntur creari, quorum materia praeexistebat: sed tum creatio non immediatam tantum illam actionem respicit, qua fit ut talia existant; sed etiam mediatam, qua factum est, ut ipsa materia existeret, ex qua illa formantur: sic fuit in creatione plantarum et animalium, Genes. 1:20". There are difficulties connected with the interpretation of this passage. But it would appear that Amesius considers the very formation that takes place through the medium of the preexisting material to be an immediate action of God and that the term "mediate" also applies to such action simply because the material upon which the action of God supervenes already existed and came to exist, of course, by the immediate action of God at the beginning. The words to be noted in this connection are: "tum creatio non immediatam tantum illam actionem respicit ... sed etiam mediatam".

the list of things *immediately* created. But prior to this action there existed the ordered heavens and earth in connection with which both immediate and mediate creation had been operative.

4. While mediate creation was conceived of as the creative action of God in which God used preexisting material, yet this action is not to be regarded as the excitation or development of potencies resident in the preexisting material. These theologians are explicit to the effect that the material used was intrinsically unfit and unapt for the effect that is wrought by the action called mediate creation. The *materia* is regarded as *inhabilis, indisposita, indisponibilis*. And these theologians are careful to distinguish between this creative action of God and the providential agency of God in the process of generation.[5] In the latter case the germ or seed is not naturally unfit or unapt for the effect that is to follow; it is, rather, naturally adapted to and fitted for that effect. In the words of the theologians themselves the germ or seed is *materia naturaliter habilis* whereas in mediate creation the preexisting material is *naturaliter inhabilis*. A good example is provided by the creation of the body of Adam. The dust of the ground used by God in the formation of man's body was not naturally and inherently "disposed" to be the body of man. It did not have any inherent aptitude to be the animated organism which man's body became and in that respect differed radically from the acorn in reference to the oak tree and the germ plasm in reference to the man. Thus in the formation of man's body from dust the omnipotent and creative action of God was manifest.

5. The distinction between mediate and immediate creation can most readily be demonstrated in the distinction between the formation of Adam's body and the creation of his soul. The former is an example of mediate creation, the latter of immediate. The soul of man is adduced as an example of

[5] *Cf*. Melchior Leydecker (*op. cit.*, Lib. II, Cap. III, §XVIII) who, in defining mediate creation, says: "*Mediata* facta est ex inhabili materia", and then adds: "Haec differt a generatione, quae materiam habilem praerequirit". In the quotation given above from Wollebius the same thought appears when he says that mediate creation is to produce something *ex materia inhabili, supra naturae vires.*

immediate creation precisely because, in the esteem of these theologians, the soul was not formed from any antecedent, prejacent, or preexisting material but brought into existence by the mere fiat of God, that is, by fiat *ex nihilo*. And the body of man is an instance of mediate creation precisely because the dust of the ground was used. Since it is the absence of prejacent material that gives to the creation of the soul the right to be called immediate as contrasted with mediate, so it is the very presence and use of prejacent material that requires us to call the formation of the body an act of mediate creation as contrasted with immediate. It would also appear that mediate creation was not conceived of as involving the interjection of any new entity immediately created by God but simply as the fashioning into something new of an entity which already existed. Thus the formation of man's body is called creation not because origination of essence in any way entered into the action of God in this case but only because the immediate and omnipotent power of God was alone adequate to form a human body out of so unfit and so unapt an entity as dust of the ground.

We also see from the distinct actions which entered into the creation of man how these theologians conceived of mediate and immediate creation as co-working to the realisation of a certain end. In the creation of man both kinds of creative activity were present, mediate in the case of his body, immediate in the case of the soul. These two perfectly coalesced in the creation of man in his unity and totality. Yet the distinctness is carefully maintained and the distinguishing feature of the one action is strictly excluded from the other.

6. Mediate creation must not be construed in terms of a succession of *ex nihilo* fiats supervening or superinduced upon preexisting material.[6] We are liable to interpret the concept

---

[6] There is, however, in Francis Junius a statement which seems to be to the opposite effect. He says: "Creatio est ratio Dei externa, qua immediate per se res a non esse ad esse, sine alteratione, pro sua libera voluntate produxit: idque aut nulla prorsus praeexistente materia fundens per verbum: aut in materiam iam a se creatam formam e nihilo creatam inducendo" (*op. cit.*, Cap. XV, Thes. 3). It will be noted that the formula *immediate per se res a non esse ad esse* applies to both types of creation, mediate as well as immediate. This is in line with what we have found

in this way, but this would be incorrect. As was indicated above, the very differentia of mediate creation is the exclusion or absence of this *ex nihilo* factor. Again, the case of Adam shows the fallacy of such an interpretation. If mediate creation consisted in the supervention of *ex nihilo* fiat upon an already existing material context, then the creation of man would be an example of mediate creation. That is to say, mediate creation would describe the whole situation of man's origin. But this is not the case. The theology concerned discriminated between Adam's body and his soul and did not conceive of mediate creation as the coalescence or combination of *ex nihilo* fiat and mediate creative action. This does not mean, of course, that God's action in the creation of the world was so conceived as to exclude repeated and successive *ex nihilo* fiats. So far from excluding such they were posited. But the point is that the concept of mediate creation does not derive its definition from these successive *ex nihilo* fiats nor was it conceived of as comprising any such *ex nihilo* fiat. Rather is it the case that its very definition strictly excludes that type of action.

already that mediate creation does not exclude immediate action on the part of God. But when Junius says that to the material already created by God is added form which, in turn, is also created *ex nihilo*, we find that the formula *creatio ex nihilo* is applied to both immediate and mediate creation. And this would imply that even in mediate creation there is *ex nihilo* fiat. If this is so, then Junius would be taking a position which runs counter to what appears to be the more characteristic viewpoint of the theologians in question. The more classic formulation of mediate creation requires a sharp contrast between *ex nihilo* and *ex materia*, and it is the latter which applies to mediate creation. There may be a way of reconciling this statement of Junius with the other viewpoint. It may be that a solution lies in the distinction which Junius makes in the preceding chapter when he distinguishes between the act of creation in which something is produced according to its whole substance without any preexisting condition and the act of creation in which something which already exists is changed for the better, not according to its substance but according to its qualities (*op. cit.*, Cap. XIV, Thes. I). The *ex nihilo* fiat which enters in mediate creation would then be not the creation *ex nihilo* of substance but the creation *ex nihilo* of the qualities with which the new form is endowed. This would tend to relieve the discrepancy but it is not at all certain that it would eliminate it. For in the more common formulation there does not appear to be room for any *ex nihilo* fiat in the action which is specifically one of mediate creation.

7. Mediate creation must not be equated with or construed in terms of God's ordinary providential control and direction.[7] In the latter God uses second causes which are suited to and endowed for the achievement of certain ends. In ordinary providence there is the operation and development of the powers which God has deposited in the world and these powers naturally exert their agency in the production of certain effects. By definition mediate creation is radically diverse; it is the creative action of God upon entities which have no intrinsic aptitude or power in the direction of the result which the creative action achieves.

CALVIN'S TEACHING

This construction of the doctrine of creation raises many questions in the mind of the student of historical theology. The question of particular interest in the present study is whether or not Calvin's thought on the subject of creation falls into the framework of the distinction between immediate and mediate creation. The question here is not the relatively simple one of determining whether or not Calvin uses such terminology. The present writer is not aware that Calvin anywhere uses these terms to distinguish one type of creative

[7] Charles Hodge does not adhere to this distinction in his use of the term "mediate creation" and consequently his concept of mediate creation is much more elastic than that of the earlier Reformed theologians. He defines mediate creation, indeed, in the usual way as "forming out of preexisting material" but then proceeds to apply this to the continuous order of providence. He says: "And the Bible constantly speaks of God as causing the grass to grow, and as being the real author or maker of all that the earth, air, or water produces. There is, therefore, according to the Scriptures, not only an immediate, instantaneous creation *ex nihilo* by the simple word of God, but a mediate, progressive creation; the power of God working in union with second causes" (*op. cit.*, p. 557). It is this extension of the term "mediate creation" to include God's activity in the course of ordinary providence that the older theologians would have disallowed. Francis Turretine, for example, says respecting mediate creation that it is "ex materia aliqua, sed plane inhabili et indisposita, nec ulla causarum secundarum vi disponibilis, si ita loqui licet, ad termini productionem, et in qua sola datur *potentia obedientialis*, seu *non repugnantiae*, in ordine ad causam primam infinita virtute agentem" (*op. cit.*, Loc. V, Quaest. I, §VI).

action from another type. The question is whether his references to God's creative action and his interpretation of what such action involved warrant the inference that he conceived of God's creative activity as taking two forms, the one corresponding to what other Protestant theologians called "immediate creation" and the other to what was called "mediate creation". Benjamin Breckinridge Warfield has devoted considerable attention to this matter and discusses the question with his characteristic erudition. He is quite emphatic to the effect that the "sequence of truly creative acts", posited by those who distinguish between immediate and mediate creation, is the very thing Calvin disallows and even directly contradicts.[8] He proceeds to argue that Calvin severely restricted the word "create" and the action denoted by it to *ex nihilo* fiat and thus set aside and repudiated the notion of "mediate creation".[9] "Calvin's sole motive", he says, "seems to be to preserve to the great word 'create' the precise significance of to 'make out of nothing,' and he will not admit that it can be applied to any production in which preexistent material is employed."[10] He regards Calvin as maintaining that God "has acted in the specific mode properly called creation only at the initial step of the process, and the result owes its right to be called a creation to that initial act by which the material of which all things consist was called into being from non-being".[11] Furthermore, according to Warfield, Calvin held that the indigested mass, which "was called into being by the simple *fiat* of God", contained the " 'promise and potency' of all that was yet to be" and "all that has come into being since — except the souls of men alone — has arisen as a modification of this original world-stuff by means of the interaction of its intrinsic forces".[12] Hence "all the modifications of the world-stuff", all the changes that took place after the original fiat, while they take place "under the directly upholding and governing

[8] B. B. Warfield: "Calvin's Doctrine of the Creation" in *Calvin and Calvinism* (New York, 1931), p. 301.
[9] *Ibid.*, pp. 302 f.
[10] *Ibid.*, p. 302.
[11] *Ibid.*, p. 300.
[12] *Ibid.*, p. 304.

hand of God, and find their account ultimately in His will",
yet "find their account proximately in 'second causes' ".
And this Warfield asserts is a "pure evolutionary scheme",[13]
that is to say, "the modification of the original world-stuff
into the varied forms which constitute the ordered world,
by the instrumentality of second causes — or as a modern
would put it, of its intrinsic forces".[14]

In this interpretation of Calvin's doctrine of creation there
are two questions: (1) whether or not it is true that Calvin
set aside and repudiated the concept of mediate creation or
rather the concept which the term "mediate creation" denotes;
and (2) whether or not Calvin regarded all the changes that
took place in the formation of the world subsequent to the
original fiat — with the exception of the soul of man — as
wrought by the instrumentality of forces intrinsic to and
resident in the world-stuff which came to exist by the initial
ex nihilo fiat. It may be that these two questions are really
reducible to one question. But, if so, it is well to bear in
mind both ways of stating the question as we proceed to
examine Calvin's own teaching on this subject.

Perhaps the two most relevant statements in Calvin's *opus
magnum, Institutes of the Christian Religion*, are found in I,
xiv, 20 and I, xv, 5. They read respectively as follows:
"Therefore to apprehend by a true faith what it behooves us
to know concerning God, it is good, first of all, to learn the
history of the creation of the world, as it is briefly set forth
by Moses . . . . From this we shall learn that God, by the
power of his word and Spirit, created out of nothing the
heaven and the earth; and thereafter produced all things,
animate and inanimate, distinguished the innumerable variety
of things in an admirable gradation, gave to each kind of
thing its proper nature, assigned its offices, and appointed
its places and stations." "It must therefore be concluded
with certainty that the souls of men, even though the divine
image is impressed upon them, were no less created than the
angels. And creation is not a transfusion but an origination
of essence out of nothing." From these quotations it is

[13] *Ibid.*, p. 305.
[14] *Ibid.*, p. 306.

obvious that Calvin defines creation in terms of origination out of nothing, that is to say, in terms of *ex nihilo* fiat, and by such fiat, he believed, originated the heavens and the earth and the souls of men. It is also apparent that he regarded all other things, animate and inanimate, as having been produced from that which came into existence by *ex nihilo* fiat, or, at least, as having been produced subsequent to the creation *ex nihilo* of the heavens and the earth.

It is not, however, clear that Calvin by such statements would be precluded thereby from affirming, in addition, what other Reformed theologians called mediate creation. Those maintaining the distinction between mediate and immediate creation could have said what Calvin says in these quotations with respect to the creation of the heavens and earth and the origin of the souls of men, the two subjects with which, in these places, Calvin is mainly concerned. And these theologians might not have demurred when Calvin says that all other things beside heaven and earth, the angels, and the souls of men were produced from the material called heaven and earth. They would define the divine method whereby these other things were produced, but they would not deny what Calvin says that they were produced from, or after, the heaven and the earth (hinc[15] omne genus . . . produxisse). We may conclude, therefore, that nothing very conclusive can be elicited from these statements in the *Institutes*. We shall have to turn, therefore, to Calvin's comments on the Mosaic account of creation.

On Genesis 1:1 he says:

> He moreover teaches by the word 'created' (creandi verbo), that what before did not exist was now made . . . . Therefore his meaning is that the world was made out of nothing (ex nihilo conditum esse) . . . . Let this then be maintained in the first place, that the world is not eternal, but was created by God (creatum a Deo fuisse). There is no doubt that Moses gives the name of heaven and earth to that confused mass (molem illam confusam) which he shortly

[15] It is difficult to know whether "hinc" at this point means that every other thing was produced "from" the heaven and earth or "after" the heaven and earth.

afterwards denominates waters. The reason of which is
that this material was to be the seed of the whole world
(ratio est, quod materia illa totius mundi semen fuerit).

The most significant statement in this comment, apart from
what has been noted already, is that the heaven and earth
of Genesis 1:1 Calvin regards as the confused mass described
in verse 2 and that this confused mass was the "seed" of the
whole world. One is distinctly liable to derive from such a
statement as this the impression that the confused mass had
inherent in it the potencies or germs which were capable of
producing the innumerable variety of things, animate and
inanimate, under the providential direction and government
of God, and that the whole subsequent ordering, fashioning,
moulding into distinct forms was by the development of
forces intrinsic to the confused mass as created by God. In
other words, the expression *semen totius mundi* would suggest
that all subsequent change — except the soul of man — was,
as Dr. Warfield proposes, a "pure evolutionism".[16]

This view would appear to be confirmed when we turn to
Calvin's comments on Genesis 1:21. He discusses the use
of the word "create" in this verse.

A question here arises out of the word *created*. For we
have before contended that the world was made out of
nothing because it was created, but now Moses says that
things which were formed out of other matter (ex alia
materia) were created. They who assert that the fishes
were truly and properly created[17] because the waters were

---

[16] *Op. cit.*, p. 305.

[17] The Latin at this point reads: "Qui dicunt vere et proprie creatos esse
pisces". John King, the Calvin Translation Society translator (Edinburgh,
1847), renders thus: "They who truly and properly assert that the fishes
were created"; B. B. Warfield, however, thus: "Those who assert that the
fishes were truly and properly created". The question is the simple one
whether the adverbs "vere" and "proprie" are to be construed with
"dicunt" or with "creatos esse". If the former alternative were followed
then Calvin would be saying that it is quite correct to say that the fishes
were created. It seems, however, to be more in accord with the construction and argument of the sentence to take "vere et proprie" with
"creatos esse", as we have done in our translation, and interpret Calvin's
argument accordingly.

in no way suitable or adapted to their production (ad procreandos ipsos idoneae aptaeque fuerint) only avoid the question: for, in the meantime, the fact would remain that the material existed previously, which the strict signification of the word (create) does not admit. I therefore do not restrict (non restringo) the creation here spoken of to the work of the fifth day but rather take it as referring to that shapeless and confused mass which was as the fountain of the whole world (scaturigo totius mundi). God therefore created the whales and other fishes, not because the beginning of their creation is to be reckoned from the moment in which they receive their form but because they are comprehended in the total matter which was made out of nothing (ex nihilo factum est). So, as regards species, form alone was then added: but creation is, nonetheless, properly used of the whole and the parts.

It might seem that Calvin here restricts creation to the original *ex nihilo* fiat by which the shapeless and confused mass came into being and that the only reason why the word "create" is used in Genesis 1:21, with reference to the specific action of that day, is that the whales or fishes derived the substance of which they were formed from the original *ex nihilo* fiat of Genesis 1:1. This would mean that the word "create" is not used at all to describe the action of the fifth day but has reference exclusively to the fiat at the beginning, and the only relevance of its use in 1:21 is that the material then being formed proceeded from an earlier act of *ex nihilo* fiat mentioned in 1:1. This would have to be the inference if it is maintained that Calvin would refuse to apply the concept of creation to any other action than that of making out of nothing.

It is clear that here Calvin recognises that the strict signification of the word "create" does not admit (verbi proprietas non admittit) of its being applied to an act of formation out of preexisting material. And it is also clear that for this reason he finds in the use of the word "create" in Genesis 1:21 an allusion to the *ex nihilo* fiat of 1:1. But what is not apparent is that here Calvin disallows altogether the propriety of the use of the word "create" with respect to the specific action of the fifth day. The case seems to be, rather, that though, in his esteem, creation, strictly understood, cannot apply to a formative action, that is, to the fashioning of something *ex materia praeëxistente*, yet *in some sense* he does regard creation as applicable to the specific action of the fifth day. When he says: "I do not restrict creation to the work of the fifth day" this is not by any means to be understood as meaning that he restricted creation to the original fiat of Genesis 1:1. The import is rather that while creation applies to the work of the fifth day yet it is not restricted to the work of that day but includes also the originative fiat. But this obviously implies that the use of the word "create" in Genesis 1:21 has some relevance to the work of God on that particular day. Furthermore, this may well be the force of what he says a little later. "So, as regards species, form alone was added: but creation is, nonetheless, properly used of the whole and the parts." It is possible, of course, that what he means at this point by "the whole and the parts" is not the original *ex nihilo* fiat and the subsequent formative acts but the whole mass of formless material of Genesis 1:2 and the various parts of that total mass out of which specific things were later formed. But the expression the "whole and the parts" may also refer to the total mass of unformed matter (which is the fountain of the whole world) and the specific things which by subsequent action were formed by the hand of God. "The parts" would thus denote the things formed, including the divine action by which they were formed. Finally, in this precise connection, there is his statement: "Therefore God created whales and other fishes, not because the beginning of their creation (initium creationis) is to be reckoned from the moment in which they receive their form . . .". Here Calvin says that the whales and fishes did not *begin* to be created when they received their form. This is apparent and is in line with his whole argument at this point. But while the fishes did not then *begin* to be created it does not at all follow that the formation on the fifth day is not included in the creation spoken of in the verse concerned. That the actual formation is included would seem to be the import.

There is one other remark of Calvin's in his comment on

this verse which is worthy of some consideration. He says: "Those who say that the fishes were truly and properly created because the waters were by no means suitable or adapted to their production only avoid the question". Here it would seem that Calvin is repudiating the notion that creation, in its strict signification, must be posited on the fifth day because the waters were not suitable to the production of fishes. And this could be interpreted as implying that Calvin was aligning himself against those who posited "mediate creation" and posited such in order to explain the formation of things out of material which was naturally unfit and unadapted for the effect produced (ex materia naturaliter inhabili). But again this inference does not necessarily follow. What Calvin is saying is that those who say fishes were *truly* and *properly* created, because the waters were in no way suited or adapted to their production, resort to a subterfuge. The adverbs "truly" and "properly" should be noted. And what Calvin may be repudiating here is simply the notion that creation *in its strict signification* must be posited on the fifth day because the waters were not adapted to the effect. If so, then his argument at this point does not exclude the exercise on the fifth day of creative activity *in some other sense.* The mediate creationists themselves excluded creation in its primary sense of *creatio ex nihilo* from the action of the fifth day. Calvin's "truly" and "properly" may have reference to this same kind of creative action.

The purpose of this extended study of Calvin's comments on Genesis 1:21 has not been to prove that Calvin held to the view called "mediate creation" and posited the presence of such creative action on the fifth day. All that has been in view is simply to show that his comments on Genesis 1:21, when carefully weighed, do not establish his repudiation of the doctrine of mediate creation and that his comments on Genesis 1:21, as also on Genesis 1:1, leave the door open. We have not yet found conclusive evidence to support B. B. Warfield's contention that Calvin repudiated the doctrine of mediate creation.

We must now turn to certain other comments which more directly bear upon the kind or quality of the divine action conceived of by Calvin as exerted in the progressive ordering and fashioning of the heavens and the earth. There are two questions in particular which should be borne in mind: (1) does Calvin conceive of the progressive action of God by which form, ornament, and perfection were given to the world as involving *creative* activity on the part of God?; (2) does he regard the rude and unpolished, empty and confused mass of Genesis 1:2 as containing within itself the forces which were developed into the ordered universe?

Calvin is insistent that although the "Word" is not expressly mentioned in Genesis 1:1,2 yet it was by the efficacy of the "Word" that the mass of heaven and earth was brought into being. Nevertheless he also maintains that God did not *put forth* his Word until he originated light (in lucis origine). It is in connection with Calvin's comments on the origin of light that we are introduced to expressions which are particularly relevant to our question. In this connection there are at least three occasions on which he uses the word "create". The first instance (*ad* Gen. 1:3) is rendered more significant by the fact that he is arguing for the eternity of the hypostatical Word by whose efficacy the mass of heaven and earth had been created and carried to its completion. The Word dwelt in God and without him God could never be. But it was with the origin of light that this became apparent — "the effect of which, however, became apparent when the light was created (quum lux creata est)". A little later he says that "the light was so created (sic creatam fuisse lucem) as to be interchanged with darkness". Then in connection with the fourth day (*ad* Gen. 1:14) he says: "He (God) had before created the light (prius lucem creaverat): but now he institutes a new order in nature, so that the sun may be the dispenser of light by day, and the moon and the stars may shine by night".

It is apparent that here Calvin applies the term "creation" to an act of God which was subsequent to the creation of the shapeless mass of Genesis 1:1,2. Light originated when God for the first time *put forth* his Word and Calvin employs the term "create" to designate this action.

Even more instructive along this line are his comments on Genesis 1:11. "Hitherto", he says, "the earth was naked and barren: now the Lord fructifies it by his word. For though it was already destined to bring forth fruits, yet, till new virtue (nova virtus) proceeded from the mouth of God, it must remain dry and empty. For neither was it naturally fit to produce anything, nor had it a germinating principle from any other source, till the mouth of the Lord was opened (neque enim ipsa naturaliter ad gignendum quicquam apta erat: nec aliunde erat germen, donec apertum est os Domini) . . . . Moreover, it did not happen fortuitously that herbs and trees were created (creatae sunt) before the sun and moon. We now see that the earth is quickened by the sun to cause it to bring forth its fruits . . . but because we are wont to include in their nature what they derive from another source, it was necessary that the vigour which they now seem to impart to the earth should exist before they were created (prius extare quam creata essent) . . . . When he says, 'Let the earth bring forth the herb . . .', he signifies not only that herbs and trees were then created (creatas fuisse), but that, at the same time, both were endowed with the power of propagation, in order that offspring might continue."

No more illuminating passage than the foregoing occurs in Calvin's exposition of Genesis 1. It is necessary to note its significant features. (1) He uses the term "create" on two occasions with reference to the production of herbs and trees on the third day and with reference to the sun on the fourth day. This exemplifies what we have found already, that Calvin freely uses this word "create" to designate the action of God subsequent to the *ex nihilo* fiat of Genesis 1:1. He has no hesitation in speaking of light, herbs, trees and the sun as having been *created*. (2) Prior to the action of the third day, he says, the earth was naked and barren (nuda et sterilis). This bare statement of itself might not establish very much in reference to our question. But the other supplementary remarks indicate what he meant by naked and barren. He adds that new virtue or power needed to be added by God, that the earth had no germinating principle, and that the herbs and trees were not only created but endowed with the power or virtue of propagation (propagationis virtutem). This description of the earth's condition and of what was requisite in order that it might bring forth fruit is in no way consonant with the notion that the earth was endowed with certain intrinsic forces which were developed by a process of "pure evolution". In other words, this description which Calvin gives of the earth's condition prior to the third day and of the divine procedure on that day is far other than one which could be defined as "the modification of the original world-stuff into the varied forms which constitute the ordered world, by the instrumentality of second causes".[18] (3) Calvin here says also that the earth was "not naturally fit to produce anything" (neque ... naturaliter ad gignendum quicquam apta erat). This reminds us quite distinctly of the language used by other theologians in connection with mediate creation. What they said was that the material upon which God's creative action supervened, in the instances of mediate creation, was *materia naturaliter inhabilis, materia non apta*. This is exactly the thought of Calvin at this point and he uses practically identical language: the earth was not naturally fit (non naturaliter apta). Yet he speaks of *creation* in this connection. And his thought is surely to the effect that creative action supervened upon this naked and barren material in endowing it with new virtue, germinating capacity, and the power of propagation. This, in essence, is the kind of creative action which was conceived of by other Protestant theologians as mediate creation in contradistinction from immediate. (4) In this same context Calvin says that "what David declares concerning the heavens ought also to be extended to the earth, that by the word of the Lord it was made and adorned and furnished by the breath of his mouth (Ps. 33:6)". In his comment on Psalm 33:6 he says: "In saying that the heavens were created (conditos) by the word of God, he greatly magnifies his power, because by his nod alone (solo nutu contentus), without summoning help from other sources, and without the expenditure of much time or labour he made so splendid and noble a work". It is therefore this creative word of God that was exemplified, according to Calvin, in the specific actions of the third day.

There are several other statements of Calvin in his expo-

[18] B. B. Warfield: *op. cit.*, p. 306.

sition of Genesis 1 which are illustrative and corroboratory of what we have found in the foregoing passages. These statements need simply to be quoted. "God . . . distributed the creation of the world (mundi creationem) into distinct stages, in order that he might claim our attention" (ad Gen. 1:5). "On the fifth day the birds and fishes are created (creantur)" (ad Gen. 1:20). "When he says 'the waters brought forth', he continues to commend the efficacy of the word, which the waters hear so promptly, that, though lifeless in themselves (mortuae in seipsis), they may suddenly teem with living offspring" (ad Gen. 1:21). "He descends to the sixth day on which the animals were created (creata sunt animalia), and then man . . . . But whence has a dead element life? Therefore there is in this respect a miracle as great as if God had begun to create out of nothing (creare ex nihilo coepisset) those things which he commanded to proceed from the earth. But he does not take material from the earth as if he needed it but that he might the better combine the several parts of the earth with the universe itself" (ad Gen. 1:24).

When we attempt to draw general conclusions from Calvin's teaching on this subject, it will have to be admitted that everything is not as clear and definite as we should wish it to be. Indeed there might appear to be incompatibility at certain points. He appears to define creation as making out of nothing, that is, the origination of essence out of nothing, and, with the exception of Adam's soul, to restrict this action to the fiat mentioned in Genesis 1:1. On the other hand, he uses the word "create" with the utmost freedom in reference to the successive acts of God by which the heavens and the earth were adorned, furnished, and perfected. Not only does he use the word "create" in these connections but also other terms which are applied to the originative ex nihilo fiat. The following observations may be made, however, on the basis of the evidence.

1. It is apparent that Calvin accords a special place in his concept of creation to the fiat mentioned in Genesis 1:1. This was ex nihilo fiat: no created entity, no material substance whatsoever, existed prior to this event. For this reason there is something absolutely specific and distinctive

about it, and any other creative act subsequent to it cannot be in precisely the same category. All subsequent acts have the context of preexistent created reality. Even though subsequent acts of creation should have brought into being new entities or essences and therefore should have involved additional *ex nihilo* fiats, yet these subsequent acts would still differ in this respect that there was already a created universe into which these new essences would have been injected or to which they would have been added. Any conclusion, therefore, which we may be compelled to draw respecting Calvin's view of the character of the subsequent creative acts need not and must not in the least deny or obscure the distinctive category to which the original fiat of Genesis 1:1 is assigned.

2. Calvin did regard the shapeless and confused mass referred to in Genesis 1:2, and which resulted from the fiat of Genesis 1:1, as the seed (semen) or fountain (scaturigo) of the whole world (*ad* Gen. 1:1 and Gen. 1:21 respectively). What, more precisely, he meant by such terms it is very difficult to ascertain. It is very likely, however, that he regarded this naked, barren, and unformed mass as containing the whole of the material substance out of which the world was shaped and formed. It is questionable if he would regard any subsequent act of God as bringing into existence any new *material* substance. At least it must be said that he regarded this confused mass as the basic substrate upon which all subsequent acts supervened and as providing material which entered into the composition of all that had been formed and fashioned later on.

3. Calvin did not regard this unformed mass as containing within itself the living germs and potencies or the intrinsic forces by the development or evolution of which the various forms of life were subsequently produced. His statements, as we found, are explicitly and emphatically to the contrary. The earth as waste and void was "naked and barren", it was not "naturally fit to produce anything", it had no "germinating principle", it needed "new virtue". We must not, therefore, be misled into thinking that when Calvin called the shapeless mass the seed or fountain of the whole world he meant by this that it contained the seeds, the germs, the

potencies, which, by potentialities and forces resident in them, produced, under the proper providential conditions, the innumerable variety of forms which the created world, when perfected, assumed. It may well be that his thought is properly expressed by saying that the unformed mass was the *seed-bed* of the whole world. That it was the seed, in the sense of possessing the germinal principles or capacities, Calvin denies.

4. Calvin does not use the term "mediate creation" with reference to the creative acts which were subsequent to the original fiat. Though he does not use the term it does not appear that there is any essential or principial difference between the conception Calvin entertained with respect to these subsequent acts and the conception entertained by the theologians who described these acts in terms of mediate creation. The fact is that he uses terms which are distinctly similar to those which were used by these theologians to describe what they designated as acts of mediate creation, namely, that these were acts of formation *ex materia naturaliter inhabili*, and acts, therefore, which were to be carefully distinguished from those of immediate creation. The latter were not acts of formation *ex materia praeëxistente* but *ex nihilo* fiats. It may be said with good warrant that the later Reformed theologians had adopted terminology which Calvin did not use but that, nevertheless, the conceptions they entertained and developed were not essentially different from those which had been expressed by their precursor in the Reformed tradition.

It seems to the present writer, therefore, that B. B. Warfield's inferences with respect to Calvin's doctrine of creation are not supported by the relevant evidence. It is not apparent that Calvin repudiated the notion of mediate creation, even though he does not use such a term. More particularly, and of much greater importance, it is not by any means apparent that Calvin's position was, that after the original fiat "all that has come into being since — except the souls of men alone — has arisen as a modification of this original world-stuff by means of the interaction of its intrinsic forces".[19]

[19] *Ibid.*, p. 304.

In fact it seems far removed from the terms in which Calvin describes the process by which the heavens and the earth were adorned, fashioned, and perfected to say that he "ascribed the entire series of modifications by which the primal 'indigested mass,' called 'heaven and earth,' has passed into the form of the ordered world which we see, including the origination of all forms of life, vegetable and animal alike, inclusive doubtless of the bodily form of man, to second causes as their proximate account".[20] In other words, Calvin conceived of creative factors as entering into the process by which the heavens and the earth were perfected so that we are not able to characterise the process, as he conceived of it, as "a very pure evolutionary scheme".[21]

CONCLUDING OBSERVATIONS

If we were to venture a judgment with respect to the notion of mediate creation a few things would have to be said.

(1) It must be admitted that the term itself is not a felicitous or lucid one. The terminology tends to confuse the mediate and immediate agency of God. While it is true that God is present and active in every event, which is just saying that God's providence embraces all that occurs, yet it is all-important to distinguish the differing modes of the divine agency. And the most basic distinction is that between God's immediate action and his action through the mediacy of other agencies. It would be more in the interests of clarity and precision to reserve the word "creation" for the strictly originative activity of God, that is to say, to the bringing into being of something, solely by the will and fiat of God. The word "creation" would then be restricted to what has been called *creatio ex nihilo*. The term "mediate", as applied to creation, is liable to be interpreted as qualifying "creation" in a way that is inconsistent with its real meaning.

(2) There is no good reason why the kind of divine action denoted by the word creation in this its precise and strict

[20] *Ibid.*, p. 305.
[21] *Idem.*

signification should be restricted to the action spoken of in Genesis 1:1. There may have been a succession of truly creative acts in the process depicted for us in Genesis 1 and 2. It does no prejudice whatsoever to the idea of creation to suppose a succession of truly creative acts over the course of the six days. In the formation of man (Gen. 2:7) we have an example of a truly creative act supervening upon an existing entity in order to produce a result which is wrought by the combination of two factors, namely, the preexistent material called "dust from the ground" and the inbreathing of the breath of life by which man became living creature (Gen. 2:7; *cf.* Gen. 5:1,2). If this occurred in the formation of man, there is no *a priori* reason why this kind of action should not have occurred in other cases.

(3) It is necessary to distinguish between the first creative fiat by which being other than God himself began to be and all subsequent truly *creative* fiats. The distinction arises from the fact that before the originative creative fiat there was no created context or entity. But once the originative fiat is posited all subsequent creative fiats presuppose an already existent created context. That is to say, the first creative fiat presupposes no created reality as its context; subsequent creative fiats do presuppose a created context in relation to which they occur. What terms we might use to express this distinction is a matter simply of terminology. We must remember, however, that, if we are to use the term "creation" in its strict sense, there is no proper distinction in the precise mode of the divine action. For creation is always the strictly originative action of God in which by the fiat of his will he calls into being that which did not exist prior to such action. It is for this reason that the term "mediate creation" is misleading. Creation as act is not mediate. And if Calvin refrained from the use of the designation "mediate creation" it is to his credit.

Westminster Theological Seminary, Philadelphia

What one misses in this informative and scholarly work is the admission that all societies and cultures — ours as well as African — are equally in need of redemption and transformation. If we need the message, and perhaps some of us do, we should acknowledge the stupidity of terms such as "savage," "primitive," and even "pagan" in reference to Africa. At the same time, we should be instructed by a work such as this, and recognize that our "religion," even our "Reformed Faith," has not been totally scriptural, but far too much culturally biased.

WM. E. WELMERS

University of California,
Los Angeles

CALVIN ON ASTROLOGY

CHRISTINE McCALL PROBES

"THERE has been for a long time a foolish curiosity which consists of judging by the stars all that should happen to men, and of inquiring of them what course to take . . . . Rejected in the past as pernicious to the human race this phenomenon is in full revival today, with the result that many people who believe themselves to be of sound mind and who indeed have the reputation of being so are almost bewitched."[1]

The quotation from Calvin indicates a resurgence of interest in astrology during the Renaissance. Eugène Defrance in his book on the astrologers and magicians of Catherine de Medici says that thirty thousand sorcerers, alchemists, diviners and astrologers lived on the credulity of sixteenth-century Paris. Astrology flourished everywhere, even in the study of the theologian. Michael Servetus was found discussing astrology in his lectures on geography and astronomy at the medical faculty of Paris. His formal defense, published in 1538 in answer to the dean's criticism and burned less than a year later by decree of Parliament, was the *Apologetica disceptatio pro astrologia.*[2] The eminent reformer Melanchton has been judged perhaps the most important defender of astrology in the mid-sixteenth century. Don Cameron Allen in chapter two of his excellent monograph *The Star-Crossed Renaissance* summarizes Melanchthon's claims for astrology as a probable science and places the reformer among its more moderate exponents.[3] Luther, who himself cast the superstition of his time aside, mockingly said that Melanchthon

---

[1] John Calvin, *Avertissement contre l'astrologie judiciaire* in *Johannis Calvini Opera*, ed. Baum, Cunitz, Reuss (Brunswick, 1863–1900), VII, 515–516. My own translation.

[2] Eugène Defrance, *Catherine de Medicis, ses astrologues et ses magiciens-envouteurs* (Paris, 1911), p. 15.

[3] Don Cameron Allen, *The Star-Crossed Renaissance* (New York: Octagon, 1973), pp. 60–61.

24

pursued the study of astrology, "as I take a drink of strong beer when I am troubled with grievous thoughts."[4]

John Calvin's views on astrology are found principally in his treatise *Admonitio adversus astrologiam, quam Judiciariam vocant* and in some twenty-one passages of his *Commentaries*.[5] The treatise in relatively unknown and unavailable today except for a 1962 reprint of the French edition.[6] No English version since the initial one of 1549 is recorded in the Erichson and Niesel Bibliographies.[7] Neither of the recent English collections of tracts and treatises include it (neither the Library of Christian Classics volume of 1954 nor Eerdmans' three-volume set of 1958).

More surprising is the fact that, according to the standard bibliographies, no monograph or article on Calvin's views concerning astrology has been published. Scholars and authors of lives of Calvin have of course briefly characterized and summarized the content of the treatise.[8] Contemporary theologians who have included some mention of it are A. Mitchell Hunter, Albert-Marie Schmidt, W. Stanford Reid and Nigel Lee.[9]

The present study will, it is hoped, begin to fill the obvious need for a full-fledged systematic treatment of Calvin on astrology which would take into account not only the treatise but also other passages in Calvin which deal with the subject.

Calvin's 8500-word book, described by Théodore de Bèze as "a very elegant little treatise [in which] he exposed the falsehood and vanity of what is called Judicial Astrology, in which not a few seemed to put too much faith,"[10] is directed to the

[4] *Ibid.*, pp. 64, 65.

[5] *Table Talk* I, 17 as cited by Heinrich Bornkamm, *Luther's World of Thought*, trans. Martin H. Bertram (St. Louis: Concordia, 1965), p. 185.

[6] The original editions are the Latin and French ones of 1549; the standard edition is the one found in volume seven of the *Johannis Calvini Opera* (*Corpus Reformatorum*), (above, note 1).

[7] John Calvin, *Avertissement contre l'astrologie* (Paris: A. Colin, 1962).

[8] Don Cameron Allen (above, note 3) has evidently consulted a 1563 English edition. I am presently preparing, in consultation with the original French and Latin versions, a modern English translation.

[9] The eminent Renaissance scholar Don Cameron Allen includes probably the best short summary of the tract in his *The Star-Crossed Renaissance* (above, note 8), pp. 71–73.

[10] A. Mitchell Hunter, *The Teaching of Calvin* (London: James Clarke and Co., 1950), pp. 290–293; Albert-Marie Schmidt, *Jean Calvin et la*

"simple and unlettered who could easily be seduced because they do not know how to distinguish between true astrology and this superstition of magicians and sorcerers."[11] Calvin accommodates his style to the recipients by the use of amusing stories, easily grasped comparisons, concrete examples, common expressions and maxims, illustrations from everyday life and contemporary events.

The stories, as indeed most of the other devices, operate not only to amuse and keep the attention of the reader but also to point to a high spiritual truth. Such is the case, for example, in Calvin's tale of an old philosopher and his chambermaid.[12] The old philosopher, watching the stars and not his feet, made a mis-step and landed in a ditch. The chambermaid said to him, "There is nothing so good as to think of whatever is nearest us." The French expression for nearest, "le plus prochain," is picked up again in a play on words and reinforces Calvin's application of the story to a spiritual end. The "speculative fools" who, with their heads in the clouds, wander from the path God has shown them also forget their duty to their neighbor, "leur prochain" (VII, 523–524). Illustrations from everyday life include things such as Calvin's description of impiety, "hidden like the venom in the tail of a snake" (VII, 533) and his distinction between the correct and incorrect use of astrology illustrated by the moderate use of wine versus drunkenness (VII, 529). Fire and water are used to show the incompatibility of false astrology and Christianity (VII, 539). In reference to some of God's pro-nouncements against diviners Calvin says it should make our hair stand on end (VII, 538). In speaking of priorities, we should be careful not to put the "cart before the horse" (VII, 541). Mention of the frequent wars of the time is found among the contemporary allusions which made the message more topical for the reader of the sixteenth century (VII, 522). Contempo-

tradition calvinienne (Paris: Seuil, 1957), pp. 62–65; W. Stanford Reid, Christianity and Scholarship (Nutley: Craig Press, 1966), pp. 61, 66, 69; Nigel Lee, Calvin on the Sciences (England: Sovereign Grace Union, 1969), p. 42.

[11] John Calvin, Tracts and Treatises on the Reformation of the Church, trans. Henry Beveridge (Grand Rapids: Eerdmans, 1958), I, xci.

[12] John Calvin, Avertissement in Johannis Calvini Opera (above, note 1), VII, 516. Subsequent references to the treatise will appear in the text and will indicate only volume and column number.

rary allusions are not present in sufficient quantity to detract
from the timeless appeal of the treatise.

Proverbial sayings or maxims which enable Calvin to reach
the simple and unlettered are used to condemn the "masked
mathematicians" who are "good for emptying purses and filling
ears" (VII, 521). Calvin accuses these same counterfeit astrologers of taking a true maxim and applying it very badly. Here it
is the generally admitted truth of lunar influences which they
immoderately extend to all areas of life including business affairs
(VII, 518).[13]

The treatise is not devoid of subtleties and figurative language
but they are either explained or relieved by the amusement they
provoke. One of Calvin's arguments points out the unlikelihood
that all who die in battle possess the same horoscope. In his
description of the battle, where some 300,000 are killed, he identifies the combatants with their astrological signs and proceeds
to describe the order of battle accordingly (VII, 522).

Calvin's warning is, as the title indicates, "against judicial
astrology and other curiosities that rule today in the world." He
reserves for those against whom the attack is directed the nouns
and adjectives that he uses for his most formidable adversaries.
They are called "fantastic," "deceitful," "erratic," "audacious,"
and "presumptuous." The art of these "masked mathematicians,"
is nothing but "bastard astrology," "foolishness" [the French
"bêtise" is very appropriate etymologically], and "without a
grain of sense." The "Chaldeans" of his day are compared to
"little streams" which have their source in the fountain of Babylon (VII, 527). The "speculative fools" (VII, 523) practice an
"evil curiosity reproved by God" (VII, 536) and a "sorcery
invented by the devil" (VII, 529).

Intent on attacking this "diabolical superstition" (VII, 515–
516), Calvin is nevertheless careful to distinguish between what
he calls the true science of astrology and the art of astrology;
natural astrology is admitted but judicial astrology is condemned. More will be said further on about Calvin's own position, but briefly the true astrology may be said to include the

---

[13] The effect of lunar rhythms on the biological clocks controlling the
activity of living creatures has been the subject of investigation by one
of today's outstanding American biologists, Frank A. Brown of North-
western. Gauquelin, (above, note 4), pp. 50, 182, 192–194, 197, 241–242.

knowledge of the natural order and disposition God has made of the stars and planets, and additionally their effects such as rains, frosts, snows and so forth. Some degree of influence on earthly and human bodies is also included (VII, 518–519). The credo of judicial astrology (judicial meaning "predictive" or "that which judges or divines") consists in the main of two principal articles: first, "of knowing [from the stars] not only the nature and disposition of men, but also all their adventures, and all that they must do or suffer in their life," and second, the success or failure of their undertakings, thereby extending itself to include the whole state of the world (VII, 518).

To combat the false astrology Calvin uses some eight weapons from his arsenal. Reason, experience, common sense, and science prove to be effective in the attack.[14] The "bastard astrology" is shown to be "without a grain of sense" (French, "raison") (VII, 521, 535). The reader is asked to judge according to "reason and verisimilitude" the claims of the casters of horoscopes, for example, that a person's nativity is a mirror in which may be contemplated all the events of life (VII, 521). Common experience is appealed to as Calvin alleges the importance of sex and what we call today "genes" over the influence of the stars at the moment of birth (VII, 518–519). In inter-personal relationships the will of others is placed above the stars (VII, 521). In business and judicial matters the law should govern, not astrology (VII, 523). Even poetry is used by Calvin to defeat his enemies. The verse of the Latin satirist Persius, carefully translated by Calvin for his readers, strengthens the argument for heredity (VII, 519).[15] These seemingly human weapons used so effectively by Calvin and recommended by him for the use of his individual readers have God as their provenance. Calvin warns

[14] The importance of Calvin's appeal to common sense has been mentioned by Francis M. Higman in his excellent study *The Style of John Calvin in his French Polemical Treatises* (London: Oxford University Press, 1967), pp. 21–22.

[15] It has been alleged that "there is no evidence that poetry or art were media which stirred [Calvin's] sensibilities" and that his "artistic imagination is confined to his prose writing." John Dillenberger, *John Calvin* (New York: Doubleday, 1971), p. 11. While it is not possible to assert the opposite view from this one use of Persius, the example may be added to those found in the books of A. Mitchell Hunter (above, note 15) and Quirinus Breen, *John Calvin: A Study in French Humanism* (Hamden: Archon, 1968).

that God can take away all reason and common sense, even wisdom, if it is not used profitably (VII, 515).

More frequent and more effective than the human weapons is the two-edged sword of the word of God (VII, 513–514). The treatise begins with a warning from St. Paul and concludes with a recommendation from the same apostle. In the intervening pages more than thirty biblical references are found.[16] Old Testament passages which speak of astrology predominate, but fourteen references are from the New Testament.

Calvin's method of refutation is both offensive and defensive, both positive and negative; our discussion of it will point toward the next section of our study, that of the structure or organization of the treatise. The method is an almost evenly balanced one. Negatively, biblical authorities are invoked to warn against dangers and vain imaginations (VII, 513, 527) and to cite Old Testament laws against diviners (VII, 536). Four references to Scripture are used to qaulify Calvin's concession to the influence of the stars in the area of so-called natural disasters (VII, 524–525). At one point the author takes up three scriptural passages used by the astrologers themselves to assert God's approval of their art and defeats them by the very same passages (VII, 530–531). Both negative and positive emphases may be made from the same biblical authority. For example, Calvin finds in Daniel 2:27 the basis for his condemnation of false astrology and his praise of the revelation of God (VII, 526–527).

Positively, the biblical citations are used to support and define Calvin's concept of true astrology (VII, 516, 530). New Testament passages may corroborate what he deduces from Old Testament examples (VII, 525). Several references instruct by describing the effects of regeneration and of conversion (VII, 520 514). Allusion is made to Jacob and Esau as examples of God's reforming grace which breaks the common order of nature (VII, 520). Calvin's suggestion of a correct response and a proper remedy to the astrological folly is taken from Scripture (VII, 539). His argument for a positive course of action finds its authority in St. Paul (VII, 513, 514, 515, 516, 540).

The positive-negative balance so vividly seen in Calvin's use of biblical citations is found throughout the entire treatise. Calvin

[16] The count is my own; only sixteen are identified in the definitive edition.

opposes key words and concepts themselves sometimes related etymologically such as "to lead" and "to be led" ("amener au point" vs. "se laisser mener") (VII, 530). The attack on false astrology is balanced by praise of true astrology; Calvin's warnings are balanced by his proposed remedies. Even the remedy itself may be balanced although it is in a two-fold rather than a positive-negative manner. The double impulse of faith and service is recommended: "Whoever, in the first place, gives himself to the fear of God, and studies to discover His will, putting into practice above all what Scripture teaches; then secondly, who applies his mind to his vocation or at least to good and useful things, [he] will not have time to flit about . . . among the clouds" (VII, 540).

The treatise may be said to be organized according to five divisions.[17] The first section or introduction (VII, 513–515) begins with a warning from St. Paul and Calvin's exposition of it. The warning itself consists of a paraphrase of two passages from the apostle's first letter to Timothy (I Tim. 1:5–6 and 1:19). Calvin often chose to paraphrase or combine these two passages in some manner, for example in the *Institutes*: III, ii, 12; III, xix, 16 and IV, x, 4. The introduction continues by establishing the sacredness of the word of God and its proper transforming use (Hebrews 4:12 and II Timothy 3:16–17). The fruits of conversion are described according to Ephesians 4:28, which fruits are found to be sadly lacking in "those who call themselves Christians today" (VII, 514). Calvin ends the introduction by bringing forward his adversaries, the extravagances and foolish opinions of the day which originate in arrogance, according to him, the root of all heresy. Francis Higman has shown his biblically-oriented introduction to be typical of Calvin's polemical treatises. It provides the reader a perspective from which to view the ensuing argument or doctrinal discussion.[18]

In the second section (VII, 515–526) Calvin fully identifies and describes his opponent, taking care to differentiate as he does throughout the treatise between "the true astrology" and "this superstition of magicians and sorcerers." He announces

[17] This is my own method of structuring the treatise. Other critics have found only two sections or the obvious three: introduction, body, conclusion.

[18] *The Style of John Calvin in his French Polemical Treatises* (above, note 20), p. 15.

his intention: to show that the superstition is a diabolical one. After identifying the recipients or potential readers of the treatise, Calvin begins his attack proper of the credo of the judicial astrologers. The attack is one of ascending structure beginning with the somewhat admissible influence of the stars on terrestrial bodies and ending with the highly controversial influence, their determining effect at birth and from day to day. The second section of the treatise and part one of the attack proper closes with an affirmation of the sovereignty of God even in the areas of admissible influences, such as weather forecasting and natural disasters.

Section three (VII, 526–534) consists of Calvin's strong condemnation of the art and its adherents in biblical terms. Here the very passages alleged to be in support of the astrologers are turned against them. A case in point is the astrologers' appeal to Joseph, Moses, and Daniel as "taught in the school of the Egyptians and Chaldeans." Joseph's divining is shown to be feigned, for purposes of disguisement. His prediction of famine was by way of revelation rather than by the stars. In the case of Moses, "instructed in all the wisdom of Egypt," Calvin asks if that wisdom necessarily included superstitions, the worst of which is "that curiosity of divining by the stars." The conduct of Moses is examined; guidance by God rather than the stars is seen. As for the art of Daniel, there is no evidence of any knowledge other than natural astrology. A reminder of God's express condemnation of the superstition (Calvin previously or subsequently cites Isa. 47:12–15, Deut. 13:1–5, 18:10–14) should put an end to the matter (VII, 531).

The fourth section of the treatise and the last of the attack proper (VII, 534–539) is composed of Calvin's reply to certain historical examples alleged by the false astrologers. His treatment of predictions involving, for example, Domitian, Julius Caesar, and Caesar Augustus is based here as elsewhere on reason, common sense, and humour. He wryly states that if the Roman Empire had been given to all those born at the same moment as Augustus, there would have been very little left for him (VII, 536). Strong condemnations from the Bible provide the final argument (Deut. 13:1–5 and 18:10–14).

The proposal and exposition of a positive remedy based on I Tim. 3:8–9 forms the fifth division and conclusion of Calvin's treatise (VII, 540–542).

Although the treatise may be said to be composed of as many as five divisions there is a pervasive sense of unity that must be observed. Repeated use of certain key expressions helps to tie the sections together; one such vivid and frequent expression is "walking" ("cheminer," "le chemin"). Calvin's intent is constantly before the reader. The continual appeal to Scripture is highly unifying, particularly as concerns the use of St. Paul's first letter to Timothy at both beginning and end.

The final point of our study will be a definition of Calvin's position on astrology according to the treatise and a statement concerning its relation to the testimony of the *Commentaries*. It might be said that with one or two exceptions, the province of Calvin's "true science of astrology" corresponds to astronomy as it has been defined since the seventeenth century. It consists primarily of the study of the constitution, relative positions, motions, and relationships of the celestial bodies, of their causes and their effects. Beyond this is included some dependence on or at least correspondence with the stars as concerns earthly bodies and character, for example the constitution of a man or woman.[19] Natural astrology can calculate and predict only in the area of natural phenomena, and even then with no absolute certainty; anything more is condemned, as has been shown, as a "sorcery invented by the devil" (VII, 529). Calvin sees the labour of the true astrologer to be that of learning the secrets of the heavens "in order to glorify God and be useful to man" (VII, 523).

Calvin's views on astrology as set forth in the treatise find their complement and corroboration in his *Commentaries*.[20] With

[19] If the stars do condition the character of a man, then the significant time for their observation is the moment of conception rather than birth (VII, 518–519). At least one famous incidence of this has been recorded, that of France's most glorious king, Louis XIV, who hid the celebrated astrologer Jean-Baptiste Morin de Villefranche in his apartment on his wedding night with Anne of Austria, to draw up the horoscope of the future prince. L.-F. A. Maury, *La Magie et l'astrologie dans l'antiquité et un moyen âge* (Paris, 1877), p. 217.

Women's lib would be proud of Calvin on at least one point where he argues for the right of a woman to her own star, or proper nativity. He asks the "bastard astrologers" how they find in the husband's star the birth of his first wife, to know how long she will live (VII, 521).

[20] The *Commentaries* contain sufficient material on astrology for several full-length studies.

one exception, that of *Romans*, the commentaries containing the twenty-one references to astrology follow the treatise in date of publication. Calvin's position, however, shows little if any further development. Isaiah 19:12, for example, gives him the occasion to inveigh against idle and false astrologers, "a vast number of whom, at the present day, endeavor to insinuate themselves into the minds of princes and subjects, as if they possessed a knowledge of everything, both present and future. Such men resemble the imposters of whom the prophet speaks."[21] Judicial astrology is castigated in the same virulent terms as it is in the treatise. One expression which occurs throughout both the treatise and the commentaries and which finds similar exposition in each is the term "περίεργα," (VII, 539 and in the commentary on Acts 19:19). Calvin explains that it is a word used by the Greeks to describe "whatever things do not contain any solid usefulness in themselves, but waste men's minds and efforts, diverting them through a variety of roundabout ways. Such [he concludes] is so-called judicial astrology and all the divinations for the future that foolish men invent for themselves."[22]

True astrology is identified with natural astrology and is praised as contributing to high reverence for God. Calvin calls it the "alphabet of theology" in his treatment of Jeremiah 10:1–2.[23] In his commentary on Genesis 1:16 Calvin speaks against those members of the anti-astrology movement who condemned the true astrology along with the false: "This study is not to be reprobated, nor this science condemned because some frantic persons are wont boldly to reject whatever is unknown to them. For astronomy [*astrologia*] is not only pleasant, but also very useful to be known: it cannot be denied that this art unfolds the admirable wisdom of God."[24]

Princeton, New Jersey

[21] John Calvin, *Commentary on the Prophet Isaiah*, trans. Rev. William Pringle (Grand Rapids: Eerdmans, 1961), II, 61.

[22] John Calvin, *Commentary on the Acts of the Apostles*, trans. John W. Fraser (Grand Rapids: Eerdmans, 1966), II, 159.

[23] John Calvin, *Commentaries on the Book of the Prophet Jeremiah*, trans. John Owen (Grand Rapids: Eerdmans, 1950), II, 8.

[24] John Calvin, *Commentaries on the First Book of Moses*, trans. Rev. John King (Grand Rapids: Eerdmans, 1963), I, 30.

CALVIN AND COPERNICUS: THE PROBLEM RECONSIDERED

by ROBERT WHITE

The sixteenth century, which saw the emergence of a new theology, a new piety and new church structures, saw also the beginnings of a new astronomy which appeared to revolutionize the medieval world-picture. Less than three decades separate the publication of Luther's Ninety-Five Theses (1517) and the appearance of Copernicus' *De Revolutionibus orbium coelestium* (1543). While Copernicanism as such posed no direct intellectual threat to the Reformation, the proximity of the two movements in time and the geocentrism largely presupposed by the cosmology of the Bible suggested at least the possibility of tension between the two. Both Luther and Melanchthon, in fact, condemned Copernican theory as incompatible with Scripture. Luther's dismissal of the Polish astronomer as a "fool" is probably apocryphal, but of his general attitude there is little doubt: "This fellow...wishes to turn the whole of astronomy upside down. Even in these things that are thrown into disorder, I believe the Holy Scriptures, for Joshua commanded the sun to stand still and not the earth" (Jos. 10:12-14).[1]

Not unnaturally, Calvin was assumed to have shared the same strong biblicism as his German counterparts. Thus British philosopher Bertrand Russell, after citing the example of Luther, comments in *Religion and Science* (1935): "Melanchthon was equally emphatic; so was Calvin, who, after quoting the text: 'The world also is stablished, that it cannot be moved' (Ps. 93:1), triumphantly concluded: 'Who will venture to place the authority of Copernicus above that of the Holy Spirit?' "[2]

---

[1] Luther, *Table Talk*, No. 4638, in *Works*, ed. by J. Pelikan and H.T. Lehmann, Vol. 54 (Philadelphia: Fortress Press, 1967), pp. 358-59. For a fuller discussion, see John Dillenberger, *Protestant Thought and Natural Science* (London: Collins, 1961), pp. 37-39; B.A. Gerrish, "The Reformation and the Rise of Modern Science," *The Impact of the Church upon Its Culture*, J.C. Brauer, ed. (Chicago: University of Chicago Press, 1968), pp. 241-55.

[2] *Religion and Science* (London: Oxford University Press, 1935), p. 23. Russell's statement

131

Russell supplies no source for his quotation, and it was only twenty years later that Thomas S. Kuhn traced it to Andrew Dickson White, first president of Cornell University and author of the highly popular *History of the Warfare of Science with Theology* (1896).[3] White's text reads as follows:

> Calvin took the lead, in his *Commentary on Genesis*, by condemning all who asserted that the earth is not at the centre of the universe. He clinched the matter by the usual reference to the first verse of the ninety-third Psalm, and asked, "Who will venture to place the authority of Copernicus above that of the Holy Spirit?"[4]

More recently, Edward Rosen has shown that White in turn drew on an earlier work by F.W. Farrar, Anglican canon of Westminster, *History of Interpretation* (1886).[5] In the preface to his work, Farrar contrasted what he regarded as the Protestant right of private judgment with the obscurantism of earlier divines, wedded to primitive views of the universe. His catalogue of errors includes the rhetorical question found in White and Russell, and attributed to Calvin.

Farrar, like White and Russell, fails to identify the source from which he is quoting, and all attempts to discover the original in the Reformer's writings have been unsuccessful. It is hard not to agree with Rosen that the text ascribed to Calvin is pure invention on the part of a "non-intensive scholar, overburdened with work, facile in expression, and relying on a 'marvelous memory' for his quotations."[6]

Implicit in the discussion outlined so far has been the assumption that Calvin had either read Copernicus or was intelligently acquainted with his ideas. Since the main elements of Copernicus' system had been known in Lutheran Germany as early as 1539, four years before the

---

is repeated almost verbatim in his *History of Western Philosophy* (London: Allen and Unwin, 1946), p. 550.

[3]T.S. Kuhn, *The Copernican Revolution* (Cambridge, MA: Harvard University Press, 1957), pp. 192, 281.

[4]A.D. White, *History of the Warfare of Science with Theology*, Vol. 1 (New York: Appleton, 1896), p. 127. The work has been frequently reprinted; latest complete edition: New York: Dover Publications, 1960.

[5]E. Rosen, "Calvin's Attitude toward Copernicus," *Journal of the History of Ideas*, 21 (1960), 431-41. Cf. F.W. Farrar, *History of Interpretation* (London: Macmillan, 1886), p. xviii.

[6]Rosen, "Calvin's Attitude," p. 435.

publication of the definitive work, that assumption appears reasonable. It has, however, been vigorously challenged by Rosen, who, after examining Calvin's exegesis of a number of key biblical texts concerned with creation and cosmology, found no allusion, positive or negative, to heliocentrism as a system, nor to Copernicus as its originator.[7] Calvin's *Institutes*, his treatises and correspondence similarly yield no firm evidence. Rosen concludes, somewhat hastily perhaps, that "never having heard of him, Calvin had no attitude toward Copernicus."[8]

Arguments from silence are, unfortunately, seldom decisive, and Joseph Ratner, in an aggressive reply to Rosen, shows that the weight of circumstantial evidence supports the opposite view. How, he asks, could Calvin have ignored the existence of Copernicus up to his death in 1564, when Luther had been initiated twenty-five years earlier? How could the constant exchanges between Wittenberg (home of Coprnicus' editor and disciple, the Lutheran Rheticus) and Geneva have left the Swiss Reformer in a state of total ignorance? "It is incredible that Calvin 'never heard' of Copernicus...[Rosen] simply argues from Calvin's 'silence' to Calvin's 'ignorance', and this is to be guilty of an elementary fallacy."[9]

Even granting the force of Ratner's argument, however—and there is no reason to believe that Calvin was intellectually less curious or less well informed than Luther or Melanchthon—there remains the problem of his reticence on the subject of Copernicus.[10] Working independently of Rosen and Ratner, Pierre Marcel in 1966 advanced the idea that, while Calvin may safely be said to have read Copernicus and to have known his system, it was not within his province to pass judgment on it.[11] Ger-

---

[7]Ibid., pp. 438-41. Among the texts considered by Rosen are Calvin's commentaries on Gen. 1:16 (together with the "Argument," presumably referred to by A.D. White), Jos. 10:12-14, Ps. 75:3, 93:1 (again referred to by White), 104:5, 136:7, and his sermons on Job 26:7 and Ps. 119:90. Quirinus Breen (*John Calvin: a Study in French Humanism* [Grand Rapids: Eerdmans, 1931], p. 155) suggests that Calvin's "only possible reference to Copernicus is in his comments on Ps. 46." But the astronomer is not mentioned by name, and the Reformer's exegesis is no more "Copernican" than the biblical text ("We will not fear though the earth be removed.").

[8]Rosen, "Calvin's Attitude," p. 441.

[9]J. Ratner, "Some Comments on Rosen's 'Calvin's Attitude toward Copernicus'," *Journal of the History of Ideas*, 22 (1961), 382-85.

[10]A point ably made by Rosen in his "Reply to Dr. Ratner," ibid., pp. 386-88.

[11]P. Marcel, "Calvin et la science: comment on fait l'histoire," *La Revue Réformée*, 68 (1966), 50-51. There is, on the other hand, no evidence to support Marcel's suggestion that

rish reaches much the same conclusion: "It is hardly necessary to suppose that Calvin had never heard of Copernicus. What is plain, however, is that, if he knew of Copernicus, he felt no compelling need to quarrel with him."[12]

The value of the debate between Rosen and Ratner was that it finally disposed of the frivolous remark attributed by Farrar to Calvin, and shifted interest from the always dubious question of whether the Reformer had read the *De Revolutionibus* to that of whether, by whatever means and to whatever degree, he was aware of the heliocentric hypothesis.

The search for documentary proof of Calvin's attitude to the new astronomy—proof that in Rosen and Gerrish's experience was wholly elusive—bore fruit in 1971 with the publication by a French scholar, Richard Stauffer, of an important text overlooked by previous critics.[13] Stauffer drew attention to Calvin's eighth sermon (probably preached in 1556) on 1 Corinthians 10 and 11. In his exegesis of 10:19-24, the Reformer warns his hearers against imitating the behavior of first century Christians who, for reasons of expediency, participated in idol-sacrifices. The believer must not, he explains, compromise in such a way as to disguise good and evil; instead, let him freely acknowledge whatever is good and praiseworthy, and thus avoid the error of

> those dreamers who have a spirit of bitterness and contradiction, who reprove everything and pervert the order of nature. We will see some who are so deranged, not only in religion but who in all things reveal their monstrous nature, that they will say that the sun does not move, and that it is the earth which shifts and turns. When we see such minds we must indeed confess that the devil possesses them, and that God sets them before us as mirrors, in order to keep us in his fear. So it is with all who argue out of pure malice, and who happily make a show of their impudence. When they are told: "That is hot," they will reply: "No, it is plainly cold." When they are shown an object that is black, they will say that it is white, or vice versa. Just like the man who said that snow was black; for although it is perceived and known by all to

Italian pastor and scholar Girolamo Zanchi may have introduced Calvin to Copernican astronomy.

[12]Gerrish, "The Reformation," p. 247.

[13]R. Stauffer, "Calvin et Copernic," *Revue de l'Histoire des Religions*, 179 (1971), 31-40.

be white, yet he clearly wished to contradict the fact. And so it is that there are madmen who would try to change the natural order, and even to dazzle men's eyes and benumb their senses.[14]

Stauffer attaches the greatest importance to this text, and since his is the most significant recent contribution, we may look at it in some detail.

Although Copernicus is not mentioned by name, his partisans are, in Stauffer's view, "clearly condemned." The descriptions applied to them are those reserved by the Reformer for his worst enemies—"dreamers," "madmen." It is nevertheless surprising, if such was Calvin's feeling, that he did not condemn Copernican theory at other times and in more explicit terms. Even supposing he did not discover the theory until 1556, he had ample opportunity to allude to and combat it in the years that followed. Stauffer is not, in fact, convinced that Calvin's works have been thoroughly enough sifted for us to say that they contain no further reference to heliocentrism. Scholars like Rosen have traditionally looked to passages of obvious cosmological import; however, as the example of 1 Corinthians 10 shows, quite different contexts may contain unexpected yet vital developments. Only a patient and systematic reading of the fifty-nine tomes of the *Calvini Opera*, and of the *Supplementa Calviniana* volumes currently being edited, will lead to a satisfactory resolution of the problem.[15]

What may be said of Stauffer's thesis? His argument is convincing to the extent that even Rosen is obliged to recognize that Calvin was not, after all, a stranger to the new astronomy: the reference to the proponents of the earth's mobility is too specific to be brushed aside.[16] We should heed, too, the suggestion that more remains to be learned from closer scrutiny of Calvin's writings, particularly of his homiletic works,

---

[14]Sermon on 1 Cor. 10:19-24, *Ioannis Calvini Opera quae supersunt omnis* [= *CO*], 49:677, in *Corpus Reformatorum*, ed. by Baum, Cunitz and Reuss (Brunswick and Berlin, 1863-1900). Our translation.

[15]Interestingly, Stauffer indicates that Calvin's unpublished sermons on Genesis which he is preparing for publication in the *Supplementa Calviniana* series contain no reference to either Copernicus or the Copernicans. ("Calvin et Copernic," p. 40, n.1.)

[16]See Rosen's reply to Stauffer, "Calvin n'a pas lu Copernic", *Revue de l'Histoire des Religions*, 182 (1972) 183-85. Much of Rosen's argument, which seeks to prove that because Calvin's sermon omits any mention of the earth's axial movement he cannot have read Copernicus, is irrelevant. Stauffer merely affirms a general acquaintance on Calvin's part with Copernican ideas.

whose relevance to the study of Reformed theology Stauffer has ably demonstrated elsewhere.[17] The prejudice that Calvin is the man of a single book, the *Institutes*, containing the sum total of his thought, has had its day. Stauffer is right to remind us of this. That said, however, criticism may be made of his methodology and his conclusions.

In the first place, it may be argued, there is something defective about a method which, isolating from Calvin's vast corpus a mere half-sentence, uses it confidently to found a theory which can be established in no other way. The elementary hermeneutic principle whereby text is compared with like text is doubtless inapplicable here, but the very absence of "like text" ought to suggest the need for greater caution than Stauffer in fact exercises. Indeed, if one considers Stauffer's restatement of his position in a paper of 1973, his language appears even less circumspect.[18] The sermon which, in 1971, was said to condemn the advocates of heliocentrism is two years later roundly described as "beyond any doubt, anti-Copernican."[19] This is unfortunate, for caution is doubly necessary in the case of a text intended for oral delivery. Calvin's sermons, premeditated in the privacy of the study, were nevertheless given extempore, without notes. Hence the vast difference in style and tone, immediately observable, between the Reformer's preaching and his written commentaries. To regard his remarks about the Copernicans (if such they were) as a *lapsus linguae*, a chance aside prompted by what Stauffer himself calls a "flurry of polemic," is at least a possibility that should be allowed for.[20] It is a fundamental weakness in Stauffer's approach that he nowhere asks, still less answers, the question of the status of the text on which so much is made to hang.

In the second place, it may be objected, Stauffer's conclusions fail to do full justice to Calvin's text or its context. Neither Copernicus nor Copernicanism, as we have seen, is designated by name. If the sermon in question is "anti-Copernican," its anti-Copernicanism is incidental, not

---

[17]Notably in his most recent work, *Dieu, la création et la providence dans la prédication de Calvin* (Bern: Peter Lang, 1979).

[18]Stauffer, "L'Attitude des Réformateurs a l'égard de Copernic," in *Avant, avec, apres Copernic* (Paris: Albert Blanchard, 1975), pp. 159-63. See also his comments in *Dieu, la création et la providence*, pp. 187-88.

[19]"L'Attitude des Réformateurs," p. 162.

[20]Stauffer, "Calvin et Copernic," pp. 37-38. Gerrish ("The Reformation," p. 255) would argue for similar restraint in the interpretation of Luther's often volatile *Table Talk*.

central, to the preacher's purpose. That purpose is briefly summed up in the prophetic text to which Calvin alludes a little earlier in his sermon: "Woe to them who call evil good and good evil, who put darkness for light and light for darkness" (Is. 5:20).[21] He proceeds to develop the theme that to cloak sins such as immorality, adultery, murder, blasphemy and theft and to excuse them as trifles is to "abolish the truth of God."[22]

Now what is truth? What will remain to God if truth is abolished? Does not God say that it is his own mark, does he not adopt the title [God of truth], to show that it would be his essence which would be abolished if his truth were not to remain whole and undiminished? And what will happen when men try to falsify truth, and change the natural order and throw restraint to the winds? Must we not conclude that all religion would be cast down, and God's essence (so far as lay in their power) trampled underfoot?[23]

It will be clear that Calvin's theme is rather more complex than would appear from a reading of Stauffer's quotation, extensive as it is. The preacher's chief concern is not with heliocentrism as a conceptual scheme, but with the "spirit of bitterness and contradiction" which he believes underlies it. That spirit is judged inacceptable, not because it overturns a particular view of the universe which the Reformer regards as true, but because it overturns truth itself. Such a spirit sanctions arbitrariness and illogicality, confuses wrong with right, guilt with innocence, and perverts what the sermon goes on to call "true religion,' "pure and holy doctrine."[24] The "spirit of contradiction" is all-embracing. Nothing is immune to its corrosive effects, which is why Calvin's argument proceeds, disconcertingly perhaps, on three different levels at once: the physical (validity of the objective evidence of the senses); the moral (reality of the distinction between good and evil); the metaphysical (vindication of God's "essence" as the Author of truth, and therefore of the possibility of a truthful, normative revelation). It is thus as the *casual* illustration of an infinitely larger, more crucial principle

[21]CO 49:676. The same verse is quoted by Calvin in Com. 1 Cor. 10:22 (CO 49:467), with reference to those who "seek one subterfuge after another" as a cloak for licentiousness.

[22]CO 49:676.

[23]CO 49:676-77. Our translation.

[24]CO 49:677.

that the heliocentric theory is here invoked. Use of the label "anti-Copernican" tends to obscure the nature of what for Calvin are the truly critical issues.[25]

There is, of course, no question of minimizing the Reformer's hostility to heliocentrism, or of evading the thrust of his words. That the whole idea appears to him erroneous is evident from the way he equates the heliocentric hypothesis with the impossible proposition, "Snow is not white but black." Both ideas are wrong because both run counter to what is "perceived and known by all." Sense-experience as clearly demonstrates that the sun moves around the earth as it does that snow is white. To deny either is, willfully and literally, to shut one's eyes to reality.

We may well conclude with Stauffer that the preacher is "a prisoner of geocentrism" or, to use Rosen's less emotive phrase, that his outlook is essentially "pre-Copernican."[26] Calvin's mistake—the mistake of his age—lay in assuming that astronomy could advance, like other sciences, on the basis of observation alone, without the help of hypothesis and of mathematical deduction. Geocentrism came clothed, moreover, with all the majesty of ancient opinion, and since it accorded fully with universal common sense, the sixteenth century layman saw little point in replacing it with an untried system, whose only advantage over the prevailing Ptolemaic model was its greater aesthetic harmony.[27]

In evaluating the Reformer's sermon of 1556, it is important to notice the heavy emphasis placed on the question of motivation. Attention is directed to the "monstrous nature" of the innovators, to their impudence and malice, their brazen disregard of established norms of conduct and debate—in a word, to the *manner* in which the new ideas are being (or may be, Calvin uses the future tense) propagated and exploited. Whether the exegete has a specific situation in view, or whether his strictures are merely those typical of unfettered Renaissance polemic, is impossible to

[25]In his brief "Note additionnelle" appended to Rosen's "Calvin n'a pas lu Copernic" (pp. 185-86), Stauffer concedes that Calvin's anti-heliocentric remarks are "only the fleeting illustration of a theological truth"; but he does not discuss the implications of this fact for his general thesis.

[26]Stauffer, "L'Attitude des Réformateurs a l'égard de Copernic," p. 162; Rosen, "Calvin's Attitude," p. 438.

[27]On this point, cf. Kuhn, "The Copernican Revolution," pp. 168-80, and Dillenberger, *Protestant Thought*, pp. 26-29. It was for Kepler, Galileo and Newton to demonstrate in the following century the validity of Copernicus' theory.

say. A detailed study of the circumstances in which the sermon was com- posed and delivered would seem to be essential. Rosen's suggestion that Calvin's understanding of Copernicanism was influenced by an "ex- tremely hostile and poorly instructed informant" is not implausible.[28] The Reformer's attribution of base motives to the heliocentrists would make better sense if they had been represented to him as lovers of novel- ty for novelty's sake, or as self-seeking manipulators of public opinion,[29] or if their ideas had found favor with old adversaries such as the astrologers, skeptics or free-thinkers. We simply do not know enough about the reception of Copernicanism in sixteenth century Geneva to make an informed judgment. Stauffer, in any case, neglects the historical context of Calvin's sermon, and thus the possibility of a more subtle in- terpretation than the one he offers.

Whether Calvin's attitude is finally to be described as anti-Copernican or as something else, there is one fact that should not be overlooked: his opposition to heliocentrism is not predicated on the idea of a clash be- tween biblical and scientific truth. In this respect the contrast with Luther could not be greater. No appeal is made to the Bible in order to "prove" the traditional cosmology. The theory of the sun's fixity is firmly set aside, not because it is a denial of Scripture, but because it is a denial of rationality; it is rejected, not as an impious doctrine unworthy of the Christian, but as an aberrant philosophy unworthy of the thinking man. Notwithstanding Breen's contention that Calvin's learning "suffered from important lacunae," that "he appears to have had no taste for the sciences" and would have regarded with "horror" the rise of "the new natural science,"[30] the fact remains that science (in the modern sense of the term) was never for Calvin the "problem" that it became for his suc- cessors. As Pierre Marcel pertinently observes, the author of the *In-*

---

[28]Rosen, "Calvin n'a pas lu Copernic," p. 184.

[29]Cf. the colorful charge of exhibitionism that Calvin levels at those possessed by the "spirit of contradiction": what they do, he asserts in the sermon on 1 Cor. 10:19-24, is to *"pisser au benoistier* (as the Papists say), in order to get people talking" (*CO* 49:677-78). In *Dieu, la création et la providence* (pp. 227-28), Stauffer examines a private suggestion by Gottfried Locher that the Corinthians sermon is directed against Andreas Osiander, who contributed the Preface to the original edition of the *De Revolutionibus.* The suggestion is, rightly, rejected as improbable.

[30]Breen, *John Calvin*, pp. 155-56. In a rare lapse, even Dillenberger sees the Reformer's biblical understanding as being incompatible with the spirit of the new science (*Protestant Thought*, p. 39).

stitutes holds science to be a revelation of God in nature which cannot be at variance with his revelation in Scripture. Truth is one, just as God its Author is one: "If we regard the Spirit of God as the sole fountain of truth, we shall neither reject the truth itself, nor despise it wherever it shall appear, unless we wish to dishonor the Spirit of God."[31]

The Calvin-Copernicus debate is not closed. Almost a century after the publication of Farrar's *History of Interpretation*, the notion that Calvin condemned Copernicanism as contrary to the Scriptures and the Spirit who inspired them, is seen to be false. On the other hand, it is clear that, from sources unknown, the Reformer had acquired at least an elementary understanding of the heliocentric hypothesis, and on at least one occasion dismissed it as a delusion. Marcel's argument that Calvin ventured no opinion because such matters were beyond his competence has now to be modified, yet some such explanation is needed to account for his general silence on the question of the new astronomy.

Irrespective, however, of the results which further research may yield, two things appear to be beyond dispute. The first is that, as Gerrish rightly remarks, there is nothing in Calvin's hermeneutics which would have prevented him assimilating Copernicus' ideas. On the contrary, the Reformer's principle of accommodation, whereby God is said graciously to reveal himself in Scripture in terms accessible to the weakest intellect, frees the exegete from the necessity of a narrow literalism.[32] Calvin's commentary on Psalm 136:7 is quite unambiguous on this point:

> The Holy Spirit had no intention to teach astronomy and, in proposing instruction meant to be common to the simplest and most uneducated persons (*rudissimis quibusque idiotis*), he made use of Moses and the other prophets of popular language, that none might shelter himself under the pretext of obscurity. . . . Accordingly, the Holy Spirit would rather speak childishly (*balbutire*) than unintelligibly to the humble and unlearned (*plebeis et indoctis*).[33]

It must be said, secondly, that the replacement of an earth- by a sun-centered universe was far from having the dire theological consequences

---

[31]*Inst.* II.ii.15, tr. by Ford Lewis Battles (Philadelphia: Westminster Press, 1960), Vol. 1, pp. 273-74. Cf. Marcel, "Calvin et la science," p. 51.

[32]Gerrish, "The Reformation," pp. 258-62. On this question, see also Ford Lewis Battles, "God Was Accommodating Himself to Human Capacity," *Interpretation*, 31 (1977) 19-38.

[33]*Commentary on . . . Psalms*, tr. by James Anderson, Vol. 5 (Edinburgh: Calvin Translation Society, 1849), p. 184; *CO* 32:364-65. Cf. Rosen, "Calvin's Attitude," pp. 440-41.

assumed by many modern writers.[34] Geocentrism was entirely peripheral to classical Calvinism: the earth, as part of the created order, could equally well serve God's purposes when in motion as when static. As for man, the fact that he inhabited a moving planet in no way altered the duty of thankful obedience he owed to his Creator, Judge and Redeemer. In the final analysis, the only "centrism" which interested the Genevan Reformer was theocentrism. Thus Auguste Lecerf observed over forty years ago: "Geocentrism plays no vital role in Calvin's thought. . . . What establishes the value and dignity of the elect, is God's election, not the material place which man occupies in the universe." Lecerf recalls Calvin's commentary on Jeremiah 10:12 ("The centre of the earth is not the principle of creation. The earth has been suspended in space because it has so pleased God."), and adds, apropos of the geocentric system: "For Calvin, God is free, he might have decided matters differently. We know or think we know that he did decide differently; but that is all."[35]

[34]See, e.g., Bertrand Russell, *Religion and Science*, pp. 23-25; Kuhn, "The Copernican Revolution," pp. 192-93. A still more extreme opinion is that of John Herman Randall who, in *The Making of the Modern Mind* (rev. ed., New York: Houghton Mifflin, 1940, p. 226), writes that the Copernican revolution "swept man out of his proud position as the central figure and end of the universe, and made him a tiny speck on a third-rate planet revolving about a tenth-rate sun drifting in an endless cosmic ocean."

[35]A. Lecerf, "Le Calvinisme et les sciences physiques et naturelles" (1937), in *Etudes calvinistes* (Neuchatel: Delachaux et Niestlé, 1949), pp. 120-21. With Com. Jer. 10:12 (*CO* 38:75-76), compare Com. Is. 40:22: "The earth does not remain firmly and permanently in its place any further than as it is upheld by the power of God" (*Commentary on. . . Isaiah*, tr. by William Pringle, Vol. 3, Edinburgh: Calvin Translation Society, 1852, p. 227; *CO* 37:22).

Calvin's Understanding of Aristotelian Natural Philosophy: Its Extent and Possible Origins

Christopher B. Kaiser

Even though contemporary science did not have such an impact on everyday life as it does now, medieval Aristotelian cosmology was perceived in Calvin's day to be a challenge to faith in a personal God as much as Newtonian physics in the eighteenth century and evolutionary biology in the late nineteenth. Calvin did not directly confront the Aristotelian view of natural philosophy, but a careful reading of the reformer's works will show that his varied comments on scientific issues of his day demonstrate a clear faith in the providence of God in the ordering of the universe. Calvin cited the Aristotelian distribution of the elements, the system of homocentric spheres, and the problem of the stability of the earth. His understanding of the issues was limited, judged by late medieval standards. Nonetheless it played an important role in his discussions of divine providence. Its origins seem to go back to his college days in Paris.

CALVIN'S PRINCIPAL INTERESTS WERE IN THE REFORM of the Church and society, not in matters of natural philosophy.[1] The same is true of the majority of Calvin scholars today. Quite properly, most contemporary treatments of Calvin have concentrated on issues of theology, the sacraments, church discipline, and the socio-political order. Very little attention has been given to the background material made increasingly available by recent studies in the history of medieval and Renaissance science.

However, Calvin had to establish the credibility of his reform program in a culture for which natural philosophy was as much a concern as it is for us today. Though contemporary science did not have such an impact on everyday life as it does now, its findings regarding the structure of the cosmos had implications for the sacraments and were widely held to provide analogies to the ideal structure of society.

[1] In addition to logic (included in the medieval *trivium*) and the practical branches of philosophy (ethics and politics), there were three theoretical branches of Aristotelian science: metaphysics; mathematics (the medieval *quadrivium*); and natural philosophy (physics, cosmology, and meteorology); Sir David Ross, *Aristotle* (London: Methuen, 1923; fifth ed., 1949), 20, 47, 156. Here we are concerned only with natural philosophy. On Calvin's use of Aristotelian categories and logic, see Joseph C. McLelland, "Calvin and Philosophy," *Canadian Journal of Theology* 11 (1965): 46–47.

77

The paradigm for natural philosophy in the middle ages (as of the thirteenth century) and Renaissance (through most of the seventeenth century) was based on the texts of Aristotle and others, such as Sacrobosco, who popularized Aristotle's cosmology.[2] Aristotelian science was perceived by many to be a challenge to faith in a personal God much as Newtonian physics was later to become in the eighteenth century and evolutionary biology in the late nineteenth.[3] Calvin's own concern with the challenges of science was most evident in his doctrines of creation and providence (Book I, chapters xiv and xvi of the 1559 *Institutes*), but it thereby affected his concept of God and his entire theology, which was rooted in the doctrines of God, creation, and providence. The fact that we no longer subscribe to Aristotelian physics and cosmology today ought not lead us to ignore this important dimension to the articulation of religious faith in the sixteenth century.

For purposes of understanding Calvin, the physics and astronomy of Aristotle can be summarized in three points: (1) the concept of "natural place" for the four elements comprising sublunar bodies; (2) the system of revolving homocentric spheres for celestial bodies; and (3) the problem of the immobility of the earth. We shall briefly inventory Calvin's knowledge of, and attitude towards, Aristotelian natural philosophy under these three headings. An interesting paradox arose, as we shall see, concerning the dual role of the earth: on one hand, it was the heaviest and most stable of the sublunar elements; on the other hand, it was the center of the system of revolving spheres. What kept it from being moved?[4]

The Concept of Natural Place

Aristotle's treatment of sublunar bodies was based on the idea that there were four terrestrial elements—earth, water, air and fire—and that these natu-

[2]On the continued influence of Aristotelian ideas in the sixteenth century, see, e.g., Arnold Williams, *The Common Expositor: An Account of the Commentaries on Genesis, 1527-1633* (Chapel Hill: University of North Carolina Press, 1948), 47-50, 183-94; Paul Oskar Kristeller, *Renaissance Thought: The Classic, Scholastic, and Humanist Strains* (New York: Harper & Row, 1961), chap. 2; Eugene F. Rice, Jr., "Humanist Aristotelianism in France: Jacques Lefèvre d'Etaples and his Circle," in *Humanism in France at the End of the Middle Ages and in the Early Renaissance*, ed. A. H. T. Levi (Manchester: University of Manchester Press, 1970), 132-49; Charles B. Schmitt, "Towards a Reassessment of Renaissance Aristotelianism," *History of Science* 11 (1973); 159-93; idem, *Aristotle and the Renaissance* (Cambridge: Harvard University Press, 1983); Edward Grant, "Aristoteliansim and the Longevity of the Medieval World View," *History of Science* 16 (1978): 93-106.

[3]The 1277 Paris condemnation of propositions associated with Aristotelian physics and Averroist philosophy is the most dramatic instance of a conservative Christian response to Aristotelian natural philosophy. In Calvin's immediate background is Zwingli's attempt to mediate between the astronomers (whose prognostications were based on Aristotelian cosmology) and their critics, the preachers (*De providentia* 7).

[4]We still have no evidence that Calvin was concerned with or even aware of the work of Copernicus; C. B. Kaiser, "Calvin, Copernicus, and Castellio," *Calvin Theological Journal* 21 (1986): 5-31.

rally distributed themselves in spherical shells, with earth at the center, because it was the heaviest, and fire at the perimeter of the sublunar realm, just beneath the sphere of the moon. In comparison to earlier medieval cosmologies, like that of the Venerable Bede (earth, air, ether, Olympus, fire), this was a more rational, naturalistic account. Not only did it explain the distribution of the elements in terms of the concept of natural place, but it suggested that human beings were confined to the lowest sphere by nature rather than by divine ordinance.

Calvin cited the Aristotelian distribution of the elements quite frequently and seems not to have been aware of earlier systems like Bede's: earth was naturally at the center of the cosmos because it was the heaviest of all the elements;[5] the waters naturally formed a spherical shell between the earth and the atmosphere;[6] the fiery realm came last, just beneath the sphere of the moon.[7] Also following Aristotle, Calvin held that comets were formed from warm exhalations rising from the earth, those that did not go into the making of thunder, lightning, and wind.[8] Vapors rising from earth produced clouds, and these were what Moses had in mind when he referred to waters above the firmament in Genesis 1:7—this in contrast to the majority of medieval writers who took the supracelestial waters to refer to a transparent crystalline sphere beyond the sphere of the stars.[9]

But, though Calvin accepted the Aristotelian ordering of the elements and alluded to the concept of natural place, he did *not* accept the idea that a natural propensity for each element was a self-evident or a complete explanation of the elements' behavior. For example, Calvin cited the fact that the earth was not entirely covered with water but that clouds held back the rain and ocean basins contained the waters on earth. This containment could not be accounted for, he argued, on strictly Aristotelian principles; it was solely due to the ordinances of God described in Gen. 1:6 ("Let there be a firmament in the midst of the waters. . . .") and Gen. 1:9 ("Let the waters be gathered together

---

[5]Sermons on Job 26 (*Calvini Opera*, ed. William Baum et al. [hereafter *CO*; 59 vols., Brunswick and Berlin, 1863-1900] 34:430, 434); Third Sermon on Genesis (Richard Stauffer, *Dieu, la création et la Providence dans la prédication de Calvin* ([Berne: Peter Lang, 1978]), 225, n 77); Comm. Psalm 104:5 (James Anderson, trans., *Commentary on the Book of Psalms* [5 vols., Edinburgh, 1845-9] 4:148-89); Comm. Jer. 10:12-13 (John Owen, trans., *Commentaries on the Book of the Prophet Jeremiah and the Lamentations* [5 vols., Edinburgh, 1850-55] 2:34). On these and other texts on the place of the earth in relation to the sun, see Edward Rosen, "Calvin's Attitude toward Copernicus," *Journal of the History of Ideas* 21 (1960): 438–40; Stauffer, *Dieu*, 186-88.

[6]Comm. Gen. 1:9 (John King, trans., *Commentaries on the First Book of Moses* [2 vols., Edinburgh, 1847] 1:81); Comm. Psalm 104:5, 9, (Anderson, trans., 4:148-52); Comm. Jer. 5:22, (Owen, trans., 1:294).

[7]Comm. Gen. 1:15 (King, trans., 1:86); Comm. Jer. 10:12-13 (Owen, trans., 2:37).

[8]Comm. Jer. 10:12-13 (Owen, trans., 2:37); cf. Aristotle, *Meteorologica* I.4,7; II.4-5.

[9]Comm. Gen. 1:7 (King, trans., 1:79-80); cf. Basil, *Hexaemeron* III.7-9.

unto one place, and let the dry land appear").[10] In other words, Calvin wanted to show that the established order of nature was not strictly "natural" in the sense of being self-evident or determined by natural propensities. Rather, it was highly contingent, having been ordained by God in ways that would not necessarily have occurred to natural philosophers and sustained by God's direct operation or particular providence.

Even the fact that earth occupied the central position in the cosmos was not self-evident, Calvin argued, for, though earth was surely the heaviest of the four elements, the center of the cosmos was not the biggest part of creation. So why should it attract the heaviest element in the first place?[11] Here again Calvin attempted to press natural philosophers to question their own first principles and to see God as the free creator who established things that seem self-evident to us.

Calvin's varied comments on scientific issues might sound contradictory at first reading. On the one hand, Calvin used Aristotelian ideas and obviously appreciated their value as an antidote to Academic relativism and Epicurean indeterminism. On the other, he repeatedly challenged their self-evidence and pointed out gaps or contradictions in the purely naturalistic account.[12] When understood as an argument for particular providence, as distinct from strict naturalism, however, Calvin's varied comments make a good deal of sense. Calvin stressed the natural order when he felt that would strengthen faith in God; he qualified it when he felt it would become self-contained and detract from faith.

How extensive was Calvin's reading in the literature concerning Aristotle's concept of natural place? Of the problems Calvin raised, that of the elevation of dry land above sea level had been discussed most extensively by earlier scholars. Albert the Great (mid-thirteenth century) treated the problem as one of the lowering of the seas, rather than an elevation of land, in certain parts of the globe. The fact that the seas were lowered and the underlying

[10]Comm. Gen. 1:6-9; 7:11-12 (King, trans., 1:80-81, 270-71); Comm. Psalm 33:7; 104:5-9 (Anderson, trans., 1:544; 4:148-52); Second Sermon on Job 26 (*CO* 34:434-5); Third Sermon on Genesis (Stauffer, *Dieu*, 225, n 78); Comm. Jer. 5:22 (Owen, trans., 1:294-6); cf. *Institutes* I.5.6 The idea was expressed by the church fathers: e.g., Athanasius (*Contra gentes* 36) and Basil (*Hexaemeron* III.8; IV.2-3), but without the strict Aristotelian framework assumed by Calvin. Indeed, Athanasius (*Contra gentes* 9) and Gregory of Nyssa (*De opificio hominis* 3) used a system of elements more like Bede's than Aristotle's. So Calvin clearly received his Aristotelian physics and cosmology through late medieval and Renaissance sources, not from the fathers.

[11]Comm. Jer. 10:12-13 (Owen, trans., 2:34).

[12]E.g., wind, rain, thunder, and lightning are not fortuitous but subject to God's *potentia ordinata*; Comm. Psalms 104:3-4; 148:7-9 (Anderson, trans., 4:146; 5:307); Comm. Jer. 10:12-13 (Owen, trans., 2:37: "fire generates water"; "the sun attracts vapors"; etc., after Aristotle). On the other hand, "the power of God cannot be excluded, when we say that anything is done according to nature," as evidenced by the fact that winds rise suddenly even when it is calm and rain does not inundate the earth as it would on natural principles alone; Comm. Jer. 10:12-13 (Owen, trans., 36-38); cf. Comm. Gen. 1:6-8; 7:11-12 (King, trans., 1:80, 270-71).

earth exposed in the temperate and tropical zones was due to the greater intensity of sun and starlight there.

But then the waters should flow back from the polar regions to cover the land again, objected an early fourteenth-century treatise, *Quaestio de aqua et terra*. The only logical solution was that the stars above the temperate and tropical zones exerted some special elevating influence on the lands beneath them.[13]

A third suggestion was offered by John Buridan (mid-fourteenth century): once land masses had somehow risen above sea level they would be stabilized there by the drying effect of the sun: the portion of earth exposed to sunlight and air (by erosion) would become rarefied and hence lighter than water.[14] Buridan's treatment was adopted by Nicole Oresme and Albert of Saxony, among others, and must be granted the status of "best science" of the late medieval period.[15]

It is doubtful that Calvin was aware of these late medieval discussions. He gave no account of the various possible explanations and consistently referred to the gathering of the waters and the emergence of dry land as a "miracle" (*miraculum*) and "beyond nature" (*praeter naturam*)[16]. The only answer the natural philosophers could give, according to Calvin, was that the natural tendency of the waters to cover the earth is counteracted by the special providence of God.[17] Calvin's approach to Aristotle's natural philosophy appears to be a return *ad fontes* typical of the Renaissance (cf. Lefèvre, Reuchlin, Melanchthon), more than a *quaestio* typical of the late middle ages.

The System of Homocentric Spheres

The feature of Aristotle's science that had the greatest influence on the medieval doctrine of God was the cosmology of homocentric spheres as modified by the Arabic natural philosophers, Thebit (Ibn Qurra) and Alpetragius (al-Bitruji). As a rule there were thought to be nine or ten celestial spheres surrounding the earth; seven for the sun, the moon, and the five known planets; an eighth sphere containing the stars; an optional ninth sphere to allow for

[13]M. A. Orr, *Dante and the Early Astronomers* (London: Allan Wingate, 1913; rev. ed., 1956), 298-305. The relevant loci in Aristotle are *Meteorologica* II.2.23-26; *De caelo* II.4.287a.30-287b.14.

[14]*Quaestiones super libris de caelo et mundo* II.7; Ernest A. Moody, "John Buridan on the Habitability of the Earth," *Speculum* 16 (1941): 415-25 (the relevant text is given on 424-25); reprinted in idem, *Studies in Medieval Philosophy, Science, and Logic* (Berkeley: University of California Press, 1975), 111-26.

[15]E.g., Nicole Oresme's *De l'espère*; George W. Coopland, *Nicole Oresme and the Astrologers* (Liverpool: University of Liverpool Press, 1952), 17.

[16]E.g., Comm. Gen. 1:9 (*CO* 23:19); Comm. Psalm 33:7 (*CO* 31:328); Second Sermon on Job 26 (*CO* 34:435); Comm. Jer. 5:22 (*CO*37:63).

[17]Comm. Psalm 104:5 (*CO* 32:86; Anderson trans., 4:149).

anomalies ("trepidation") in the motion of the stars in the eighth; and a tenth containing the supracelestial waters of Gen. 1:7.[18]

The abode of God was located in the empyrean, beyond the outer boundary of the outermost sphere. According to Aristotle, God was the First Mover, that is, the ultimate formal and final cause, whose very presence was enough to activate the rotation of the outermost sphere of the cosmos. The latter was, therefore, the "first moved sphere" (*primum mobile*), the only object with which God was normally in any kind of immediate relationship. Inner spheres were moved by virtue of their proximity to outer ones, thus forming a chain of influence extending to the innermost celestial sphere, that of the moon, and even to the cycles of generation and corruption on earth.[19]

Since God was located, symbolically at least, beyond the outermost created heaven, the effect of the medieval assimilation of Aristotelian cosmology with its nine or ten heavens was that his action appeared to be rather more remote from terrestrial events than was traditionally thought to be the case. We are concerned here only with the normal mode of God's activity (*de potentia ordinata*), not with his occasional use of his absolute power (*de potentia absoluta*), as in miracles, or with his indirect operation through angels.

So with the influx of Aristotelian thought a spatial and causal gap threatened to open up between the normal activity of God and events on earth. Grosseteste (d. 1253), for instance, held that the diurnal rotation of the *primum mobile* was communicated to it by God in such a way that energy and motion were transmitted through the lower spheres all the way to the earth.[20] The same idea appears in Roger Bacon, William of Auvergne, Bonaventure, Albertus Magnus, and Thomas Aquinas in the thirteenth century.

The remoteness of God's providence suggested by the new cosmology, of course, had to be counterbalanced, even with respect to the normal mode of God's activity, if Aristotelian science was to be acceptable to Christian faith. This was done in several ways. Bonaventure, Albert, and Thomas all attempted to restore the balance by limiting the influence transmitted through the celestial spheres to the physical, secular aspects of life. So the configuration

---

[18]For background, see Nicholas H. Steneck, *Science and Creation in the Middle Ages* (Notre Dame: University of Notre Dame Press, 1976), 70-71; Edward Grant, "Cosmology," in *Science in the Middle Ages*, ed. David C. Lindberg (Chicago: University of Chicago Press, 1978), 273-75. A convenient source on the system of homocentric spheres in the sixteenth century was Gregorius Reisch's *Margarita philosophica* first published in 1503; A. Rupert Hall, *The Scientific Revolution* (2d ed., Boston: Beacon Press, 1966), 11-17.

[19]Aristotle, *De generatione* II.10.337a; 11.338b; *Meteorologica* II.2.354b.26-31. With the development of medieval machinery, models of the cosmos became so mechanical that they could be driven by a single weight; Coopland, *Nicole Oresme*, 15-16.

[20]Clare C. Riedl, trans., *Robert Grosseteste: On Light* (Milwaukee: Marquette University Press, 1942), 6-7, 15-16. Note that God became the efficient cause of motion for Grosseteste and other thirteenth-century scholastics, not just the formal and final cause as for Aristotle.

of the heavens was responsible for the creation of worms and insects from putrefaction, for instance, and the sun could influence the birth and death of higher animals—all, of course, under God's ultimate control. There were two channels open, however, for the more immediate influence of God in human life under normal conditions (*de potentia ordinata*): God could enlighten the soul or affect the will directly, and he could, and regularly did, infuse grace through the seven sacraments, particularly through the Eucharist.[21]

Calvin had difficulties, as did many of his contemporaries, with the Aristotelian cosmology, even in its medieval Christian version. Yet it was too well entrenched in Western thought to be dismissed altogether. Even critics of medieval Aristotelianism like Lefèvre, Reuchlin, and Melanchthon were concerned to restore the original texts and their meaning in keeping with the humanist program of bypassing scholasticism and returning to the ancient sources.

Calvin made no mention of the optional ninth sphere which was added by Arabic commentators, and, as noted, he rejected the medieval notion of a tenth (crystalline) sphere containing the supra-celestial waters. Here again his stance was consistent with that of the humanist litterati.[22] But Calvin accepted the basic outline of Aristotle's cosmology: "astronomers make a distinction of spheres," he said in his *Commentary on Genesis*, "and . . . teach that the fixed stars have their proper place in the firmament." Beneath the firmament of the fixed stars were the planetary spheres ranging from Saturn to the moon and the outer boundary of the sublunar realm.[23] The whole structure was fitted together and interlocked like a great machine with the lower spheres subordinated to and driven in various ways by the upper ones; at the outer limit was the *primum mobile*, the sphere which moved all the others and was, in turn, driven by God. God was thus the Prime Mover, the "beginning and cause of all motion," from that of the outer stars to that of the moon.[24]

---

[21]E.g., Aquinas, *Summa theologiae* Ia.115.3-4; Theodore Otto Wedel, *The Mediaeval Attitude Toward Astrology* (New Haven: Yale University Press, 1920), 64-68; N. Max Wildiers, *The Theologian and His Universe* (New York: Seabury Press, 1982), 46-48, 53-55, 64,72. Cf. Calvin's comment on the necessity of transubstantiation for a realization of the presence of Christ within the scholastic framework; *Institutes* IV.17.15.

[22]Treatises like Nicole Oresme's *L'espère* and Luther's *Lectures on Genesis* had already questioned the need for the ninth and tenth spheres; Coopland, *Nicole Oresme*, 16; *Luther's Works*, ed. Jaroslav Pelikan and Helmut Lehmann, 55 vols., (Saint Louis: Concordia and Philadelphia: Fortress, 1955-76) 1:26-29. The point is that Calvin rejected the tenth outright and did not even mention the ninth.

[23]Comm. Gen. 1:15, 16 (King, trans., 1:86); Comm. Psalm 19:4-6 (Anderson trans., 1:315).

[24]*Institutes* I.14.21; 16.1-5 (the quote is taken from Battles trans., *Institutes of the Christian Religion*, ed. John T. McNeill 2 vols., [Philadelphia: Westminster, 1960], 1:200). Here Calvin critiques the philosophers' restriction of God to the role of prime mover but does not reject the role itself as one aspect of God's operation; cf. Comm. Gen.3:17 (King, trans., 1:173); Comm. Psalm 68:31-33 (Anderson, trans., 3:43).

Here, again, we find Calvin delighting in the orderly presentation of the universe offered by the natural philosophers. But, also, we find him drawing the line in order to counteract the suggestion that God was separated from the ordinary events of life on earth by a long chain of second causes. This was one of the reasons for his opposition to judicial astrology. In astrological determinism, the chain of cause and effect was regarded as extending not only to the seasonal cycles of generation and corruption, but to all terrestrial events. Grosseteste's theory of the inward radiation of light and other material forms provided a plausible physical basis for such cosmic influences on everyday events. "The heavens," as A. M. Hunter put it, "were threatening to put their maker out of sight."[25]

Calvin, like his scholastic forebears, was quite specific in pointing out the limits of such astrological influence. Terrestrial bodies were subject to the order of the heavens, he allowed, and they drew their qualities and basic dispositions from the configurations of the celestial realm. But stellar influence could only account for events that occurred within the ordinary course of nature and not for "accidental" happenings, particularly those with possible spiritual consequences, which Calvin saw as coming under the direct control of God.[26] Examples of the latter were: (1) the determination of heredity—here God acted directly and made use of the means of parental seed more than of the stellar configurations at birth; (2) the regeneration of believers through his Spirit; and (3) the bestowal of special gifts or talents among humans for the benefit of his people. In short, Calvin limited astrological determination to the behavior of subhuman creatures and, in the case of humanity, to everyday matters of the body like physical illness and healing.[27] Stellar influences were a part of God's universal providence, but had little or nothing to do with particular providence, inner grace, or the care of the Church.

In all of these ways, Calvin, like Aquinas, Bonaventure, and others before him, tried to prevent the Aristotelian account of the massive world machine

[25]A. M. Hunter, *The Teaching of Calvin*, 2d ed. (London: James Clarke & Co., 1950), 291. Melanchthon, for example, allowed a degree of astrological determination; Clyde Manschreck, *Melanchthon, the Quiet Reformer* (Nashville: Abingdon, 1958), 102-12; Bruce Moran, "The Universe of Philip Melanchthon: Criticism and Use of the Copernican Theory," *Comitatus* 4 (1973): 8-10. On the differences between Calvin and Melanchthon, see Josef Bohatec, *Budé und Calvin* (Graz: Hermann Böhlaus Nachf., 1950), 276-78.

[26]*Advertissement contre l'astrologie* (Mary Potter, trans., "A Warning Against Judicial Astrology and Other Prevalent Curiosities, by John Calvin," *Calvin Theological Journal* 18 [1983]: 166-69, 181-83); cf. *Institutes* I.16.3, 5.

[27]*Advertissement* (Potter, trans., 170-71, 182); cf. Hunter, *Teaching*, 291-93; Wayne Shumaker, *The Occult Sciences in the Renaissance* (Berkeley: University of California Press, 1972), 44-46. The importance of natural astrology for medicine was based on, though not limited to, the humoral pathology of Galen. It had been a commonplace in Western Europe since the time of Isidore of Seville (seventh century) and was restated by Oresme among others; Wedel, *Mediaeval Attitude*, 28, 36, 67, 71-73; Coopland, *Nicole Oresme*, 23-24 (n 63 compares Calvin's *Advertissement*).

from embracing all of life and to secure a preserve for the direct action of God in human affairs. A cosmological interest and an understanding of the problematics of the Aristotelian worldview must be taken into consideration, therefore, in our interpretation of his theology.

But all of the ways just cited in which God affected human affairs directly were under the heading of special graces or *potentia Dei absoluta*.[28] If that were all, the realm of God's *potentia ordinata* would still have been governed by the great world machine, and in the everyday events of the natural world ("accidents" aside) God's activity would have seemed as remote as the distant *primum mobile*, just as it seemed (to their critics) to be in the theology of the medieval schoolmen.[29]

However, there were also several ways in which Calvin saw particular providence as affecting terrestrial events, even within the ordinary course of nature (the sphere of *potentia ordinata*) and these were wonderful signs to him that the direct expression of God's sovereignty and fatherly love were not limited to special graces but were evidenced in the basic conditions of everyday life. Two of these signs have already been discussed in our treatment of the sublunar elements: the confinement of the terrestrial waters to restricted areas and the restraint of the rain by the formation of clouds. Without these providential ordinances of God, waters would completely cover the earth in accordance with their nature, as they did in the great flood of Noah's time.[30]

Yet there was a third, even more astounding way in which God's immediate supervision affected everyday terrestrial affairs, and the evidence for this was incontrovertible. In fact, it was immediately at hand (or under foot) for everyone to see and feel—the immobility of the earth. This is the third point of Aristotelian natural philosophy that we need to consider.

The Immobility of the Earth

What Calvin noticed was that the earth played a dual role in medieval cosmology. On the one hand, earth was the heaviest of the elements; hence, it naturally settled in the center of the world system, according to Aristotle, and

---

[28]*Advertissement* (Potter, trans., 170); cf. *Institutes* I.5.11; *Comm. Gen.* 48:17; Charles Partee, *Calvin and Classical Philosophy* (Leiden: Brill, 1977), 129-30. On the relevance of the scholastic distinction between *potentia absoluta* and *potentia ordinata* to Calvin's theology, see Heiko A. Oberman, "The 'Extra' Dimension in the Theology of Calvin," *Journal of Ecclesiastical History* 21 (1970): 62-64; idem, "*Via antiqua* and *Via moderna*: Late Medieval Prolegomena to Early Reformation Thought," *Journal of the History of Ideas* 48 (1987): 38-39; Alister E. McGrath, "John Calvin and Late Medieval Thought," *Archiv für Reformationsgeschichte* 77 (1986): 77-78 with notes promising further details.

[29]The thirteenth-century scholastics also found scope in the sphere of everyday life for the immediate activity of God (*de potentia ordinata*), but this was primarily through the sacraments administered by the Church as noted earlier; see n 21. Calvin, obviously, would have to seek another solution.

[30]See n 10.

it was supposed to be stable there by nature. On the other hand, the earth was also the hub of the cosmic machine, the center of the system of homocentric spheres, with nothing but the surrounding elements of air and water to stabilize it. Why, then, should the earth not turn and twist along with the rest of the cosmic machinery?

Calvin phrased the question in two rather different ways, but, in each case, he saw the stability of the earth against any kind of rotation or wobble as a clear sign of God's continuous intervention in the regular course of nature. First, here is how Calvin put the question in his 1557 *Commentary on Psalm* 93:1, "He hath established the world; it shall not be moved":

> The psalmist proves that God will not neglect or abandon the world from the fact that he created it. A simple survey of the world should of itself suffice to attest a divine providence. The heavens revolve daily [*quotidie volvitur*], and, immense as is their fabric [*in mole tantae magnitudinis*], and inconceivable the rapidity of their revolutions [*in tante celeritate*], we experience no concussion—no disturbance in the harmony of their motion. . . . How could the earth hang suspended in the air were it not upheld by God's hand? By what means could it maintain itself unmoved [*staret immobilis*], while the heavens above are in constant rapid motion, did not its divine maker fix and establish it?[31]

In other words, Calvin argued, the massive motion of the heavenly spheres would inevitably disturb the equilibrium of the earth if God did not act continuously to keep it stationary. As the text cited shows, the issue was an existential one for Calvin: the incredible stability of the earth in the midst of the swirling heavens was a sign that God had not left terrestrial affairs to follow their own course or made them entirely subordinate to stellar influences—a sign of God's particular providence even in the everyday course of nature.

One problem with this passage is the absence of any mention of the fact that Aristotle had a simple explanation for the earth's immobility: the *primum mobile* moved all of the lower spheres by a series of mechanical linkages (with some degree of angelic supervision), but these linkages extended only as far as

---

[31]Comm. Psalm 93:1 (*CO* 32:16-17; Anderson, trans. 4:6-7; the French text is given in *Commentaires de Jehan Calvin sur le Livre des Psaumes,* 2 vols. [Paris, 1859], 2:205). Compare the following passage which first appeared in the 1543 edition of the *Institutes:* " . . . who so proportioned the inequality of days, which we daily observe [*quotidie cernimus*], that no confusion occurs. It is so too when we observe his power in sustaining so great a mass [*tanta mole*], in governing the swiftly revolving [*tam celeri . . . volutatione*] heavenly system," (*CO* 1:509; *Calvini Opera Selecta,* ed. P. Barth and W. Niesel [hereafter *OS;* 5 vols., Munich: Chr. Kaiser Verlag, 1926-36], 3:172; Battles, trans., 181). This earlier discussion of the swirling heavens may have raised the problem of the stability of the earth discussed in Calvin's later writings like the Commentary on Psalms.

the sphere of the moon. Beneath the moon, all motions were naturally up or down. Only the outermost part of the terrestrial atmosphere was dragged along with the lunar sphere. Why, then, did Calvin apparently assume that the rotational forces of the celestial spheres would extend all the way to earth? Why did he not even mention the Aristotelian explanation as he often did even if he wished to challenge the self-evidence or completeness of that explanation?[32]

Was Calvin's knowledge of Aristotelian science simply deficient at this point? Or, is it possible that he was trained to look for contradictions in the Aristotelian worldview in a speculative manner?[33] If the latter, could this critical approach to Aristotle reflect on the liberal arts instruction he received at the Collège de Montaigu in the 1520s?

There had been significant modifications in physical science since the thirteenth century, when Aristotelian physics and cosmology reigned supreme in Western thought. One of the leading arts masters at the Collège de Montaigu, John Major (1469-1550), was well known as an advocate of anti-Aristotelian concepts like an extra-cosmic void and an infinity of worlds that had developed in the fourteenth and fifteenth centuries.[34] However, I have not been able to find evidence of awareness on Calvin's part of these late medieval developments sufficient to confirm such an explanation of the apparent discrepancy in his understanding of Aristotelian cosmology.[35] There is an interesting (derogatory) reference to the idea of an extra-cosmic void in the 1559 edition of the *Institutes*,[36] but it is not specific enough to be differentiated from traditional Stoic speculations that might have been available to Calvin from

[32]See n10 above. Calvin may have been aware of passages in Aristotle's *De caelo* (II.13-14) where the possibility of the earth being swirled about by the heavens was discussed and rejected. An edition of the *De caelo* was published at Basel in 1553, the same year as Calvin's first discussion of the problem of the earth's stability (Twelfth Sermon on Psalm 119, delivered on 9 April 1553); Alexandre Ganoczy, *La Bibliotèque de l'Academie de Calvin* (Geneva: Droz, 1969), 263.

[33]Possible instances are cited in nn10-12 above.

[34]Edward Grant, *Much Ado About Nothing* (Cambridge: Cambridge University Press, 1981), 149-52. On the possibility of Major's influence on Calvin, see Alexandre Ganoczy, *Le jeune Calvin* (Wiesbaden: Franz Steiner Verlag, 1966), 186-92; A. N. S. Lane, "Calvin's Use of the Fathers and the Medievals," *Calvin Theological Journal* 16 (1981): 151-55; McGrath, "John Calvin and Late Medieval Thought," 66, 71.

[35]Compare Calvin's treatment of the rainbow which, of course, was a sign of the covenant between God and Noah. Here Calvin merely cited the classical explanation (reflection by water droplets) that had been offered by Aristotle (*Meteorologica* III.4) and repeated by Seneca (*Quaest. nat.* I.3) and Pliny (*Nat. hist.* II.1x.150) and made no mention of the new theory (refraction and internal reflection) developed by thirteenth- and fourteenth-century perspectivists like Theodoric of Freiburg (d. 1311). He merely insisted that the meaning of the rainbow was not exhausted by a naturalistic explanation, however complete: *Institutes* IV.14.18 (IV.8 in 1536 edition.); Comm. Gen. 9:13 (King, trans., 1:299). On the medieval theory of the rainbow, see A. C. Crombie, *Augustine to Galileo*, 2d ed. (Cambridge: Harvard University Press, 1961), 1:114-24.

[36]*Institutes* I.14.1. For the late medieval background of this idea, see Edward Grant, *Much Ado*, 129-52.

other sources. We do not yet know enough about the training Calvin received or about the sources he used to give a more detailed interpretation of his cosmological interests at this point.

The second way in which Calvin raised the paradox of the earth's immobility was based on the inability of the fluid elements—air and water—to provide the earth any firm support, rather than on the possible torque exerted by the whirling heavens. The two versions of the problem are logically independent and occur in different contexts, though there is no inconsistency between them, and they could quite easily be combined.

This second argument occurs in two slightly different forms both dating from the mid-1550s. First, in the *Twelfth Sermon on Psalm 119*, which was delivered on 9 April 1553 and published in 1554, we read:

> I beseech you to tell me what the foundation of the earth is. It is founded both upon the water and also upon the air: behold its foundation! . . . Behold the whole earth founded only in trembling, indeed poised above such bottomless depths that it might be turned upside down at any minute [*qu'elle pourroit renverser à chacune minute de temps*] to become disordered. Hence there must be a wonderful power of God to keep it in the condition in which it is.[37]

A second, slightly longer form appears in the corresponding passage in Calvin's *Commentary on Psalms*, which was published a few years later (Latin, 1557; French 1558). Here the ideas of the natural instability of earth and the overwhelming power of the rotating heavens are combined:

> . . . and now he [the psalmist] again teaches us, by experience, that, though the world is subject to revolutions [*quamvis volvatur mundus*; French: *combien que le monde soit sujet à révolutions*], yet in it bright and signal testimonies to the truth of God shine forth, so that the steadfastness of his word is not exclusively confined to heaven, but comes down even to us who dwell upon the earth. For this reason, it is added, that the earth continues steadfast, even as it was established by God at the beginning. . . . for, though it is suspended in the midst of the sea, yet it continues to remain in the same state. . . . for earth the which otherwise could not occupy the position it does for a single moment [*quae alioqui momento uno non staret*; French: *laquelle autrement ne pourroit subsister une seule minute*

---

[37]Twelfth Sermon on Psalm 119 (CO 32:620; Thomas Stocker, trans., *Two and Twentie Sermons . . . The Hundredth and Nineteenth Psalme* [London, 1580], fol. 99v; quoted and modernized by Edward Rosen, "Calvin's Attitude," 439); cf. Basil, *Hexaemeron* I.8 and Ambrose *Hexaemeron* I.vi.22 for the thought.

de temps], abides notwithstanding steadfast, because God's word is the foundation on which it rests.[38]

The emphases in these two passages are slightly different. The first stresses the instability of the terrestrial sphere, with clearly existential undertones ("founded in trembling," "poised above bottomless depth," etc.), as befits a sermon on the Psalms.[39] The second passage, on the other hand stresses the steadfastness of the earth, based on the care and faithfulness of God, in the midst of revolutionary cosmic forces ("subject to revolutions").

In all these ways, Calvin came to associate the apparent immobility of the earth with the immediate presence and power of God in ordinary events as a bulwark against revolution and disorder. The particular providence of God could be seen by all in the stability of the earth just as universal providence could be seen in the regular motions of the heavens. For Calvin, of course, there was a clear correlation between the concept of stability and order in the natural sphere and the sense of God's protection in the personal and social spheres. The believer could take comfort in the midst of social instability and ecclesiastical disorder knowing that God held the whole world in his hands.[40]

We have established that Calvin knew and accepted the basic tenets of Aristotelian natural philosophy, particularly those dealing with the terrestrial elements, meteorology, and the celestial spheres. The basic ideas he accepted include the concept of natural place, the natural sphericity of elemental distributions, and subordination of terrestrial cycles to the revolutions of the heavenly spheres, and the driving force of the *primum mobile.*

It should be stressed that there was nothing wrong with Calvin's ideas about natural philosophy: they had been accepted as well-established facts in the West for over three centuries and would not become "out of date" until a century later. Even Calvin's apparent ignorance (or disregard) of late medieval refinements of the Aristotelian cosmology was perfectly in keeping with Renaissance humanist efforts to bypass the subtleties of medieval scholasticism and work from original sources.

[38]Commentary on Psalm 119:90 (*CO* 32:253-4; *Commentaires sur le Livre des Psaumes* 2:419; Anderson, trans., 4:469). I take the word "world" (*mundus*) to refer to the world-system of celestial spheres (rather than to the earth) for two reasons: (1) that was the meaning of the term for late medievals like John Major; Pierre Duhem, *Medieval Cosmology* (Chicago: University of Chicago Press, 1985), 504; and (2) we have no evidence that Calvin was aware of Copernicus's work; Kaiser, "Calvin, Copernicus, and Castellio," 31. Cf. Comm. Psalm 90:2 (*volvanturomnia*; *CO* 31:834; Anderson, trans., 3: 462–63).

[39]Cf. William J. Bouwsma, "John Calvin's Anxiety," *Proceedings of the American Philosophical Society* 128 (1984): 254. I agree with Bouwsma that Calvin's sense of the instability of nature reflected his own anxieties (which had objective, as well as purely personal, grounds), but would also call attention to his concern to avoid total determination by forces (natural or ecclesiastical) other than God. See now Bouwsma's *John Calvin* (New York: Oxford University Press, 1988), 85.

[40]*Institutes* I.16.3-4; cf. Comm. Gen. 7:11 (King, trans., 1:270); Comm. Psalm 115:17 (Anderson, trans., 4:358).

The Origins of Calvin's Understanding

This leaves us with the question of when and how Calvin became interested in the specific problems of Aristotelian science. A brief review of the material cited above shows that most of Calvin's discussions of Aristotelian natural philosophy were written in the 1550s. They occur in both sermons (on Psalm 119, Job, and Genesis) and commentaries (on Genesis, the Psalms, and Jeremiah), as well as in the 1559 edition of the *Institutes*.[41]

Some of the most detailed descriptions of Aristotelian scientific issues are the meteorological material found in the *Commentary on Jeremiah*, which was begun in 1560 and published in 1563. A series of sermons on Jeremiah had been delivered as early as 1548-50, but, unfortunately, only the twenty-five sermons on Jer. 14:19 to 18:23 have survived in manuscript, whereas the meteorological material mentioned appears in the commentary on Jer. 10:12-13.[42] If the sermon on Jer. 10:12-13 dealt with problems of Aristotelian meteorology, then it may have been the earliest such discussion on Calvin's part, dating from December 1549 or January 1550.[43] The earliest surviving indications (of which I am aware) of a detailed interest in the cosmology of Aristotle occurred in the *Commentary on Genesis*, begun in July 1550 and published in 1554.[44] Here we find the first extant discussion by Calvin of the containment of terrestrial waters and the differentiation of celestial spheres.[45] The issue of the stability of the earth was first treated in the sermons and commentary on Psalms in the mid-1550s.[46]

It is difficult to know just how much significance to attach to these dates. They represent the mature Calvin, to be sure. Indeed, the publication dates all fall within five years of the last major Latin edition of the *Institutes* (1559). It may also be noted that the detailed expression of Calvin's interest in Aristotle's cosmology began just about the time Girolamo Zanchi arrived in Geneva (1552-53) and Peter Martyr Vermigli returned from Oxford to Strasbourg

---

[41]In roughly chronological order the writings cited above as discussing natural philosophy are: Commentary on Genesis (begun 1550; published 1554); Twelfth Sermon on Psalm 119 (preached 9 April 1553; published 1554); Commentary on Psalms (exposition begun 1552; published 1557); Sermons on Job (begun 1554; published 1563); *Institutes* I.14.1; 16.3-5 (1559); Sermons on Genesis (preached 1559-60; not published); and Commentary on Jeremiah (exposition begun 1560; published 1563). On the manuscripts and dates of the unpublished sermons on Genesis, see Richard Stauffer, "Les sermons inédits de Calvin sur le Livre de la Genèse," *Revue de théologie et de philosophie*, 3d ser., 15 (1965): 26-36. On the dates of the expositions or lectures related to the commentaries, see T. H. L. Parker, *Calvin's Old Testament Commentaries* (Edinburgh: T. & T. Clark, 1986), 29.

[42]See n 8.

[43]Rudolphe Peter, ed., *Sermons sur les Livres de Jérémie et des Lamentations* (*Supplementa Calviniana* 6, ed. Erwin Mülhaupt, Neukirchen-Vluyn: Neukirchener Verlag, 1971), xiv-xvi.

[44]Letter to Farel, July 1550 (*CO* 13:606). Parker ventures that Calvin wrote the first few chapters of the Genesis commentary (including Genesis 1:6-9) in his own hand in 1550; *Calvin's Old Testament Commentaries*, 25-26.

[45]See nn 10 and 23.

[46]See nn 31, 37, and 38.

(1553). Both Vermigli and Zanchi were trained in Italian Aristotelianism and lectured and wrote on Aristotelian natural philosophy, among other things.[47] It is conceivable that Calvin's interest was stimulated by their ideas, though I find no evidence of any discussions of natural philosophy in their written correspondence.

It is more likely that the appearance of passages dealing with Aristotelian physics and cosmology in the early 1550s was fortuitous. After all, it was not until the late 1540s that Calvin had his sermons systematically recorded and began regular work on his Old Testament commentaries.[48] So it would be worthwhile asking whether the ideas about natural philosophy expressed in Calvin's sermons and commentaries could have had their origins in earlier stages of his work.

Passing references to Aristotelian meteorology had occurred already in the 1532 Commentary on Seneca's *De clementia*, Calvin's first published work,[49] and in the first edition of the *Institutes* (1536).[50] The first reference (to my knowledge) to the rotation of the celestial spheres appeared in the 1543 *Institutes* along with the first extant citation of Basil's *Hexaemeron* as a model for the "history of the creation of the universe."[51] Then, Luther's first *Lectures on Genesis*, published in 1544, treated some of the same points of Aristotle and in relation to the same verses of Genesis 1 as those found in Calvin's later *Commentary on Genesis*.[52]

Based on the evidence cited here, a plausible account of the origins of Calvin's understanding of Aristotelian natural philosophy would be as follows. Calvin probably became interested in and informed about the subject

[47]Marvin Walter Anderson, *Peter Martyr: A Reformer in Exile* (Nieuwkoop: De Graaf, 1975), 175-77, 196-98, 372; John Patrick Donnelly, "Italian Influences on the Development of Calvinist Scholasticism," *Sixteenth Century Journal* 7 (1976); 86-88, 93-94.

[48]Nicolas Colladon, "Vie de Calvin" (*CO* 21:70); T. H. L. Parker, "Calvini Opera sed non Omnia," *Scottish Journal of Theology* 18 (1965): 196-97; *John Calvin: A Biography* (Philadelphia: Westminster 1975), 129-30; *Calvin's Old Testament Commentaries*, 9, 24-25.

[49]Ford Lewis Battles and André Malan Hugo, trans., *Calvin's Commentary on Seneca's "De Clementia"* (Leiden: Brill, 1969), 135. In another work, Battles concluded, "In the Commentary [on Seneca] can be seen the beginnings of Calvin the exegete. . . . The tools of exegesis: grammatical and rhetorical analysis, a wide background in history, philosophy, literature, and other studies—these characterize the young Calvin as they will more fully the later Calvin"; "The Sources of Calvin's Seneca Commentary," *John Calvin*, ed. G. E. Duffield (Appleford, Abingdon, Berkshire: Sutton Courtenay Press, 1966), 56-57.

[50]1536 *Institutes* IV.8 (IV.14.18 in 1559 ed.); cf. n 35 above.

[51]*Institutes* 1.14.20, 21 (*OS* 3:170, 172); cf. Basil, *Hexaemeron* I.11 for the ideas of the beauty of creation and God as the Artificer. The similarity of the wording of the 1543 *Institutes* passage to that in the later *Commentary on Psalms* 93:1 suggests that it may have raised in Calvin's mind the problem of the stability of the earth (also treated by Basil in *Hexaemeron* I.8) taken up in the latter; cf. nn 31 and 37 above.

[52]Luther, *Lectures on Genesis* 1:6, 9; 7:11-12 (*Luther's Works* 1:26-29, 34; 2:93-94). The Melanchthonian character of the redaction of Luther's commentary is noted by Pelikan in his Introduction to Vol. 1 of *Luther's Works*, x-xii.

during his college days in Paris; his approach to Aristotle's natural philosophy appears to be that of a humanist like Jacques Lefèvre d'Etaples or François Vatable, who may have been his Hebrew instructor at the Collège Royal in 1531-32.[53] Calvin's interest and understanding were heightened by his study of Seneca (early 1530s), his reading of Basil's *Hexaemeron* (early 1540s),[54] and by the publication of Luther's *Lectures on Genesis* (1544). This led to his first treatment of the distribution of the terrestrial elements and the mechanics of the celestial spheres. The fact that our texts do not give detailed evidence of this interest until the early 1550s is merely the result of his adopted schedule of preaching and writing.

Finally, in the mid-1550s, Calvin thought more deeply about the problem of the stability of the earth in the midst of a whirling cosmos. This further development may reflect the influence of Vermigli and Zanchius. It could also be related to Calvin's concern about the threat of Academic skepticism which was raised in his mind by the writings of Castellio and which occasioned his scornful rejection of the notion that the earth might turn in space in a sermon he preached in 1556.[55] It should be stressed that this is a tentative reconstruction. The identification of additional texts will serve to verify or improve on it.

Calvin was surely not a specialist in natural philosophy, but he did make an attempt to do justice to the subject in his biblical expositions and occasionally went into more detail than was absolutely necessary. His general stance was one of genuine dialogue reminiscent of that of one of his principal models, the *Hexaemeron* of Basil of Caesarea.

[53]Quirinius Breen, *John Calvin: A Study in French Humanism* (Grand Rapids; Eerdmans, 1931), 61-66. Vatable had translated several of Aristotle's scientific works, including the *Meteorologica*, in cooperation with Lefèvre d'Etaples in 1518; Rice, "Humanist Aristotelianism," 135-36.

[54]Calvin cited the Hexaemera of Basil and Ambrose in his *Psychopannychia* (CO 5:180, 181), written in 1534, but the earliest extant edition is that of 1545; Hughes Oliphant Old, *The Patristic Roots of Reformed Worship* (Zurich: Theologischer Verlag, 1970), 144-45.

[55]Eighth Sermon on 1 Corinthians 10-11 (CO 49:677); Kaiser, "Calvin, Copernicus, and Castellio," 23-31.

Scot. Journ. of Theol. *Vol. 38, pp. 221-240.*

THE PROTESTANT REFORMATION
AND THE RISE OF MODERN SCIENCE

by Dr G. B. DEASON

THE vast literature on the Reformation and the rise of science has produced what may be called *strong* and *weak* interpretations of their relation.[1] The strong interpretation holds that specific doctrines or attitudes affirmed by the Reformers and their followers contributed directly to the growth of science. On this view, the Reformation was among the causes of the Scientific Revolution. Without the changes in thought and values wrought by the Reformation, proponents of the strong interpretation argue, modern science would not have developed as it did. The weak interpretation, on the other hand, does not claim a direct influence of Protestantism on science. It acknowledges that modern science developed as a movement independent of the Reformation and it claims only that Protestantism offered relatively few obstacles to scientific expansion. On the weak interpretation, the absence of the Reformation would have had little, if any, effect on the

[1] In addition to the literature cited elsewhere in this article, important studies of Protestantism and science include: John Dillenberger, *Protestant Thought and Natural Science* (Nashville: Abingdon, 1960); Eugene Klaaren, *Religious Origins of Modern Science* (Grand Rapids: Eerdmans, 1977); Richard Westfall, *Science and Religion in Seventeenth Century England* (New Haven: Yale University Press, 1958); Robert S. Westman, 'The Melancthon Circle, Rheticus, and the Wittenberg Interpretation of the Copernican Theory', *Isis*, 1975, vol. 66, pp. 164-93. Studies of English Puritanism and science include: Charles Webster, *The Great Instauration: Science, Medicine and Reform, 1626-1660* (London: Duckworth, 1975); Christopher Hill, *Intellectual Origins of the English Revolution* (Oxford: Oxford University Press, 1965); R. F. Jones, *Ancients and Moderns* (Berkeley: University of California Press, 1965); Dorothy Stimson, 'Puritanism and the New Philosophy in Seventeenth Century England', *Bulletin of the Institute of the History of Medicine*, 1935, vol. 3, pp. 321-34; A. Rupert Hall, 'Merton Revisited or Science and Society in the Seventeenth Century', *History of Science*, 1963, vol. 2, pp. 1-16; T. K. Rabb, 'Puritanism and the Rise of Experimental Science in England', *Cahiers d'histoire Mondiale*, 1962, vol. 7, pp. 46-67; Richard Greaves, 'Puritanism and Science: The Anatomy of a Controversy', *Journal of the History of Ideas*, 1969, vol. 30, pp. 345-68; John Morgan, 'Puritanism and Science: A Reinterpretation', *The Historical Journal*, 1979, vol. 22, pp. 535-60; and the exchange among Hugh Kearney, Christopher Hill, and T. K. Rabb in issues 28 (July, 1964), 29 (Dec., 1964), 31 (July, 1965), 32 (Dec. 1965) of *Past and Present*.

The categories of *strong* and *weak* are useful, although they should be refined further. A more complete analysis than that given in this paper would require further distinctions to be drawn among types of *strong* interpretations in particular. A fuller analysis should appear soon in my article 'Protestantism and Science: A Typology and Criticism of Interpretations'.

221

Scientific Revolution. After brief discussion of each of these interpretations, I will argue that the strong interpretation is too strong and that the weak one can be strengthened. I will outline an *indirect* approach, which falls between the above extremes, and offers advantages not offered by either of them.

Some readers, having learned of antagonism of early Protestants toward science, may be surprised that neither of the above interpretations suggests a detrimental influence of Reformation religion on science. In fact, both interpretations reject a 'warfare' model as unfounded. Brian Gerrish, a proponent of what I have called the weak interpretation, argues against any understanding of the Reformation and the new astronomy of Copernicus which sees them in irreconcilable opposition.[2] Gerrish points out that a spurious tradition has developed about the antagonism of the Reformers toward science, which has appeared and reappeared in otherwise reputable histories. He traces the origins of five distinctive claims of Protestant opposition to science and shows that, in each case, the claims are based on hearsay, exaggerations, mistranslations, and perhaps unscrupulous motives. Gerrish properly chastises historians for repeating these claims without returning to original sources to verify them.

Many of the unfounded claims, Gerrish notes, rest on a misunderstanding of Protestant biblical hermeneutics. Considerable confusion has resulted from the assumption that the Reformers believed in the literal interpretation of Scripture, which led to direct conflict between certain biblical passages and new astronomical claims. Gerrish details several elements in Protestant hermeneutical theory which, far from leading to conflict with the claims of astronomy, allowed for rapprochement between Protestants and Copernicans. For example, Luther recognized the significance of contexts of discourse in which the same object can be described in either a religious or a scientific way. The light of the moon, he observed, can be seen by the believer as a sign of divine providence, even though the astronomer may understand it as a reflection of the sun.[3] Similarly, Calvin's influential principle of accommodation attributed a degree of poetic licence to the biblical text, by which divine truths were presented in a non-technical

---

[2] B. A. Gerrish, 'The Reformation and the Rise of Modern Science' in Jerald C. Brauer, ed., *The Impact of the Church Upon Its Culture* (Chicago: University of Chicago Press, 1968), pp. 231-75.

[3] Cited by Gerrish, 'Reformation and Rise of Science', p. 250.

language for the lay reader. In his commentary on Genesis, Calvin stated:

> Moses wrote in a popular style things which, without instruction, all ordinary persons endued with common sense, are able to understand; but astronomers investigate with great labour whatever the sagacity of the human mind can comprehend. Nevertheless, this study is not to be reprobated, nor this science to be condemned, because some frantic persons are wont boldly to reject whatever is unknown to them. For astronomy is not only pleasant, but also very useful to be known: it cannot be denied that this art unfolds the admirable wisdom of God. . . . Nor did Moses truly wish to withdraw us from this pursuit in omitting such things as are peculiar to the art; but because he was ordained a teacher as well of the unlearned and rude as of the learned, he could not otherwise fulfil his office than by descending to this grosser method of instruction . . . Moses, therefore, rather adapts his discourse to common usage.[4]

Using Calvin's principal of accommodation, Protestants were able to claim that the intention of the biblical author was to describe nature as it appears to the layman, not as it appears to the scientist. This device, Gerrish argues, allowed Protestants and scientists to avoid conflicts. Therefore, he concludes, it is fair to say that the Reformation 'did nothing to *hinder* scientific progress'.[5]

Whether or not we accept the view that Protestantism did not *hinder* science, we should recognize that Gerrish does not address the question of whether it *accelerated* science. Nor does he need to, strictly speaking, to support the weak interpretation. However, without addressing this question, he and other proponents of the weak interpretation cannot explain sociological data suggesting more rapid growth of science in Protestant countries than in Catholic ones. Reijer Hooykaas, for example, cites data showing an imbalance between numbers of Protestants and Roman Catholics belonging to the French Academy of Science from its founding in the early seventeenth century until the end of the nineteenth century.[6] Whereas the proportion of Protestants

---

[4] John Calvin, *Commentaries on the First Book of Moses called Genesis*, trans. John King, 2 volumes (Edinburgh: Calvin Translation Society, 1847-50), pp. 86-7.

[5] Gerrish, 'Reformation and Rise of Science', p. 263.

[6] R. Hooykaas, *Religion and the Rise of Modern Science* (Edinburgh: Scottish Academic Press, 1972), pp. 98-9.

to Roman Catholics in the general population averaged 6 to 27, Protestants outnumbered Roman Catholics 6 to 4 in the Academy. In Switzerland during the same period, Protestants and Roman Catholics were as 3 to 2 in the population, but Protestants contributed all of the Swiss members of the French Academy while Roman Catholics contributed none. In southern Belgium during the same period, Protestants were a very small minority of the population, but they comprised a large majority of the scientists. Since the weak interpretation does not claim that Protestantism accelerated science more than Catholicism, it offers no basis for explaining this data. This does not make it wrong, but suggests that it is a less than adequate account of the relation of Protestantism and science.

The strong interpretation, on the other hand, while having its own problems, explains the greater popularity of science in Protestant countries by claiming that the Reformation had a direct influence on science. The most vocal advocates of the strong interpretation of Protestantism and science have followed the lines of Max Weber's argument about Protestantism and capitalism.[7] Weber argued that the 'worldly asceticism' of the Reformers created a climate of thought and values that enhanced capitalistic interests. He traced the origins of worldly asceticism to a special form of the Calvinist doctrine of election in which disciplined activity in the world, such as exhibited by the rising merchant class, became a sign of divine election. Robert K. Merton extended Weber's argument to the growth of science in a classic formulation of the strong interpretation. His *Science, Technology, and Society in Seventeenth Century England* claimed that the search for a sign of election among English Puritans was epitomized in their admonition to work 'for the glory of God and the good of mankind'. Having these goals, Puritans turned to science as a means to fulfill them. It promised to reveal the intricacies of creation and to improve the standard of living. As a result, between 1640 and 1660, when Puritans were influential in English government, natural science became for the first time an attractive vocation. Merton cited figures showing a sharp rise in numbers of students entering scientific fields during and shortly after this period and concluded that Puritan values had contributed significantly to the growth of science in mid-seventeenth century England.

A variety of criticisms of Weber and Merton have been made.

[7] Max Weber, *The Protestant Ethic and the Spirit of Capitalism*, trans. Talcott Parsons (New York: Scribner's, 1958).

Weber's grounds for associating worldly asceticism with the doctrine of election have been questioned. Quakers, Independents, Mennonites, and Pietists were as worldly ascetic as other Protestant groups, but were not characterized by belief in the doctrine of election described by Weber. Merton has been criticized for restricting his study to the period 1640-60 and for focussing on Richard Baxter, whom several critics argue not to be a representative Puritan. The most telling criticism of the Merton thesis, however, is its difficulty in accounting for scientific interests in Roman Catholic countries. Merton does not explain the scientific interests, for example, of Galileo, Mersenne, Descartes, or Gassendi, who presumably had not been influenced by the Protestant values described by him. Perhaps more important, Merton and other proponents of the strong interpretation fail to account for the appearance of scientific academies in France and Italy even before their appearance in Protestant countries.

There is a second version of the strong interpretation which has not been as influential as the Merton thesis, but which deserves mention here because, among other problems, it also fails to account for scientific interests among Roman Catholics. This view holds that the Calvinist doctrine of predestination led to naturalistic determinism, and that the latter made science possible. As formulated first by Abraham Kuyper and advanced later by Stephen Mason, the view maintains that Calvin's emphasis on divine decrees in his doctrine of predestination enabled science to see nature as an orderly, unified system of events following laws prescribed by God.[8] On this account, God's decrees, as defined by Calvin, became the laws of nature of seventeenth century science. As a result of Calvin's theology, Mason writes, God 'now governed directly as an Absolute Ruler by means of decrees decided upon at the beginning. These decrees were nothing other than the laws of nature, the theological doctrine of predestination thus preparing the way for the philosophy of mechanical determinism.'[9]

There are several problems with this view. First, it represents a

---

[8] Abraham Kuyper, *Calvinism: Six Lectures Delivered in the Theological Seminary at Princeton* (New York: Revell Co., 1900), pp. 146-53; and Stephen F. Mason, *A History of the Sciences*, rev. ed. (New York: MacMillan, 1962), pp. 180-2. While this interpretation resembles Merton's in holding that Protestantism was necessary for the rise of science, it differs in claiming that Protestantism made *scientific thinking* possible, whereas Merton claims that it made possible the *social acceptance* of science. This is an example of the finer distinctions that would be drawn if a complete analysis of interpretations were to be given.   [9] Mason, *History of Sciences*, p. 182.

misunderstanding of Calvin's analysis of God's relation to nature. As discussed further below, Calvin did not see the laws of nature as autonomous causes acting independently of God. Rather, God caused every event in nature *directly*. Second, as Reijer Hooykaas points out, historical research has not confirmed the presumption that naturalistic determinism provided a philosophy of nature conducive to scientific investigation.[10] Quite the opposite: the sense of the dependence of nature on God, not of its autonomy, gave the greater stimulus to science. Finally, this version of the strong interpretation, like Merton's version, makes a direct connection between Protestantism and science at the expense of acknowledging the existence and importance of science among Roman Catholics. Kuyper and Mason claim that science was not possible without the concept of laws of nature based on Calvin's view of divine decrees, but surely Descartes or Gassendi, for example, did not form their views of the laws of nature under Calvin's influence.

The problem of the strong interpretation is that it views the relation between Protestantism and science on a causal model, whereas the complex interrelationships among different groups and ideas in this period require a more sophisticated model of interpretation. The Reformation and the Scientific Revolution were multi-faceted events influenced by the profound changes in European society, politics, and thought between 1500 and 1700. Any account of their relationship must acknowledge that the historical situation was a web of institutional, societal, political, and intellectual threads. Under these circumstances, no simplistic cause-effect model of historical explanation will suffice. We are not dealing with Protestant causes and scientific effects, as though the Scientific Revolution simply rebounded from the impact of the Reformation.

Given such a difficult subject, can any general claims be made about it without undue exaggerations or endless caveats? In this paper, I will try to show that some general claims can be made about the Reformation and the Scientific Revolution, if we are willing to impose certain limits on our inquiry that are appropriate to the complexity of its object. In particular, we must adopt an *indirect* model. I will approach the topic by recognizing that the development of modern science occurred in a polemical context — the polemic between the new, mechanical philosophy and the old, Aristotelian philosophy. Protestantism contributed to the rise of the mechanical philosophy

[10] Hooykaas, *Religion and Rise of Science*, pp. 107-8.

largely by helping to undermine Aristotelian philosophy. I will suggest that the Protestant Reformation influenced the rise of science *indirectly*, by providing new ideas and arguments opposed to Aristotelian philosophy, which were adopted by proponents of the new science to strengthen their own position against Aristotle. The combined effect of the Protestant and the scientific criticism of Aristotle accelerated the transformation from the ancient to the modern world-view more rapidly among Protestants than among Roman Catholics which (unlike the *weak* interpretation) accounts for the greater incidence of scientific interests among those touched most closely by the Reformation.

The *indirect* approach, moreover, recognizes that first-class scientific work was done by Roman Catholics in Catholic countries. If we try to locate the *cause* of modern science in the Reformation, as the strong interpretation does, the achievement of these scientists remains an enigma. On the other hand, if we see the primary role of the Reformation as contributing along with the new science to the tide of change that eventually overwhelmed Aristotelianism, then we ought only to expect that science proceeded *relatively* more rapidly among Protestants, not that it proceeded *only* among Protestants.

Moreover, it should be remembered that some facets of the Reformation were not anti-Aristotelian. Melanchthon, for example, quickly returned Lutheranism to Aristotle and there arose in Germany a significant form of Protestant Aristotelianism, usually referred to as Protestant Scholasticism. The existence of Protestant Scholasticism, however, does not so much count against the *indirect* interpretation as for it. If we were to say that Protestantism *caused* the advent of modern science, then we would be hard pressed to explain the retrenchment of some parts of the Reformation into Aristotelianism. On the *strong* interpretation, the existence of Protestant Aristotelianism is just as hard to explain as the existence of Roman Catholic science. My claim, however, is only that the anti-Aristotelian dimension of Protestantism helped to confirm the anti-Aristotelianism of the Scientific Revolution. If some Protestant traditions remained Aristotelian, it makes little difference to the indirect approach as long as we do not see science developing more rapidly where those traditions prevail. In fact, we do not. Areas of Germany characterized by Protestant Aristotelian thought did not produce the high incidence of modern scientific activity that was seen, for example, in Holland and England where Protestants and scientists joined hands against Aristotle.

Now let us turn to the main discussion. I will suggest that Protestant arguments made against Aristotle, primarily for religious purposes, reinforced (and in some cases, informed) scientific arguments made against Aristotle. The arguments that I will consider cluster into three areas: (1) the locus of authority (2) the necessity of empirical methods and (3) the radical sovereignty of God.

(1) *The locus of authority*

The Roman Catholic church's understanding of religious authority at the time of the Reformation and the Scientific Revolution included three elements: scripture, tradition, and the church. How each of these elements functioned with respect to science can be illustrated by reference to the Galileo affair. After his telescopic discoveries of 1609-10, Galileo became convinced of the truth of Copernicus' theory that the sun occupied the center of the universe and that the earth was a planet circling it. In seeking to make his views public, Galileo encountered opposition on three fronts, each of which represented one of these elements in the understanding of authority. First, a number of theologians argued that *scripture* opposed belief in a central sun and a moving earth. Passages such as Joshua 10.12-13, in which Joshua was said to have commanded the sun to stand still in the midst of the heavens, implied strongly that the sun was moving, not standing still as Copernicus claimed. Other passages, such as Psalm 103.5, implied that the earth was not a planet by stating that God 'fixed the earth on its foundation, not to be moved forever'. Second, Galileo's opponents observed that the *tradition* of interpretation of these passages supported their anti-Copernican views. Citing church fathers from Augustine to Aquinas, they claimed that the authority of tradition supported Aristotelian geocentrism, not Copernican heliocentrism. Finally, in 1616 and again in 1633, Galileo encountered the authority of the *institutional church*. On the earlier date, a committee of theological consultors pronounced Copernicanism contrary to the Catholic faith and the Commissary General issued an injunction against its teaching. On the latter date, Galileo stood trial before a special commission for having defended the motion of the earth by attributing the motion of the tides to it and for having broken the injunction of 1616 against teaching the truth of Copernicanism.[11]

My purpose in referring to these events is *not* to suggest that the

[11] For discussions of Galileo's conflict with the church, see Jerome J. Langford, *Galileo, Science and the Church*, rev. ed. (Ann Arbor: University of Michigan Press, 1971); and Giorgio de Santillana, *The Crime of Galileo* (Chicago: University of Chicago Press, 1955).

Roman Catholic Church stood obstinately or blindly against science. It did not. Much of the church's position can be justified on grounds that Galileo had insufficient evidence to proclaim, as vehemently as he did, the truth of Copernicanism. My only purpose in pointing to the Galileo affair is to contrast the understanding of authority in the Roman Catholic Church to its understanding among Protestants, and to state that the difference is significant for the swiftness of the rejection of Aristotle by the new science in Protestant countries.

In place of scripture, tradition, and the church as elements constituting religious authority, the Protestant reformers concentrated authority in the Word of God revealed in scripture. The elimination of tradition as an authoritative standard was important for the new science since the largest part of church tradition assumed the Aristotelian-Ptolemaic cosmology. By denying tradition an authoritative role, the reformers did not *reject* the truth of the old cosmology (indeed, their scattered remarks about nature often reflect it), but they did eliminate the need to consult authorities who had assumed its truth. As a result, when the Copernican hypothesis was discussed in Protestant countries, as it was in England in the late 1500's and early 1600's, there was no need to refer to the cosmology of Lactantius, Basil, or Augustine because it was no longer relevant to do so. By contrast, a great deal of the discussion in Roman Catholic circles about Copernicanism, for example, Galileo's exchanges with Bellarmine, centered on the Fathers' interpretation of key biblical passages.[12] By denying authority to tradition, the Reformation undermined the preeminence afforded Aristotle by virtue of his longevity and eased the way for acceptance of ideas that disagreed with his.

The shift from the institutional church as a religious authority to scripture played an equally important role in facilitating the acceptance of new scientific ideas. Whereas Galileo encountered theological consultors and special commissions charged with establishing the church's position on Copernicanism, no such bureaucratic machinery existed in Protestant countries. In Protestantism, the church was no longer the guardian of secular and political affairs, at least not to the same extent as in Catholicism, and this meant that the door was left open for other institutions — such as the State and

[12] For example, Cardinal Bellarmine's correspondence with Galileo and Galileo's 'Letter to the Grand Duchess Christina' repeatedly address the question of the Fathers' interpretation of key biblical passages. See Langford, *Galileo, Science, and the Church*, pp. 50-78.

Science — to fill the vacuum of authority left by the departure of the church. Roman Catholic ecclesiology had required the church to reconcile the *lex dei* and the *lex naturae* in a coherent, working synthesis. This role included the *active reconciliation* of scientific claims with scriptural or theological claims to show that they were consistent and part of the same truth. Part of the attraction of Thomism was that it provided an intellectual framework in which the church could accomplish this role. Protestantism, on the other hand, did not give the church any such role. Protestant theology recognized the ultimate compatibility of the *lex dei* and the *lex naturae*, but the church was not required to demonstrate or to enforce their consistency. In most Protestant countries, no official machinery existed for guaranteeing the relation between things divine and things earthly. Their reconciliation was still a concern, but one that was left largely up to the individual conscience and not up to the church. Lacking such a role, the Protestant church required no theology (such as Thomism) built upon an extensive philosophy (such as Aristotelianism), making it easier to break the influence of past intellectual traditions and assimilate new ideas.[13]

(2) *The necessity of empirical methods*

Rejecting the tripartite division of religious authority, the Reformation claimed that tradition and the church had corrupted the truth of Scripture by empty and erroneous speculations. 'The disputations of the Scholastics,' Luther said, 'are nothing but empty fictions, the dreams of idle men; yet the entire papacy is founded on these non-existent things and depends on them to this day.'[14] Virtually every Protestant thinker after Luther castigated the Roman Church and the theological tradition for having replaced the objective and simple truth of scripture with the subjective, obscure, and erroneous opinions of human beings. Calvin went so far as to suggest that Roman theologians 'attempt nothing in life but to enshroud and obscure the simplicity of Scripture'.[15] Heinrich Bullinger called Roman Catholic

[13] A fuller discussion of the type of analysis presented in this paragraph can be found in Ernst Troeltsch, *Protestantism and Progress*, trans. W. Montgomery (Boston: Beacon Press, 1958), pp. 89-127 and 155-64.

[14] Martin Luther, 'Lectures on Galatians (1535)', in *Luther's Works*, eds. Jaroslav Pelikan and Helmut T. Lehman, 56 vols. (St. Louis: Concordia Publishing House, 1955-), vol. 26, p. 126.

[15] John Calvin, *Institutes of the Christian Religion*, ed. John T. McNeill and trans. Ford Lewis Battles, in *The Library of Christian Classics*, 26 vols. (Philadelphia: Westminster Press, 1960), vol. 20, p. 22.

exegesis the 'vain cogitations' of men and likened it to a 'plague' that afflicts God's word. England left the Roman faith, John Jewel wrote, because she came to recognize that 'error, superstition, idolatry, and men's inventions disagreed with Holy Scripture' and displeased God.[16]

In the course of the development of Protestant thought, there emerged an ideology which claimed that the natural operation of reason led to vain speculations and idle inventions. The mind operating on its own produced nothing but errors. Protestants adopted this ideology as one of their primary weapons in the attack on Roman Catholicism. Beginning with Luther, they never tired of accusing Roman Catholics of idolatry. By allowing reason too much of a role in theology, Roman Catholic thought had created an idol of God and now worshipped it instead of the true God revealed in scripture.

Implicit in this Protestant view was an understanding of reason that tied Aristotelian philosophy to the downfall of theology and that promoted a new form of biblical empiricism in the place of Aristotelian speculation. Protestants claimed that Aristotle provided a deductive model for theology, but that their theology was built inductively out of scripture. For example, Luther strongly criticized the Aristotelian assumption that human virtue could be improved by habitual practice. This assumption, he said, has ruined theology because Roman theologians used it to claim that human beings must practice virtue to attain salvation. They conformed scripture to Aristotelian ethics and, by doing so, destroyed the pre-eminence of faith in the process of salvation. The remedy, according to Luther and the Protestants, was to eliminate speculation by carefully constructing theology out of the Bible. Only direct investigation of the biblical text according to strictly inductive methods could save theology from the empty inventions of human reason and from the idle speculations of Aristotelian reason in particular.

Protestant criticism of Aristotelian rationalism and insistence that theology must begin with the direct study of scripture proved a useful precedent for seventeenth century scientists arguing against Aristotle's deductive methods and in favor of the empirical study of nature. One thinks, of course, of Francis Bacon, who sharply turned natural philosophy in an empirical direction by his vehement criticism of the Aristotelian syllogism and his advocacy of inductive methods. A close look at Bacon's assumptions and his language reveals the importance

[16] John Jewel, *An Apology of the Church of England*, ed. J. E. Booty (Ithaca, N.Y.: Cornell University Press, 1963), pp. 68-9.

of the anti-Aristotelian precedent set by the Reformation. Like the Reformers, Bacon assumed that reason operating on its own produced empty dreams or vain imaginations and not truth. When reason deduced what nature must be like, Bacon said, it produced 'empty dogmas instead of the true signatures and marks set upon the works of creation as they are found in nature'. 'Unless we recognize the difference,' he continued, 'between the Idols of the human mind and the Ideas of the divine', we will continue to acquiesce in sterile, self-serving rationalism and fail to achieve progress in the knowledge of nature.'[17] Just as Protestants had argued against the idolatry of Roman Catholic theology, Bacon argued that Aristotelian natural philosophy had aborted progress in the sciences by substituting an idol of nature for the true works of God in creation.

To remedy the ills of the sciences, moreover, Bacon recommended specific steps analogous to Protestant reform. Just as Protestants advocated careful study of the Book of Scripture to rid theology of empty speculations, so Bacon believed that science must begin with observation and classification of the great Book of Nature in order to free itself from the idols of Aristotelian philosophy. For Bacon, the method of induction had this power: 'The formation of ideas and axioms by true induction,' he said, 'is no doubt the proper remedy to be applied for keeping off and clearing away idols.'[18] By following the guidelines of Bacon's method, the interpreter could understand nature according to the order of nature and not according to the order imposed by the mind.

The parallel that I have drawn between biblical empiricism and scientific empiricism did not go unnoticed in the seventeenth century. The acceptance of science in Protestant countries rested in part on the perceived similarity between inductive study of scripture and inductive study of nature, both in opposition to the deductivism of Aristotle. The new science appeared to follow the lead of the Reformation by turning directly to the original, by-passing the corruptions introduced by the Greek philosophical tradition. In the words of Thomas Spratt, first historian of the Royal Society,

Protestantism and science ... both may lay equal claim to the word *Reformation*: the one having compass'd it in *Religion*, the

[17] Francis Bacon, 'The New Organon', in *The Works of Francis Bacon*, comp. and ed. James Spedding, Robert Leslie Ellis, and Douglas Denon Heath, 15 vols. (Boston: Taggard and Thompson, 1860-4), vol. 8, p. 72.
[18] ibid., p. 76.

other purposing it in *Philosophy*. They both have taken a like course to bring this about; each of them passing by the *corrupt Copies*, and referring themselves to the *perfect Originals* for their instruction; the one to the *Scripture*, the other to the large Volume of the *Creatures*.[19]

Of course, it would be foolish to claim that the advent of modern science involved nothing but the acceptance of empirical methods. To do so would be to overlook the singular importance of mathematical methods for the Scientific Revolution. The point here, however, is not that empiricism alone made modern science, but rather that seventeenth century scientists argued that the new science was more empirical than Aristotle, and that their arguments were corroborated by Protestant criticism of Aristotle.

(3) *The radical sovereignty of God*

By *radical* sovereignty of God, I mean an understanding of sovereignty peculiar to the Reformers and to some of their followers which held that God's sovereignty excluded the active contribution of human beings or of Nature to his work.[20] According to Luther, human beings are not justified by actively endeavoring to become righteous, but by accepting on faith that God through Christ has made them righteous. Luther drew a sharp distinction between 'active righteousness' (trying to become righteous through actions) and 'passive righteousness' (accepting on faith the righteousness offered by God). Active righteousness, he maintained, had a role in everyday affairs, but no place in the gospel. The gospel of Christ concerned only passive righteousness.

According to the Reformers, Roman Catholic soteriology presumed active righteousness. It claimed that God rewarded only believers who made an active effort. The Reformers argued that this made salvation contingent on human actions and detracted from God's glory. 'For God is He who dispenses His gifts freely to all,' Luther wrote, 'and this is the praise of His deity. But He cannot defend this deity of His against the self-righteous people who are unwilling to accept grace and eternal

[19] Thomas Spratt, *The History of the Royal Society of London for the Improving of Natural Knowledge* (London, 1687), p. 345.
[20] This discussion of the implications of the Protestant doctrine of radical sovereignty of God for the rise of science is dealt with more fully in my 'Reformation Theology and the Mechanistic Conception of Nature' in *God and Nature: A History of the Encounter between Christianity and Science*, eds. David C. Lindberg and Ronald L. Numbers (forthcoming).

life from Him freely but want to earn it by their own works. They
simply want to rob Him of the glory of His deity.'[21] To maintain God's
glory, the Reformers emphasized his radical sovereignty. Salvation did
not depend on human actions, but on God alone. Against common
sense and church tradition, Luther boldly proclaimed this conclusion
about salvation: God does everything, human beings do nothing.

The same concept of radical sovereignty can be seen in the
Reformers' descriptions of God's relation to nature: God does
everything, Nature does nothing. In creating the firmament and
giving motion to the celestial bodies, God did not depend on Nature
which, Luther said, 'is incapable of such an achievement'.[22] By his
Word, he called the heavens into existence, and by the same Word he
created the things of the earth. Luther chided physicians and
philosophers for ascribing procreation to 'a matching mixture of
qualities which are active in predisposed matter'. 'Aristotle,' he
claimed, 'prates in vain that man and the sun bring man into existence.
Although the heat of the sun warms our bodies, nevertheless the cause
of their coming into existence is something far different, namely the
Word of God.'[23]

In his discussion of providence in the *Institute*, Calvin formulated
what could be called a systematic view of God's relation to the natural
world. He made clear that God's activity in nature is ever-present and
that nothing in nature can be attributed to natural causes alone. God
sustained the existence of creatures, he invigorated created beings with
power and movement, and he determined the ends of natural things
and of nature as a whole. Under no circumstances can nature be seen
as an independent entity running under its own power toward
inherent ends. Natural things were only instruments through which
God acted; he could choose different instruments, or none at all. For
example, in discussing the sun as a cause of propagation of plants,
Calvin pointed out that Genesis describes the creation of herbs and
fruits *before* the creation of the sun. He concluded, 'Therefore a godly
man will not make the sun either the principal or the necessary cause of
these things which existed before the creation of the sun, but merely the
instrument that God uses because he so wills; for with no more
difficulty he might abandon it, and act through himself.'[24]

[21] Luther, *Luther's Works*, vol. 26, p. 127.
[22] Luther, *Luther's Works*, vol. 1, p. 25.
[23] ibid., p. 127.
[24] Calvin, *Institute*, vol. 2, p. 199.

Protestant belief in the radical sovereignty of God opposed Aristotelian philosophy in two ways, and in each of these the Protestant doctrine indirectly supported the world-view of the new science. The radical sovereignty of God opposed (a) Aristotle's hierarchical cosmology and (b) his conception of nature as a being having intrinsic powers.

(a) *Cosmology*

It is well known that Dante's *Divine Comedy* incorporated Aristotle's view of the cosmos as an ordered hierarchy of concentric celestial spheres having earth at the center, encircled by the spheres of the moon, Mercury, Venus, the sun, Mars, Jupiter, and Saturn, the outer sphere of the fixed stars, the *primum mobile*, and finally the Empyrean Heaven where God dwelt. In much of medieval thought and popular literature, this cosmic hierarchy was a continuation of the hierarchy of nature existing on earth. Together, the celestial and terrestrial hierarchies constituted the great chain of being, extending in gradations from God, through angels, rational souls, animals and vegetables, to inanimate objects. The Deity delegated power to angelic beings who moved the heavenly bodies, whose motion was communicated through the nesting system of spheres to the earth, where the divine power trickled down the scale of nature to the most homely creatures of God's creation.

Paralleling this cosmic hierarchy was the hierarchy of the church. Ecclesiology in the Middle Ages justified the hierarchical structure of the church in part by appeal to the cosmic hierarchy, an appeal made as early as the fifth century by Pseudo-Dionysius. The pope, cardinals, archbishops, bishops, and priests formed the conduit through which divine law and grace reached the common person. Each station in the hierarchy stood below the one above it and above the one below it in a neatly ordered chain of command.

The frontal attack made by the Reformation on the hierarchical structure of the Roman Catholic Church is well known. Not so well known is the role played by the doctrine of God's radical sovereignty or its subsequent implications for cosmology. Throughout his writings, Luther argued that the Roman Catholic understanding of the church weakened God's power and glory by dissipating it through a series of intermediaries. On Luther's view, the power given church officials by this ecclesiology detracted from the power that was rightly God's

173

alone. For Reformation theology, God's sovereignty could not tolerate an institutional hierarchy having any power independent or even semi-independent of him. No church official could absolve sin or transform bread and wine into the body and blood of Christ without challenging the sovereignty of God. For this reason, the Reformers held that divine power was communicated by God's immediate, direct action without the use of intermediary officials. Luther's doctrine of the real presence of Christ in the Eucharist is an example of this immediacy. God's radical sovereignty demanded that no human being could act as an intermediary between heaven and earth. For the Reformers, Christ was the only mediator; his mediation did not challenge God's sovereignty or his glory.

From this analysis, it is easy to see how readily belief in the radical sovereignty of God spilled over into the debate between the Aristotelian and Copernican cosmologies. Defenders of the old view clung to the belief that God accommodated his sovereignty so as to act through intermediaries: angels, celestial spheres, and church officials. Defenders of the new cosmology argued that Copernicanism freed God from dependence on cosmic intermediaries, just as the Reformers had freed him from ecclesiastical intermediaries. The removal of both types of intermediaries, Protestant Copernicans claimed, did full justice to the radical sovereignty of God. In the church and in the world, God's action came to be seen as direct. In his *Discourse Concerning a New Planet*, a defense of Copernicanism published in 1640, John Wilkens not only reconciled Copernican doctrine with passages of scripture that appeared to oppose it, but also argued that the new cosmology was consistent with Protestant theology because it recognized that God acts directly without need of intermediaries. 'Those who make angels move the orbs,' Wilkins wrote, fail to recognize 'that it were a needless thing for Providence to have appointed Angels unto this business, which might have been done just as well by the only will of God.'[25]

(b) *The Concept of Nature*

On the basis of the earlier discussion of God's sovereignty over nature in Reformation thought, we may draw several conclusions here about the erosion of the Aristotelian conception of nature in Protestant thought. As a result of their belief in the radical sovereignty of God, the Reformers undermined Aristotle's view of nature as a being having

[25] Cited by Mason, *History of Science*, pp. 187-8.

intrinsic powers. In place of the Aristotelian definition of nature as 'the principle of motion and change' (*Physics* 200b), the Reformers conceived of nature as entirely passive. For them, the Word or command of God was the only active principle in the world. 'Secondary causes,' Calvin said, 'have no power in themselves,' but 'derive their power from Him'.[26]

By contrast to the Aristotelian view of nature and consistent with the Protestant view, the mechanistic conception of nature rested on a single, fundamental assumption: *matter is passive*. It possessed no active, internal forces. Nothing in matter compelled it to develop or to move toward an ultimate goal. The matter of the seventeenth century possessed only the passive qualities of size, shape, and impenetrability. Change did not result from the operation of internal principles and powers, as in the Aristotelian view; instead, motion was explained with the new concept of *inertia* by which a body remained at rest or acquired motion from other bodies. The seventeenth century replaced Aristotle's conception of nature as an organic being achieving maturation through self-development with the view of nature as a machine whose parts made different movements in response to other parts doing the same thing.

The mechanical philosophers turned to the Protestant doctrine of the radical sovereignty of God in arguing for their belief in the passivity of matter. The conviction that matter could not possess active powers if God were sovereign (in the Reformation sense of sovereignty) helped the mechanical philosophers in constructing arguments for mechanism and against Aristotelianism. For example, the English chemist, Robert Boyle, was a prolific critic of the Aristotelian concept of nature and one of the strongest advocates of the mechanical philosophy. In *A True Inquiry into the Vulgarly Received Notion of Nature* (1686), he argued that the Aristotelian view of nature 'has been injurious to the glory of God'. 'It seems to detract,' he said, 'from the honor of the great author and governor of the world, that men should ascribe most of the admirable things, that are to be met with in it, not to Him, but to a certain nature.'[27] Seeing nature as a living, active being, he added, 'seems not to me very suitable to the profound reverence we owe the divine majesty'. Insofar as active qualities were attributed to nature,

[26] Jean Calvin, *Calvin's New Testament Commentaries*, eds. David W. and Thomas F. Torrance, 12 vols. (Grand Rapids: Eerdmans, 1960–   ), vol. 12, pp. 362-3.
[27] Robert Boyle, *The Works of the Honorable Robert Boyle*, ed. Thomas Birch, 5 vols. (London, 1744), vol. IV, p. 361.

they detracted from God's sovereignty. According to Boyle, Aristotle's view of nature denied 'the ability of the sovereign Lord and Governor of the world to administer his dominion over all things'. 'For my part,' Boyle said, 'I see no need to acknowledge any architectonic being besides God . . .'. 'Those things which the school philosophers ascribe directly to the agency of nature, I ascribe to the wisdom of God. . . .'[28]

In addition to Boyle, Isaac Newton referred to the sovereignty of God as a reason for rejecting views of nature that attributed activity to matter. Following the publication of the *Principia* (1687), when the cause of gravity became a heated issue, Newton vehemently rejected the possibility that matter inherently possessed powers such as gravity. 'I desired that you not ascribe innate gravity to me,' he told Bentley in 1693. 'That gravity should be innate, inherent and essential to matter . . . is to me so great an Absurdity, that I believe no Man who has in philosophical Matters a competent Faculty of thinking, can ever fall into it.'[29] In making this denial Newton appears to have had two reasons. First like other mechanists, he accepted the doctrine of the passivity of matter. Second, the radical sovereignty of God required that the animation of nature come from God alone and not from matter.[30]

Consistently maintaining these two commitments, Newton struggled between the publication of the *Principia* in 1687 and the *Opticks* in 1704 to arrive at a satisfactory solution to the problem of gravity. Although he never accomplished his aim, in the course of these struggles he developed a view that separated the phenomena of nature into two fundamental principles: a 'passive' principle, which he associated with matter, and an 'active' principle, which he associated with God. Given only the passive principle, the world as we know it never could have formed, nor could it continue. From the passivity of matter alone, neither motion nor the conservation of motion was possible. Active principles, on the other hand, initiated and conserved motion. Newton identified them with such forces as gravity, fermentation, and cohesion.

[28] ibid., pp. 372 and 362.
[29] 'Isaac Newton to Richard Bentley, February 25, 1692-3' in *Isaac Newton's Papers and Letters on Natural Philosophy*, 2nd edition, ed. I. Bernard Cohen (Cambridge, Mass.: Harvard University Press, 1978), pp. 302-3.
[30] These two reasons underlying Newton's conception of matter are discussed in Ernan McMullin, *Newton on Matter and Activity* (Notre Dame: University of Notre Dame Press, 1978).

Bifurcating the world into passive and active principles, Newton came to see nature as a lifeless world permeated by the life of God. Active principles became a manifestation of God's sovereign power, providing vitality to senseless, inert matter. In attempting to portray the mechanism of divine sufficiency, Newton returned to the conception of space and the model of mind-body interaction which he had developed in an early essay entitled *De gravitatione et aequipondio fluidorium*. He imagined God immediately present in the world, constituting space itself, and the Divine Will acting on matter in a way analogous to the movement of the human body by the will. In the early essay, he wrote, 'Since each man is conscious that he can move his body at will, and believes further that all men enjoy the same power of similarly moving their bodies by thought alone; the free power of moving bodies at will can by no means be denied to God, whose facility of thought is infinitely greater and more swift.'[31] Because of God's omnipresence, he is able to act in every part of the world without exception. 'God ... is everywhere present,' Newton wrote in the General Scholium, 'He is omnipresent not *virtually* only, but *substantially* . . . In him are all things contained and moved.'[32]

Thus between 1687 and 1704, as he wrestled with the explanation of gravity, Newton came to see not only gravity, but also the other animating forces of nature, as a manifestation of the immediate presence of God in the world. Even though he never committed himself publicly to an explanation of the cause of gravity, for much of his career he held privately to the view that God caused gravitational attraction by his omnipresent activity according to principles which he had established and which Newton called 'active principles' or 'laws of motion'. Working in accord with these principles, God animated nature, providing life to a world of dead matter. Without him, there would be no vital force in the world. Samuel Clarke, with whom Newton was in close contact, summed up the latter's view in a letter to Leibniz. There are, Clarke said, 'no powers of nature independent of God'.[33]

[31] Isaac Newton, *Unpublished Scientific Papers of Isaac Newton*, eds. A. Rupert Hall and Marie Boas Hall (Cambridge: Cambridge University Press, 1962), pp. 138-9.
[32] Isaac Newton, *Sir Isaac Newton's Mathematical Principles of Natural Philosophy and His System of the World*, trans. Andrew Motte, rev. Florian Cajori, 2 vols. (Berkeley: University of California Press, 1934), vol. 2, p. 545.
[33] Samuel Clarke, *The Leibniz-Clarke Correspondence*, ed. H. G. Alexander (New York: Philosophical Library, 1956), p. 22.

Conclusion

The world as Newton described it appeared to be the product of God's action on mindless, inchoate matter. Unlike the world conceived by Aristotle in which inherent principles imbued matter with purposive development, the Newtonian world possessed no inherent activity and no inherent direction. Apart from God's direct action, the world would languish inert and purposeless. If our analysis has been correct, Newton's view, like Boyle's before him, represented the adaptation of the Protestant conception of the radical sovereignty of God to the needs of the mechanical philosophy. As the Reformers had appealed to divine sovereignty to oppose active righteousness in theology, so the mechanists made a similar appeal in excluding active powers from natural philosophy. The examples of Boyle and Newton provide further confirmation of the general thesis of this paper, that the Protestant Reformation contributed *indirectly* to the rise of science by providing a precedent for opposition to Aristotle and by providing some of the specific arguments used later by scientists against Aristotle's conception of nature. The three topics which we have discussed, (1) the locus of authority (2) the necessity of empirical methods and (3) the radical sovereignty of God, do not exhaust the complex relation between the Reformation and the Scientific Revolution. However, they offer partial explanation of why modern science after the sixteenth century appeared to accelerate more in Protestant countries than in Roman Catholic ones, while acknowledging that science also developed in Roman Catholic countries and that it would have continued to develop had the Reformation not occurred.

GARY B. DEASON

St. Olaf College
Northfield, Minnesota 55057

〈〈〈-〈〈〈

Natural Science in Sixteenth-Century Calvinistic Thought

W. STANFORD REID

IN recent years historians of science have pushed the beginnings of the so-called "scientific revolution" from the middle of the seventeenth century into the last half of the sixteenth, and have even traced some of its roots as far as Robert Grosseteste of the thirteenth.[1] Yet, as A. C. Crombie has admitted, these same historians are at a loss to provide a unified explanation for the fact that the new scientific outlook appears to have had its beginnings in the latter half of the 1500's. He has suggested various reasons such as economic and social conditions, while others have mentioned new patterns of thought that came into conflict with the accepted humanism of the Renaissance and similar intellectual movements.[2] In general, however, the interpreters of the scientific development have either ignored or specifically denied the influence of the Reformation, a movement widespread and influential in the very geographic areas where natural science later attained some of its greatest achievements.[3] For this reason the present paper will endeavour to set forth some of the scientific concepts which Calvin and his followers developed and which seem to have contributed to the seventeenth-century scientific development, in this way forming a stage on the way to Newton's *Principia*.

Historians of science have stated more than once that the scientific movement of the sixteenth century brought no sudden change in thought, but only carried the medieval and Renaissance thinking somewhat farther.[4] While this point of view in some ways has considerable truth, one must always bear in mind that medieval scientific endeavour from 1250 on usually followed the lead of Aristotle in stressing the metaphysical background of physics by laying its stress on final causes, in searching for qualitative rather than quantitative attributes, and in employing the form-substance dialectical

[This was part of a session on Theologians and Science. See also pp. 251 and 283.]

[1] Cf. A. C. Crombie, *Robert Grosseteste and the Origins of Experimental Science, 1100–1700* (Oxford, 1953).

[2] *Augustine to Galileo* (London, 1957), p. 275.

[3] H. Haydn, *The Counter-Renaissance* (New York, 1960), p. 245, declares that Luther and Calvin both disliked the arts and sciences since they laid all their stress upon salvation, while W. C. D. Dampier-Whethan, *A History of Science* (New York, 1930), p. 118, believes that the only importance of the Reformation for science was that it unintentionally broke ecclesiastical control over European thought.

[4] H. Brown, "The Renaissance Historians of Science," *Studies in the Renaissance* (New York), VII (1960), 27ff., holds that the scientific revolution "cannot be said to begin much before the very end of the sixteenth century, and it dates properly from the seventeenth" (p. 36), Cf. also A. R. Hall, *The Scientific Revolution, 1500–1800* (London, 1954) pp. 68ff.; N. W. Gilbert, *The Renaissance Concept of Method* (New York, 1960), pp. 223f.

explanation for nature which soon came to be equated with the theological grace-nature motive.[5] Although the work of Grosseteste and some of his followers pointed in the direction of a more empirical, experimental type of method, their influence died out under the impact of Renaissance humanism.[6] The humanists revived the study of the classical scientific tests and commentaries, but generally speaking they did little to stimulate an interest in what one today would call scientific investigation.[7] Even Vesalius and Copernicus, although they had largely broken from the ancient traditions, still showed little appreciation of the modern point of view.[8]

Probably the chief stimulus to change in accepted interpretations of nature came as a result of practical technical discoveries and inventions. The medieval scholar had thought primarily in terms of arranging a curriculum for teaching, but increasingly craftsmen, surgeons, navigators and the like, seeking some limited, practical objective which would help with their work, discovered new facts and invented new machines or instruments. Theoretical interpretation then had to accommodate itself to these novelties which because of their increase became something of a problem in the sixteenth century.[9] Aristotle could not be discharged from his place of predominance until some new interpretation, as all-inclusive as his, had been established. Yet at the same time, he and even more his disciples were proving less and less satisfactory as interpreters of the new knowledge. Consequently the more advanced "scientific thinkers" began to reject the Aristotelian pattern of the universe.[10] Of these quite a number turned to the pre-Aristotelian philosophers for their explanations as did Paracelsus, while others such as William Gilbert employed a good many ideas derived

[5]T. F. Torrance, "The Influence of Reformed Thought on the Development of Scientific Method," *Dialogue: A Journal of Theology*, II (1963), 42; E. A. Burtt, *The Metaphysical Foundations of Modern Science* (rev. ed., New York, 1931), pp. 17ff.; J. Dillenberger, *Protestant Thought and Natural Science* (London, 1961), p. 23; P. O. Kristeller, *Renaissance Thought* (New York, 1961), p. 31.

[6]Crombie, *Grosseteste*, pp. 290ff.; Kristeller, *op. cit.*, p. 33. W. J. Ong, *Ramus Method and the Decay of Dialogue* (Harvard University Press, 1958), p. 142, believes that many of the Roman Catholic theologians of the sixteenth century were beginning to enter the field of natural science but the Reformation forced them back to biblical studies. This would hardly seem to have been very general.

[7]The principal Renaissance contribution came in the form of a revived study of "method," on classical lines, but the humanists never devised a "scientific method" as such. Their main stress lay upon the study of classical texts. Gilbert, *op. cit.*, p. 231; Kristeller, *op. cit.*, pp. 40ff.; cf. R. Hooykaas, "Humanisme, science et reforme," *Free University Quarterly*, Amsterdam, V (1958), 171.

[8]This statement would not in any sense deny the value of their contributions, but when analysed their work did not follow nor did it have as its mainspring a modern "scientific" approach. Vesalius seems to have regarded his work primarily as a matter of technique while Copernicus sought an explanation different from that of Ptolemy because the latter's system did not manifest the simplicity which Copernicus thought should be implicit in nature. M. Boas, *The Scientific Renaissance, 1450–1630* (London, 1962), p. 77; Hall, *op cit.*, chap. II; Hooykaas, *op cit.*, p. 177; Burtt, *op cit.*, pp. 38ff.; H. Butterfield, *The Origins of Modern Science* (London, 1950), pp. 22ff.

[9]Butterfield, *ibid.*, pp. 210ff.; Ong, *op. cit.*, pp. 224ff.; Gilbert, *op. cit.*, p. 230.

[10]Boas, *op. cit.*, pp. 238ff.; Kristeller, *op. cit.*, p. 44.

from magic and naturalistic mysticism.[11] And yet neither of these approaches met the need for an all-inclusive theory, with the result that others like Peter Ramus, in his early work, although strongly anti-Aristotelian had no adequate system to put in the place of the accepted interpretation.[12]

Because of this situation, the Protestant Reformation, particularly its Calvinistic phase, had a special appeal for the philosophically homeless students of nature. The primary reason for this was Luther's and particularly Calvin's opposition to the whole medieval-Aristotelian Scholastic synthesis with its rationalistic attempt to place everything in nature in logical and hierarchical relationships.[13] Furthermore, the rejection of the idea of church control and the stress upon vocation even in scientific studies no doubt also had their influence.[14] Consequently one finds that a number of sixteenth-century "scientific" practitioners, thinkers and writers, such as Peter Ramus,[15] Bernard Palissy,[16] Ambrose Paré,[17] and Francis Bacon[18] accepted Calvinism which in turn seems to have stimulated them to further efforts in their studies.[19] To understand this, however, one must see how Calvinism provided them with the structure of thought of which they felt in need and how they employed it in their scientific thinking.

[11]Hooykaas, op. cit., p. 171; Boas, op. cit., p. 190.

[12]Boas, ibid., p. 238. Peter Ramus, in his pre-Protestant days before 1562, seems to have sought a philosophic system in dialectic by which he could co-ordinate all his thought, but he never seems to have felt that he had achieved his aim. Vide infra.

[13]A. S. Nash, The University and the Modern World (New York, 1944), pp. 62f.; Torrance, op. cit., p. 42; Hooykaas, op. cit., pp. 169, 263.

[14]Nash, op. cit., p. 64f.; A Lecerf, Etudes calvinistes (Paris, 1949), pp. 116ff., points out that "pour le Calvinisme, il n'y a rien de profane que le mal," consequently the study of natural science might well be a man's God-given vocation, in which he would fulfil his calling as much as the minister did in his.

[15]Peter Ramus (1515–1572) became an influential philosopher and "methodologist" in the Université de France. W. J. Ong feels that his influence led to sterility of thought, but Ong does not seriously consider the changes which came in his views after his conversion to Protestantism, particularly his insistence upon his freedom over against the Aristotelianism of the Sorbonne. He was killed on the third day of the Massacre of St. Bartholomew's Eve.

[16]Bernard Palissy (1510–1590), a potter of Saintes, by dint of experimentation succeeded in producing an enamel similar to that of Majolica. He became a special favourite of the French court and so escaped the St. Bartholomew's Eve massacre. He died in the Bastille for his Protestantism in 1590.

[17]Ambrose Paré (1510–1590) became probably the most famous French surgeon of his day. He also escaped the Massacre of St. Bartholomew's Eve through royal protection. He was noted for his empirical approach to matters medical. Cf. F. R. Packard, Life and Times of Ambrose Paré (New York, 1921), pp. 80ff.

[18]Francis Bacon in the history of science is not usually considered as particularly religious owing to the fact that his confession of faith is often ignored. Yet when one reads his statements in his Advancement of Learning and similar works in conjunction with his confession, one can see that a strong Calvinism coloured all his scientific thinking. For Bacon's confession see Works, ed. J. Spedding and R. L. Ellis (London, 1870), VII, 215ff.

[19]Both Calvin and Ramus more than once referred to the fact that there seemed to be a relationship between the rise of Protestantism and the growth of the knowledge of natural science. J. Calvin, "Advertissement contre l'astrologie judiciare," Opera Omnia, ed. G. Baum et al. (Brunswick, 1868), VII, 516; Hooykaas, op. cit., p. 252.

I. The Nature of Nature

Calvin as a theologian did not spend much of his time discussing natural science, but both his doctrinal and his exegetical works reveal a very well-defined view of nature and of man's understanding of it. In this, his doctrine of creation holds pride of place for by his stress upon the fact that everything beyond God comes from the divine creative activity in Jesus Christ, he rejects any idea of one "great chain of being." Thus, even in its ideal structure, creation has a qualitatively different essence from that of God.[20] Neither are form nor substance, universals nor particulars, co-eternal with God. Rather there exist two levels of reality, the Eternal and the temporal, the uncreated and the created, and though man made in the image of God spiritually and intellectually stands halfway between, he still forms part of the dependent, space-time condition reality.[21]

Yet with all his stress upon the difference between the Creator and the creature, Calvin never adopted a deistic interpretation of reality.[22] God continually orders, upholds and governs creation by the "secret power" of His Holy Spirit who brought order out of original chaos and who keeps all things in existence even now. Calvin also insisted that all things operate usually according to the laws with which God has endowed nature and which the Holy Spirit continually maintains and activates.[23]   Only on special occasions, i.e. on occasions of special revelation or special redemptive action, does God act directly: above or contrary to secondary causes.[24] Thus law, established and continued by God's Spirit, binds the whole of creation together.

It can hardly cause any surprise, therefore, that Calvin insisted that the created-temporal reality forms one vast system, not of substantial forms but of phenomena and laws. More than once Calvin devoted his attention to the magnificent order of the whole of the universe which operates without the slightest sign of confusion according to the laws which God sustains and governs at all times. The "ordo naturae" to Calvin forms one grand machine which manifests the wonderful divine wisdom, power and

[20]J. Calvin, *Commentary on Genesis* (Grand Rapids, 1948), I, xxxi: "le premiere livre de Moyse merite d'estre tenu pour un thresor inestimable, lequel pour le moins nous donne certitude infaillible de la creation du monde: sans lequelle, nous ne sommes pas dignes quen la terre nous soustiene." Cf. also J. Bohatec, *Budé und Calvin* (Graz, 1950), p. 269; E. A. Dowey, *The Knowledge of God in Calvin's Theology* (New York, 1952), pp. 73ff.

[21]Torrance, *op. cit.*, p. 41; Bohatec, *op. cit.*, pp. 264f.; Hall, *op. cit.*, p. xvi.

[22]Hall, *ibid.*, p. xvii.

[23]Calvin's views on God's providential care of nature through the Holy Spirit appear in many places in his commentaries although he seems to sum up the whole matter in his words concerning Acts 17:28: "For the power of the Spirit is spread abroad throughout all the parts of the world, that it may preserve them in their state; that he may minister unto the heaven and earth that force and vigour which we see, and motion to all living creatures." Cf. also: Ps. 19:1, 2; Jeremiah 10:12, 13; Isaiah 40:22; *Institutes of the Christian Religion*, I, xvi, 4ff.

[24]W. Keusche, *Das Wirken des Heiligen Geistes nach Calvin* (Göttingen, 1957), pp. 25ff.; "Avertissement," *Opera*, VII, 532.

goodness. Contrary to what many seem to think, therefore, nature in his mind was something to be considered and enjoyed, for it radiates the glory of the sovereign God.[25]

To summarize Calvin's thought and to show how he applied it, one should examine his views on astrology to which he gave expression in 1549 by the publication of *Admonitio Adversus Astrologiam, quam Iudiciariam Vocant*. In this tractate he maintains that the study of the heavens by man is a proper and legitimate occupation, as long as man limits himself to the study of the motions and relationships of the celestial bodies. In his statements concerning this aspect of "astrology" he shows no sign of ever having heard of Copernicus, which is hardly surprising seeing that he wrote only four years after the publication of the *De Revolutionibus*. When he turns to the judicial astrologers, he bases his criticism primarily upon empirical evidence, rejecting all ideas of heavenly intelligences, the harmony of the spheres and the difference of heavenly from terrestrial substances. While he accepts generally Ptolemy's system of crystalline spheres his views differ radically from those of Dante as expressed in *The Banquet*. Moreover, although the heavenly host may influence man's body in some ways, they have no control over his actions or his fortunes. God alone governs by the laws of His universe.[26]

All of those who professed to be followers of Calvin during the forty years following his death in 1564 did not succeed in remaining as free from Aristotelian influences as did he. Beza, Calvin's successor in Geneva, and many others accepted whole-heartedly Aristotle's guidance in matters scientific.[27] And yet even convinced Aristotelians could hardly follow Aristotle entirely, as long as they maintained Calvin's doctrine of creation, which most of them did. Jerome Zanchi, an Italian theologian at Heidelberg University, for instance, in his *De Operibus Dei intra Spaciam Sex Diebus Creatis* written around 1570, spends considerable time attacking Aristotle's views on the eternality of matter, and even alters the Philosopher's teachings concerning the relation of form and substance by insisting that diversity and distinctions in the natural world arise solely out of the sovereign creative will of God.[28] Similarly Peter Ramus in his *Scholae Mathematicae* (1569) stresses that God had created all things, particularly the heavens, on a mathematical pattern.[29] In the same way Bernard Palissy sought in his art

[25]*Institutes*, I, xiv, 20, 21; Ps. 104:1–4; Ps. 19:2; Dowey, *op. cit.*, p. 66; Krusche, *op. cit.*, pp. 15ff. "Therefore, if any smatterer in philosophy, with a view to ridicule the simplicity of our faith, contend that such a variety of colours [in a rainbow] is the natural result of the refraction of the solar rays on an opposite cloud, we must immediately acknowledge it, but we may smile at his stupidity in not acknowledging God as the Lord and Governor of nature, who uses all the elements according to his nature for the promotion of His own glory." *Institutes*, IV, xiv, 18.
[26]Calvin's tractate also appeared for popular consumption in a French translation in the same year as "L'avertissement contre l'astrologie judiciaire." His views on astrology also appear at appropriate places in his biblical commentaries. Cf. Bohatec, *op. cit.*, pp. 268ff.; Lecerf, *op. cit.*, pp. 119f.
[27]Dillenberger, *op. cit.*, p. 62; Hooykaas, *op. cit.*, p. 177.
[28]2nd ed., Hanover, 1597, Part I, Lib. i, chap. iii.   [29]Hooykaas, *op. cit.*, pp. 250ff.

to reproduce "the works of God as they came from His hands,"[30] while Francis Bacon continually refers to God's creation of all things, and like the others takes for granted Calvin's "two level" interpretation of all reality.[31]

When one studies the thought of Calvin's followers with regard to providence, natural law and secondary causes one finds again rather complete unanimity. Zanchi spends much time setting forth the Reformed doctrine of providence as the basis for the idea of natural law and the validity of secondary causes;[32] while in Palissy one even hears echoes of the very phraseology and examples cited by Calvin.[33] Bacon sums the whole matter up when, after pointing out that final causes are matters properly metaphysical and physical causes relate only to this world, he insists that "neither doth this [distinction] call in question, or derogate from Divine Providence, but highly confirm and exalt it."[34] To these men as to Calvin the relationships of things arose out of natural law, created and sustained by God's sovereign power.

Similarly they all laid great stress upon the fact that this world of nature formed one vast machine, a term used numerous times by Zanchi and others. Even the smallest and most vile phenomena of creation form part of the great whole.[35] Palissy in his pottery continually modelled his ornaments on lizards, molluscs and fish, because he held that these all form part of God's great and grand design of creation.[36] In this way the concept of "system" dominated their understanding of nature of which no part was too small or too unimportant for consideration and study. On the other hand, they never accepted the idea of a static universe. Zanchi insisted more than once that the physical universe continually moves forward to the completion of God's purpose, while Palissy held that it did so by natural processes as revealed by the fact that many rocks were laid down by both sedimentary and volcanic action.[37] Ramus and Bacon likewise subscribed to this continual purposive movement of all things physical.[38] But always the movement arose out of God's action and according to His natural laws.

What did these men hold concerning the heavens? Most of them accepted completely Calvin's views on astrology, rejecting any mystical or magical influence of the heavenly bodies and denying any such things as heavenly

[30]A. Dumesnil, *Gernard Pallissy* (Paris, 1851), pp. 38ff., 53; H. Morley, *Palissy the Potter* (London, 1852), II, 240ff.; *Les Oeuvres de Bernard Palissy*, ed. Anatole France (Paris, 1880), pp. 106ff.

[31]*The Advancement of Learning*, ed., G. W. Kitchin (London, 1915), p. 8.

[32]*De Operibus*, Pt. I, Lib. I, cap. iii; Pt. II, Lib. II, cap. iv.

[33]Dumesnil, *op. cit.*, pp. 50ff.; Morley, *op. cit.*, pp. 133, 140, 158.

[34]*Advancement*, p. 98.

[35]*De Operibus*, Pt. I, Lib. I, cap. iii, p. 54, "Nihil vero tam vile atque exiguum esse in mundo, quod non suum habeat usum ad totius machinae, tamquam totius corporis conservationem, ornatum, formam."

[36]*Oeuvres*, pp. 231ff.; 446ff.

[37]*De Operibus*, Pt. I, Lib. I, cap. iii, p. 54; Morley, *op. cit.*, p. 158.

[38]Hooykaas, *op. cit.*, pp. 232ff.; Bacon, *Advancement*, p. 93.

intelligences or spheric harmonies.[39] With regard to Copernicus's theories those who dealt with the subject seem to have been divided.[40] Zanchi, for instance, took the Ptolemaic structure for granted.[41] Bacon seems to have put Ptolemy and Copernicus on a par, for although he held no brief for Ptolemy he felt that Copernicus had endeavoured to over-simplify matters and both theories would have to await further confirmation.[42] Ramus, on the other hand, supported the Copernican ideas largely because he rejected Ptolemy's epicycles as too complicated, but as a result of Osiander's unsigned introduction to the De Revolutionibus he also criticized Copernicus strongly for setting forth his theory merely as a mathematical hypothesis for calculation. He felt that he should have maintained that it conformed to the facts.[43] In general one may say that with their view of the universe and the sovereignty of God over all, they had no need to worry if this planet did cease to be the physical centre of all things.[44]

To the Calvinist, then, nature is not a servant to be exploited or a temptress to be avoided. Rather, God has created nature that He might show forth His glory which man alone may recognize. Man with a "natural" body, but created in the image of God, has received the commission of God to "subdue the world and rule over it." The Calvinist saw nature as something objective to himself which he must endeavour to understand and use in order that he might truly fulfil his task upon earth. This provided him with an effective stimulus to scientific investigation.[45]

II. THE SCIENCE OF NATURE

As pointed out at the beginning of this paper, science in the Middle Ages and Renaissance had, despite some opposition, largely accepted Aristotle as its guide. This meant that not only his description of the physical universe but also his deductive, syllogistic method as the only proper method for scientific study, dominated men's minds. This was the heritage of the sixteenth century and in many cases even those who rebelled against the medieval theological and religious outlook continued to adhere closely to Aristotle's scientific method.[46] Yet as in the case of the explana-

39Cf. Zanchi, De Operibus, Pt. II, Lib. VI, cap. ii; Bacon, Advancement, p. 29.

40As pointed out by Boas, op. cit., pp. 101ff., Copernicus's theory did not receive unanimous support before the first quarter of the seventeenth century. Guillaume du Bartas, Jean Bodin, Michel de Montaigne and John Donne all either rejected Copernicus or had very great doubts concerning his views.

41De Operibus, Pt. I, Lib. I, cap. II, p. 19.

42Bacon, Advancement, p. 104.

43Hooykaas, op. cit., pp. 230.

44Calvin, while holding "that the circuit of the heavens is finite, and that the earth like a little globe is placed in the centre," also held that "in comparison with the boundless waste which remains empty, the heaven and earth occupy but a small space." Commentary on Genesis, The Argument.

45Ibid.; Bohatec, op. cit., p. 269; Dumesnil, op. cit., p. 64.

46Hooykaas, op. cit., p. 177; Dillenberger, op. cit., p. 62; C. Waddington, Ramus, sa vie, ses écrits et ses opinions (Paris, 1855), pp. 190ff.

tion of nature, the practice of scientific method during the century kept well ahead of the theory. The craftsmen and artisans as well as many others working in practical affairs began to develop increasingly an empirical approach for which they needed theoretical justification and explanation.[47] Aristotelianism did not provide the answer, but Calvinism offered a rationale which opened the way towards seventeenth-century developments.

In order to understand Calvin's influence on the scientific method, one must look first at his theological technique. Seeking to reform the church, he turned back to the original Christian source, the biblical text, which he believed to be the Word of God. His method of approach to the Scriptures was basically empirical for he rejected all speculation and all philosophizing in favour of a strict grammatico-historical exegesis under the guidance of God's spirit, which limits one to what the text actually says.[48] This method had wielded a strong influence on Calvinists down to the present day, but in the late sixteenth century it completely dominated their thinking. Even an Aristotelian such as Zanchi adhered rigorously to it, while Ramus and Bacon made it the very heart of their approach to Holy Writ.[49]

Calvin, however, did not stop with a theological method, for he held that God also revealed Himself in his works of creation and providence. These latter man comes to know not by studying the Scriptures, but by investigating nature itself.[50] Here the two-level theory of reality came into play, for he insisted that one must investigate the things of this earth by appropriate mundane means, the only limitation being that unless men see this earth "in the light of eternity," by which he means in the perspective of faith in Christ, they will neither understand it truly nor use it properly.[51] At the same time he also insisted that since God is the creator and sustainer man can never understand all His works; he can only analyse their relationships and material causes recognizing that even the *ordo naturae* because of its divine origin is never wholly subject to human rational analysis.[52]

In the light of this interpretation how did Calvin regard non-Christian scientific endeavours? The answer to this question is that although he held that by the Fall man had lost all capacity for the knowledge of both God and the creation, God in His grace through the Holy Spirit does give even to unbelievers certain gifts by which they may investigate and understand

[47]Hooykaas, *op. cit.*, p. 257.

[48]Calvin's attitude to the writings of Dionysius the Areopagite illustrates his approach: "No one will deny that Dionysius, whoever he was, subtly and skilfully discussed many things in his *Celestial Hierarchy*. But if anyone studied it more closely, he will find it for the most part nothing but talk. . . . If you read that book, you would think a man fallen from heaven recounted, not what he had learned, but what he had seen with his own eyes." (*Institutes*, I, xiv, 34), Cf. Haydn, *op. cit.*, p. 212; Lecerf, *op. cit.*, pp. 121f.

[49]Bacon, *Advancement*, pp. 209ff., 214f.; "Religious Meditations," *Works*, VII, 252ff.; Gilbert, *op. cit.*, p. 110; Hooykaas, *op. cit.*, p. 287.

[50]"Avertissement," *Opera*, VII, 523f., 529f., 540f. Cf. also his comments on Ps. 148:3; 1 Cor. 1:17. Lecerf, *op. cit.*, p. 123.

[51]*Instruction in Faith* (1537), ed. P. T. Fuhrmann (Philadelphia, 1949), p. 20; Comment on 1 Cor. 1:20 Dowey, *op. cit.*, pp. 77, 131ff.; Bohatec, *op. cit.*, pp. 265ff.

[52]*Instruction*, p. 19: Comment on Jeremiah 10:12, 13; *Institutes*, I, v, 9; II, ii, 13ff.

this world.[53] This knowledge and ability he never said was "natural" but came from God's special benevolence, so that even the Christian had to acknowledge and thank God for what he calls the ancient philosophers' "fine observation and careful description of nature."[54] In this way he accepted all scientific investigation as God-given for the use and profit of man.[55]

Here again, once they had accepted his basic theological presuppositions, even Calvin's most Aristotelian disciples found it necessary to follow. Zanchi repeatedly praises the study of nature as the study of God's work, although he has as his objective the establishment of a perfect science such as that set forth in Aristotle's *Physics*.[56] Similarly Ramus made repeated calls for the study of nature, holding that man's "natural reason" if properly guided would lead to the truth.[57] The clearest statement of the Calvinistic position, however, comes from Francis Bacon:

To conclude therefore, let no man upon a weak conceit of sobriety or an ill-applied moderation think or maintain that a man can search too far, or be too well studied in the book of God's word or in the book of God's works; divinity or philosophy: but rather let men endeavour an endless progress and proficiency in both; only let them beware that they apply both to charity, and not to swelling; to use not to ostentation; and again that they do not unwisely mingle or confound these learnings together.[58]

This naturally brings one face to face with the question of the statements of the Scriptures concerning natural phenomena and happenings. Is the Bible the final authority on matters scientific? To this Calvin replied that when the Spirit of God speaks through the Law and the Prophets He does so not with rigorous exactness, "but in a style suited to the common capacities of man."[59] This of course would not involve the question of miracles, for they are special occurrences for some particular purpose, but

[53]*Institutes*, II, ii, 12ff.; Comment on Jno. 4:36; Dowey, *op. cit.*, p. 139f.; Krusche, *op. cit.*, p. 104.
[54]*Institutes*, II, ii, 15.
[55]*Ibid.*, II, ii, 12. If we say, according to Calvin, that the unbeliever cannot know anything "we not only go against God's Word, but also run contrary to the experience of common sense."
[56]Zanchi, *De Operibus*, Epistle Dedicatory, had this to say: "there is nothing more noble, nothing more in accordance with the dignity of man, including Christians, nothing which gives more solid pleasure, nothing more useful and therefore by the theologian to be least neglected but rather most accurately studied, than the attentive and diligent contemplation of the works established by God." Cf. Pt. I, Lib. I, cap. i; Pt. II, Lib. IV, cap. iv. His position on creation and providence obviously prevented him from holding to a thorough Aristotelianism.
[57]Hooykaas, *op. cit.*, p. 186. Ramus, it would seem, did not feel that sin had corrupted man's "natural reason" so that he could not think without divine grace. In this he did not go as far as his fellow Calvinists who believed that the Fall wrecked man's thinking capacity to the extent that he needed divine assistance for a true understanding of nature.
[58]*Advancement*, p. 8. Cf. also pp. 88ff., 186.
[59]In his comment on Ps. 19:4, Calvin points out that David "accommodating himself to the rudest and dullest ... confines himself to the ordinary appearances of the eye. . . ." Comment on Jer. 1:12, 13; Torrance, *op. cit.*, p. 45; Dillenberger, *op. cit.*, pp. 32ff.

for the knowledge of all normal natural happenings the study of the
phenomena, not of the Scriptures, brings man true knowledge.[60] Of this
point of view one finds many echoes in most Calvinistic writings down into
the seventeenth century.[61]

Such an attitude to the Bible and nature meant that Calvin and his
followers flatly rejected any form of biblicistic rationalism or mysticism. As
Calvin put it: "He who would learn astronomy and other recondite arts,
let him go elsewhere."[62] This anti-rationalist approach lay at the basis of his
rejection of judicial astrology. Similarly Ramus and Bacon spent considerable time blasting at astrology, alchemy, and the esoteric philosophy
of Paracelsus who attempted to deduce all scientific truth by means of
rationalization from the Scriptures, and declared all other knowledge of
nature false. Even philosophical rationalism came under attack. Ramus and
Bacon flatly rejected the deductive-syllogistic method as inadequate for
science, since it dealt with notions rather than with facts of nature,[63] while
Palissy and Paré defended their practices on grounds of experience alone.[64]

It is through the facts of nature that one learns about nature. In his
tractate on astrology and in his pamphlet advocating the creation of an
inventory of all religious relics in Europe,[65] Calvin continually pointed to the
need for ascertaining the facts, even as in a theological argument he continually went back to what the Bible said. "Je ne veux rejetter l'art qui est
tiré de l'ordre de nature, mais que je le prise et loue comme un don singulier
de Dieu."[66] This in turn became the central theme of Calvin's "scientific"
disciples. Ramus made a considerable reputation for himself by rejecting
every "hypothesis" which did not keep strictly to the facts.[67] Palissy attacked
Paracelsus, Raymond Lull and the alchemists on the same grounds, preparing a cabinet of geological specimens to support his case.[68] And again
Bacon sums up the whole matter in his preface to the *Novum Organon*
when he expresses the hope that he has brought about the marriage of "the
empirical and rational faculties," in order that God may enable him to
present further gifts to the family of men.[69]

[60]Comment on Genesis 1:16.
[61]Zanchi, *De Operibus*, Pt. III, Lib. I, cap. i; Waddington, *op. cit.*, pp. 359f.; Dillenberger, *op. cit.*, p. 61.
[62]Comment on Gen. 1:6.
[63]Hooykaas, *op. cit.*, pp. 218, 247, 274f., 278f.; Bacon, *Advancement*, pp. 100, 216ff.
and Aphorism XXIII, *Novum Organon, Works*, V, 51: "There is a great difference
between the Idols of the human mind and the Ideas of the divine. That is to say between
certain empty dogmas, and the true signatures and marks set upon the works of creation
as they are found in nature."
[64]Morley, *op. cit.*, II, 101; Ambrose Paré, "Apology and Treatise." in F. R. Packard,
op. cit., pp. 129ff.
[65]"An Admonition showing the advantage which Christendom might derive from an
Inventory of Relics," *Tracts Relating to the Reformation*, ed., H. Beveridge (Edinburgh,
1860), I, 255.
[66]"Avertissement," Coll. 529.
[67]Hooykaas, *op. cit.*, pp. 178ff., 183ff., 269; Waddington, *op. cit.*, p. 355.
[68]*Oeuvres*, pp. 394ff.; Morley, *op. cit.*, II, 101; J. Huizinga, *Men and Ideas* (New
York, 1959), p. 304.
[69]*Novum Organon, Works*, IV, 19.

This emphasis upon the factual and empirical raises an important question. How did they propose to find the "fact"? In the development which took place between 1570 and 1620 one sees a change in the answers offered. The earlier and more humanistically inclined writers such as Zanchi and Ramus thought not in terms of experimentation, but in terms of the statements of ancient authorities: Aristotle's *Meteors*, Pliny's *Natural History* and the like.[70] With Palissy who prided himself on knowing no Latin or Greek, and with Paré the military surgeon, practical experience predominated. They found their facts through rudimentary experimentation, whether in the firing of pottery vessels or in the testing out of new methods of tying up wounds.[71] By the time Bacon wrote, under the influence of such men as Ramus and Palissy experimentation albeit of a somewhat haphazard type had begun to become the principal means of "invention and discovery" in the study of nature.[72]

Then came the problem of the way in which the facts discovered should be treated or as they said "judged." Calvin, while stressing the importance of facts, had said little on this subject, but he had in his biblical-theological studies developed a method. One might call it the method of logical arrangement and relationship, by which he placed his biblical material in certain theological loci or topics set in an order of progression. For instance, he began his *Institutes of the Christian Religion* with the doctrine of the knowledge of God and ended with a discussion of the outward form of the church and the nature of civil government. In this he seems to have thought primarily of a teaching technique which led in logical fashion from knowledge to action. In matters relating to physical science, however, although he spoke in terms of natural law and natural order, he never developed any specific pattern of method.

Consequently one finds that "method" developed only very gradually. Zanchi worked out a kind of Protestant scholasticism, but this satisfied few.[73] Most of those in the Calvinistic stream of thought sought a single method

[70]Zanchi, *De Operibus, passim* continually quotes the ancients as authorities who record what they saw happening. In this he revealed clearly the influence of the Renaissance humanistic method. (Gilbert, *op. cit.*, p. 110.) W. J. Ong, *op. cit.*, p. 268, seems to fail to understand that Ramus in following the same method felt that he was being truly empirical. True, he did not perform experiments himself, but, under the influence of contemporary humanism, he believed that he could trust Aristotle's observations completely, despite his repeated and vigorous rejection of the Philosopher's theories. As Hooykaas, *op. cit.*, pp. 199ff., has pointed out, while Ramus felt that experimentation was beneath a scholar's dignity he stressed the importance of the careful observation and measurement of phenomena. In this sense he helped to lay the groundwork for experimental investigation.

[71]Palissey has caused considerable discussion since his nineteenth-century biographers such as Morley, *op. cit.*, pp. 26ff. and Dumesnil, *op. cit.*, p. 19, hold that he employed a truly empirical method while a later writer such as H. Brown, *op. cit.*, p. 35, maintains that his whole method was "hit and miss." Perhaps Huizinga's interpretation lies nearest the truth when he states that Palissy's "place is among those minds who enthusiastically hunted and grubbed in nature to discover its secrets and thus prepared the way for a positivistic natural science" (*op. cit.*, p. 304). Paré obviously followed the same pattern of thought and action. Packard, *op. cit.*, pp. 129ff.

[72]Bacon, *Advancement*, pp. 122ff.; Huizinga, *op. cit.*, p. 304.

[73]Gilbert, *op. cit.*, pp. 110f.

which would do away with Aristotle completely and would produce results firmly based upon facts alone. In this attempt Peter Ramus took a major share, for he taught that the arts arise out of the facts. Man's natural reason takes the facts, sorts them according to their natural order into groups, loci or topics, and gradually combining them eventually produces general principles or precepts. Thus he does not begin with hypotheses but with the facts, allowing them to lead him naturally to certain conclusions.[74] Bacon, accepting a good part of this, carried the matter farther by insisting that such examination or judgment should lead on to the discovery of new facts and new relationships. This he termed "magistral" judgment.[75] Thus, as W. J. Ong has pointed out, the method was based on the idea of space and arrangement which themselves were part of nature, a method very closely linked to that of the theologian and his *loci theologici*.[76]

The influence of the theologian and his teaching methods appears even more clearly when one examines what Bacon calls "the method of tradition" or exposition. From Calvin down to Bacon the primary purpose of the scholar was that of teaching. All Calvin's writings show this and those who followed him in the scientific field have the same approach.[77] Palissy wrote and collected his geological specimens for this purpose[78] and Ramus thought much more of a "teaching" than a "research" method. The latter usually came in only as an afterthought. This would seem to be the reason for Ramus's reputation as a man who mixed rhetoric and dialectic, although in point of fact the rhetorical aspect of his method formed only a small part of his whole system.[79] It remained for Francis Bacon to distinguish clearly between the two types of method and to insist that they should not be confused.[80] Yet in their teaching or rhetorical methods both Ramus and Bacon insisted fervently that everything must find its basis in solid facts as one moves from the better known to the less known. Even in this, however, the topical order was to govern as one set forth one's ideas as convincingly as possible.[81]

---

[74]Hooykaas, *op. cit.*, pp. 188ff., 218ff., points out that Ramus insisted upon beginning with the facts in any attempt to build up a science, although he stressed the necessity of commencing from the most general principles in teaching. Cf. Gilbert, *op. cit.*, p. 1.

[75]Bacon, *op. cit.*, pp. 93ff.; Boas, *op. cit.*, pp. 250ff.

[76]Ong, in his criticism of Ramus, seems to have overlooked the fact that the "geometrical" method was regarded by many as the most "natural," and this method in a sense was that of the typical logic of the theologians. *Op. cit.*, pp. 196f., 288, 354f.; Gilbert, *op. cit.*, pp. 84ff.

[77]Cf. the full title of Calvin's major work, *Christianae Religionis Institutio Totam Fere Pietatis Summam et Quiquid est in Doctrina Salutis Cognitu Necessarium Complectens Omnibus Pietatis Studiosis Lectu Dignissimum Opus ac Recens Editum*. Cf. H. Obendiek, "Die Institutio Calvins als 'Confessio' und 'Apologie,' " *Theologische Aufsätze*, Karl Barth zum 50 Geburtstag, ed., M. Lempp and E. Wolf (Munich, 1936), pp. 418ff.

[78]Dumesnil, *op. cit.*, pp. 24ff.; Morley, *op. cit.*, pp. 102f.; Palissy, *Oeuvres*, pp. 434ff.

[79]Ong, *op. cit.*, pp. 283f.; Gilbert, *op. cit.*, pp. 136, 221; Hooykaas, *op. cit.*, pp. 222ff.

[80]*Advancement*, p. 140.

[81]*Ibid.*, pp. 141ff.; Hooykaas, *op. cit.*, pp. 195f.; Gilbert, *op. cit.*, pp. 134–143.

At this point one feels obliged to ask whether mathematics played any part in this concept of method. As far as one can tell, Calvin, Zanchi, Beza and the others had little interest in such matters. Francis Bacon went even further, expressing a fear of the subject since he felt that the mathematician always tended to over-simplify for the benefit of a neat numerical scheme. This provided part of the reason for his doubts concerning Copernicus.[82] Ramus, on the other hand, from the time of his open conversion to Protestantism increasingly stressed the need for mathematical studies and their application to the science of nature. Seeing that he had little or no interest in actual experimentation, this may appear strange, but if one remembers that his basic method was one of arrangement in space, one can understand perhaps why geometry and arithmetic played such an important part in his scheme of things.[83] Thus in Calvinistic thought relating to nature and natural phenomena, although the stress still lay on the qualitative rather than on the quantitative, the tendency to regard the geometrical arranging of the facts as the truly "scientific" method became increasingly prominent. In this way mathematics almost imperceptibly entered the picture.

Although mathematics obtained no great recognition, Calvinistic thinking concerning nature possessed another characteristic still very important: a stress upon objectivity. Calvin held that God had objectified His revelation in the Scriptures and in nature, so that man could comprehend both by a proper analysis in the light of eternity. This forced him to avoid speculation in order that he might truly hear God speaking. He rejected any idea of a creative tradition and of a concept of dialogue with the world. Man's dialogue is with God.[84] The realism of Palissy's "rustic pieces" and Ramus's stress upon the study of nature external to man along with his insistence that rhetoric involved only ornament and delivery while reason dealt with the understanding of the facts, both came out of this tradition. Ramus clearly feared, as Ong has said, "the obtrusion of voices and persons in scientific issues."[85] This same attitude appears in Bacon when he speaks of God framing "the mind of man as a mirror or glass, capable of the image of the universal world, and joyful to receive the impression thereof, as the

[82]*Advancement*, pp. 98f., 129ff.; *Novum Organon*, pp. 47ff.; S. F. Mason, A *History of the Sciences* (London, 1953), p. 114.

[83]Although Melancthon and Agricola both favoured the study of mathematics, they never attempted to apply it universally. John Sturm of Strasburg did to a certain extent, and through his influence Ramus sought to apply it to the quadrivium of the medieval curriculum. His interest in physical science and in particular in mathematics seems to have arisen at the time of his conversion to Protestantism, a point which Waddington, Hooykaas and Ong all miss. Ramus left an endowment for the establishment of a chair of mathematics in the Université de France. Waddington, *op. cit.*, pp. 246ff.; Hooykaas, *op. cit.*, pp. 196–251; Ong, *op. cit.*, pp. 30ff., 196 f., Gilbert, *op. cit.*, pp. 84ff.

[84]*Institutes*, I, v, 5. "We must therefore admit in God's individual works—but especially in them as a whole—that God's powers actually appear as in a painting" (I, v, 10). Cf. Torrance, *op. cit.*, p. 44.

[85]Ong, *op. cit.*, pp. 287ff.; Waddington, *op. cit.*, p. 346; Hooykaas, *op. cit.*, pp. 183f., 221.

eye joyeth to receive light. . . ."[86] Without bias caused by rhetoric, there-fore, man should seek to know and to interpret nature. Objective investiga-tion alone could adequately set forth the truth.

The ultimate goal of all scientific method is the establishment of the most general principles by establishing an all-inclusive system. So thought Calvin, whether dealing with matters theological or matters physical, and his successors felt much the same way.[87] And yet they also admitted that both in theology and in natural science there always remains for man an ultimate surd which man cannot break down for analysis. This does not result from some obduracy of nature, but rather from the mystery of God the creator and upholder of all things. One must seek as far as possible to discover the system in the universe by empirical means, but at the same time must acknowledge that some parts will always remain unknown. In this way and by these means the Calvinists endeavoured to provide an understanding of nature which would supplant that of Aristotle.

III. The Use of Nature

One cannot speak about the Calvinistic concept of nature and of scientific method without at least referring to one other important facet of thought. Neither Calvin nor those who came after him held any brief for mere learning as such. Man's knowledge and abilities must be applied to use. This idea was by no means Calvin's invention, but it fitted in well with his point of view and received support from those who followed him.[88]

Calvin held on biblical-theological grounds that God had placed man upon this earth to subdue and use it. Thus man should employ the good gifts of God for his own physical and emotional well-being.[89] This utilitarian approach one finds in the others who have been mentioned as following in his footsteps: Zanchi, Palissy, Paré, Ramus and Bacon as well as many others.[90] But the highest end of all scientific, as well as theological, studies is ultimately the glory of God. As all of creation is the handiwork of God, the study, the analysis and synthesis of it, and the explanation of its wonders all have as their ultimate end and purpose the manifestation and revelation of the infinite wisdom, power and grace of the Tri-une Godhead.[91]

[86]*Advancement*, p. 5. Cf. also pp. 23f., 121, 129ff., 141, 146.
[87]Calvin, *Institutes*, I, v, 5, 11, 12; Zanchi, *De Operibus*, Epistle Dedicatory; Hooykaas, *op. cit.*, p. 240; Bacon, *Novum Organon*, pp. 47ff.; *Advancement*, pp. 5, 95ff., 215; Haydn, *op. cit.*, pp. 267ff.; Hall, *op. cit.*, p. xvi.
[88]Bohatec, *op. cit.*, pp. 263; Gilbert, *op. cit.*, pp. 69f.; Hooykaas, *op. cit.*, pp. 187ff.; Ong, *op. cit.*, pp. 224f.
[89]Comment on 1 Cor. 1:17; Bohatec, *op. cit.*, pp. 263; Nash, *op. cit.*, pp. 67f.
[90]Zanchi, *op. cit.*, pp. 329f.; Hooykaas, *op. cit.*, pp. 222ff.; Palissy, *op. cit.*, pp. 231ff.
[91]Calvin in his attack on Astrology states the Reformed position most clearly: "Surquoi je dis brievement, que nulle bonne science n'est repugnante à la crainte de Dieu mis à la doctrine qu'il nous donne pour nous mener en la vie eternelle, moyennant que nous ne mettions la charrue devant les boeufs: c'est à dire que nous ayens cette prudence de nous servit des arts tant liberaux que mechaniques en passant par ce monde, pour tendre toujours au Royaume celeste." (*Avertissement*, p. 540f.) Zanchi, *De Operibus*, Epistle Dedicatory; Bacon, *Advancement*, pp. 7, 36.

How much influence did the Calvinistic school of thought exercise? It would seem that in some areas—France, Holland, Western Germany, England and Scotland—it gained a very considerable following. Calvin's writings themselves were wide spread, laying the foundation for this point of view.[92] The works of Ramus, also translated into many different languages, made their impress in various places. The English Puritans and the Scottish Presbyterians, for instance, accepted most of his ideas with the result Gresham College in England, Edinburgh University in Scotland and Harvard College in Massachusetts all began their existences primarily as Ramist institutions. Added to this Ramus received much attention in the Netherlands and Germany.[93] Similarly Bacon had his adherents not only in England but also on the Continent. Thus, the Calvinistic schools of thought exercised an important influence on the development of scientific thought in the sixteenth century.

Yet one must recognize that the Calvinistic tradition had its serious weaknesses. Its interest more in teaching than in experimental research, its failure to use mathematics, and its continued thinking in qualitative rather than quantitative terms concerning natural phenomena show this. Furthermore, because of these deficiencies it never really devised an effective method of research. Consequently, it did not directly force a scientific advance.

Despite these limitations, however, it played an important part in the breaking down of the old scientific order. It undermined the medieval synthesis at every level with its stress upon the factual and its insistence on objective analysis of phenomena in order that all things might be subordinated to law and formed into a system. Moreover, the use of a "special" method, instead of a search for purpose and final causes in nature, helped to give a new view of nature so that men began to ask different questions of nature with startling results.[94]

Thus Calvinism's influence, while not leading necessarily to the scientific revolution, was one of the important movements which helped to prepare the way for seventeenth-century developments in the work of such men as Kepler, van Huygens and Newton, and provides us today with an integration of religion and science in the ultimate Christian theistic environment of all created reality.

[92]Lecerf, *op. cit.*, p. 118.
[93]Kristeller, *op. cit.*, p. 43; Hooykaas, *op. cit.*, pp. 279f.
[94]Crombie, *Augustine to Galileo*, pp. 274f.; Hooykaas, *op. cit.*, pp. 288ff.; Ong, *op. cit.*, p. 268; Burtt, *op. cit.*, pp. 27ff.

Acknowledgments

Gerrish, B.A. "The Reformation and the Rise of Modern Science: Luther, Calvin and Copernicus." In *The Old Protestantism and the New* (1982): 163–78. Reprinted with the permission of the University of Chicago Press, publisher. Copyright 1982 by the University of Chicago. All rights reserved. Courtesy of Yale University Sterling Memorial Library.

Rosen, Edward. "Calvin's Attitude Toward Copernicus." *Journal of the History of Ideas* 21 (1960): 431–41. Reprinted with the permission of the *Journal of the History of Ideas*. Courtesy of Yale University Sterling Memorial Library.

Ratner, Joseph. "Some Comments on Rosen's 'Calvin's Attitude Toward Copernicus,'" and Edward Rosen, "A Reply to Dr. Ratner." *Journal of the History of Ideas* 22 (1961): 382–8. Reprinted with the permission of the *Journal of the History of Ideas*. Courtesy of Yale University Sterling Memorial Library.

Hooykaas, R. "Calvin and Copernicus." *Organon* 10 (1974): 139–48. Courtesy of Yale University Sterling Memorial Library.

Kaiser, Christopher B. "Calvin, Copernicus, and Castellio." *Calvin Theological Journal* 21 (1986): 5–31. Reprinted with the permission of the *Calvin Theological Journal*. Courtesy of the *Calvin Theological Journal*.

Marcel, Pierre Ch. "Calvin and Copernicus." *Philosophia Reformata* 46 (1981): 14–36. Courtesy of *Philosophia Reformata*.

Murray, John. "Calvin's Doctrine of Creation." *Westminster Theological Journal* 17 (1954): 21–43. Reprinted with the permission of the Westminster Theological Seminary. Courtesy of Yale University Divinity Library.

Probes, Christine McCall. "Calvin on Astrology." *Westminster Theological Journal* 37 (1974–75): 24–33. Reprinted with the permission of the Westminster Theological Seminary. Courtesy of Yale University Divinity Library.

White, Robert. "Calvin and Copernicus: The Problem Reconsidered." *Calvin Theological Journal* 15 (1980): 233–43. Reprinted with the permission of the *Calvin Theological Journal*. Courtesy of the *Calvin Theological Journal*.

Kaiser, Christopher B. "Calvin's Understanding of Aristotelian Natural Philosophy: Its Extent and Possible Origins." In Robert V. Schnucker, ed., *Calviniana: Ideas and Influence of Jean Calvin* (Kirksville, MO: Sixteenth Century Journal Publishers, Inc., 1988): 77–92. Reprinted with the permission of the Sixteenth Century Journal Publishers, Inc. Courtesy of Yale University Divinity Library.

Deason, G.B. "The Protestant Reformation and the Rise of Modern Science." *Scottish Journal of Theology* 38 (1985): 221–40. Reprinted with the permission of T&T Clark Ltd. Courtesy of Yale University Divinity Library.

Reid, W. Stanford. "Natural Science in Sixteenth-Century Calvinistic Thought." *Proceedings and Transactions of Royal Society of Canada* 1 (1963): 305–319. Reprinted with the permission of the Royal Society of Canada. Courtesy of Yale University Sterling Memorial Library.